Dutcn

lonely planet

phrasebooks
and
Annelies Mertens

Dutch phrasebook
1st edition – September 2007

Published by
Lonely Planet Publications Pty Ltd ABN 36 005 607 983
90 Maribyrnong St, Footscray, Victoria 3011, Australia

Lonely Planet Offices
Australia Locked Bag 1, Footscray, Victoria 3011
USA 150 Linden St, Oakland CA 94607
UK 72-82 Rosebery Ave, London, EC1R 4RW

Cover illustration
Gallery gas by Wendy Wright

ISBN 978 1 74179-180-8

text © Lonely Planet Publications Pty Ltd 2007
cover illustration © Lonely Planet Publications Pty Ltd 2007

10 9 8 7 6 5 4 3 2

Printed through The Bookmaker International Ltd
Printed in Hong Kong

acknowledgments

Editor Branislava Vladisavljevic would like to acknowledge the following people for their contributions to this phrasebook:

Annelies Mertens for the comprehensive translations and the cultural information.

Annelies is a native Dutch speaker hailing from the Kempen region in Belgium. At the age of 18 she moved to the Flemish 'student city' of Leuven to study Arts and Linguistics. After obtaining her Honours in Romance studies and graduating as a French and Spanish teacher, she moved to the baroque port city of Antwerp to sample more of the good things life (and Belgium) have on offer. Having travelled the length and breadth of Europe as a kid with mum and dad, Annelies has continued to travel as often as she can to all corners of the world, and now lives in Melbourne, Australia with husband Tony, and works at Lonely Planet as a Managing Editor. During her visits to Belgium she indulges in the cuisine, the vibrant cultural life, the most *gezellige* pubs imaginable, the beers, the chocolates, and can be seen wandering seemingly aimlessly through its historic cities.

Annelies would like to thank colleague and fellow native Dutch speaker Barbara Delissen, originally from Gouda, the Netherlands, for providing extra Dutch language and cultural expertise, as well as support during the production of this book. Thanks also to editor Brana Vladisavljevic with whom the manuscript was in super-safe and capable hands. Last but not least, a big thank you to Moeke, Katleen, Tony, Els, Dirk and Jules – you all know why!

Thanks also to Wendy Wright for the inside illustrations.

Lonely Planet Language Products

Publishing Manager: Ben Handicott

Series Designer: Yukiyoshi Kamimura

Commissioning Editor: Karin Vidstrup Monk

Editor: Branislava Vladisavljevic

Assisting Editors: Vanessa Battersby & Francesca Coles

Managing Editors: Annelies Mertens & Barbara Delissen

Layout Designers: Clara Monitto & Katie Thuy Bui

Managing Layout Designer: Sally Darmody

Cartographer: Wayne Murphy

make the most of this phrasebook ...

Anyone can speak another language! It's all about confidence. Don't worry if you can't remember your school language lessons or if you've never learnt a language before. Even if you learn the very basics (on the inside covers of this book), your travel experience will be the better for it. You have nothing to lose and everything to gain when the locals hear you making an effort.

finding things in this book

For easy navigation, this book is in sections. The Tools chapters are the ones you'll thumb through time and again. The Practical section covers basic travel situations like catching transport and finding a bed. The Social section gives you conversational phrases, pick-up lines, the ability to express opinions – so you can get to know people. Food has a section all of its own: gourmets and vegetarians are covered and local dishes feature. Safe Travel equips you with health and police phrases, just in case. Remember the colours of each section and you'll find everything easily; or use the comprehensive Index. Otherwise, check the two-way traveller's Dictionary for the word you need.

being understood

Throughout this book you'll see coloured phrases on each page. They're phonetic guides to help you pronounce the language. Start with them to get a feel for how the language sounds. The pronunciation chapter in Tools will explain more, but you can be confident that if you read the coloured phrase, you'll be understood. As you become familiar with the spoken language, move on to using the actual text in the language which will help you perfect your pronunciation.

communication tips

Body language, ways of doing things, sense of humour – all have a role to play in every culture. 'Local talk' boxes show you common ways of saying things, or everyday language to drop into conversation. 'Listen for ...' boxes supply the phrases you may hear. They start with the language (so a local can find the phrase they want and point it out to you) and then lead in to the phonetic guide and the English translation.

CONTENTS

5

social 107

dutch

NORTH SEA

Schiermonnikoog
Ameland
Terschelling
Vlieland
Leeuwarden • Groningen
Texel Waddenzee
Drachten
Sneek • Assen
Den
Helder
Emmen
Alkmaar Hoorn
IJsselmeer
Purmerend • Lelystad • Zwolle
Haarlem ★ **Amsterdam**
Leiden Amersfoort • Apeldoorn Enschede
Den • Utrecht
Haag
NETHERLANDS Arnhem
Rotterdam
NORTH SEA Nijmegen
Schouwen-
Duiveland Den Bosch
Noord-Beveland Breda • Tilburg **Germany**
Zuid-
Vlissingen Beveland Eindhoven • Helmond
Zeebrugge Zeeuws-
Oostende Vlaanderen
Brugge Antwerpen • Herentals
Gent Aalst Heerlen
Ieper Leuven Hasselt
Kortrijk Maastricht
Brussel/
Bruxelles **BELGIUM**
Tournai • Liège
France Mons
• Namur
Charleroi

Bastogne

BELGIUM
★
Brussel/
Bruxelles
Luxembourg
Arlon

EUROPE

0 ⌐──── 50 km
0 ⌐──── 30 mi

■ Dutch-speaking
areas
■ French-speaking
areas
■ German-speaking
areas

For more details, see the **introduction**

When it comes to Dutch, you can safely put aside those negative stereotypes about 'double Dutch'. The reality is that Dutch and English are closely related, both being members of the Germanic family of languages. Such are the similarities that Bill Bryson was moved to remark in *Neither Here Nor There* that 'when one hears Dutch, one feels one ought to be able to understand it.'

The connection between English and Dutch has been reinforced by numerous word borrowings – some 2000 English words are said to be of Dutch origin. The impetus behind this phenomenon was the Dutch Golden Age (1584–1702), when the Dutch sailed across the seven seas founding colonies and establishing a trading empire. As you might expect, many of the adopted words are of maritime origin: buoy, dock, skipper, whiting and yacht are only a few.

at a glance ...

language name:
Dutch

name in language:
Nederlands
ney·duhr·lants

language family:
Germanic

approximate number of speakers: 20 million

close relatives:
Afrikaans, English, Frisian, German

donations to English:
buoy, cookie, cruise, dock, landscape (among many others)

Dutch is more than just the language spoken in the Netherlands. Flemish (*Vlaams* vlaams), spoken in the northern part of Belgium (known as Flanders), is really the same language as Dutch, but for historical and cultural reasons the name 'Flemish' is often used. Officially, eg in the school curriculum, it's always referred to as *Nederlands* ney·duhr·lants (Dutch). There are slight differences in pronunciation and vocabulary between Flemish and the Dutch spoken in the Netherlands. In this phrasebook, the differences are indicated with Ⓝ and Ⓑ

introduction

9

(signifying the Netherlands and Belgium). Both countries are members of the *Nederlandse Taalunie* (Dutch Language Union), the supreme authority on modern language standards. The same rules for spelling and grammar are followed throughout both countries and the same dictionaries are used as reference. There are also some dialect divisions within the language as a result of historical circumstances, but they are limited to the spoken language and informal surroundings only. Everyone is taught standard Dutch at school. The standard language is based on the northern dialects, mainly as spoken around Amsterdam. Due to historical events, Dutch is also spoken by a few thousand mainly older people in the very northeastern corner of France, around the city of Dunkirk.

With over 20 million speakers, Dutch has a strong presence on the world linguistic stage. The explorers and traders of the Dutch Golden Age, who brought their language to many corners of the globe, helped establish it as an official language in Aruba, the Dutch Antilles and Suriname. The greatest achievement of the Dutch linguistic expansion is its famous offspring, Afrikaans, now considered a separate language and spoken by around six million people in South Africa.

Some travellers might wonder about the necessity of using Dutch when so many Dutch and Flemish people seem to speak excellent English. While it's true that the Dutch and Flemish are avid linguists, a little effort on your part to speak the local language will be warmly received as a sign of goodwill. And remember that a country's language is also a key to its culture. Taking this book with you will open the door to a truly *gezellige* khuh·*ze*·li·khuh travel experience. If you want to discover firsthand the true meaning of this quintessentially Dutch word ('convivial' just doesn't do it justice), then don't leave home without this little book!

abbreviations used in this book

a	adjective	m	masculine
adv	adverb	n	neuter (after Dutch)
⑧	Belgium	n	noun (after English)
f	feminine	⑩	the Netherlands
Ind	Indonesian (food)	pl	plural
inf	informal	pol	polite
lit	literal	sg	singular

TOOLS > pronunciation
uitspraak

To most foreigners, Dutch has a delightfully distinctive sound – with its guttural r and kh sounds and its array of vowels.

If you put aside your inhibitions and read our coloured pronunciation guides as if you're speaking English, you'll have no trouble getting your message across. It's such a rarity for foreigners to make the effort to speak Dutch that when you do, you'll win friends quicker than you can say *Nederlands* ney·duhr·lants (Dutch).

vowel sounds

Dutch has a rich reservoir of vowel sounds. Most vowels have a long and a short version, which simply means that you hold vowels for a greater or lesser length of time. It's important to make the distinction between long and short versions, as they can distinguish meaning – eg *maan* m**aa**n means 'moon' but *man* m**a**n means 'man'.

There are also a few vowel sounds that are a bit trickier for English speakers to pronounce as they have no equivalent in English, such as the öy and eu sounds. The many-hued Dutch vowels often merge together into swooping diphthongs (vowel sound combinations). While the vowels might take a little practice, they're a key part of the unique flavour of spoken Dutch. If you listen carefully to native speakers and follow our coloured pronunciation guides, you shouldn't have any problems being understood.

symbol	english equivalent	dutch example	transliteration
a	run (but more clearly pronounced, as in 'pasta')	*vak*	vak
aa	father	*vaak, maken*	vaak, *maa*·kuhn
aw	saw	*lauw, koud*	law, kawt
e	bet	*bed*	bet
ee	see	*niet*	neet
eu	nurse	*leuk*	leuk
ew	ee pronounced with rounded lips	*u, uur*	ew, ewr
ey	as in 'bet', but longer	*beet, reis, mijn*	beyt, reys, meyn
i	hit	*ik*	ik
o	pot	*bot*	bot
oh	note	*boot*	boht
oo	zoo	*boer*	boor
öy	her year (without the 'r')	*buik*	böyk
u	put	*geluk*	khuh·*luk*
uh	ago	*het, een*	huht, uhn

consonant sounds

Dutch consonants are pretty straightforward to pronounce as they're also found in English. You might need a little practice with the kh sound, which is guttural and harsher than the English 'h' (although in Flanders it's a lot 'softer' than in Holland). The distinctive trilled r sound is traditionally made with the tongue forward, although these days a lot of people pronounce it more like a French 'r' – held back and restricting the flow of air in the throat.

symbol	english equivalent	dutch example	transliteration
b	bed	*bed*	bet
ch	cheat	*kindje*	*kin*·chuh
d	dog	*dag*	dakh
f	fat	*fiets*	feets
g	go	*gate*	geyt
h	hat	*hoed*	hoot
k	kit	*klok*	klok
kh	as the 'ch' in the Scottish *loch*	*goed, schat*	khoot, skhat
l	lot	*lied*	leet
m	man	*man*	man
n	not	*niet*	neet
ng	ring	*haring*	*haa*·ring
p	pet	*pot*	pot
r	red (trilled)	*rechts*	rekhs
s	sun	*slapen*	*slaa*·puhn
sh	shot	*alsjeblieft*	a·*shuh*·bleeft
t	top	*tafel*	*taa*·fuhl
v	very	*vlucht*	vlukht
w	win	*water*	*waa*·tuhr
y	yes	*je*	yuh
z	zero	*zomer*	*zoh*·muhr
zh	pleasure	*garage*	kha·*raa*·zhuh

word stress

There are no universal rules on stress in Dutch. Just follow our pronunciation guides, in which the stressed syllables are always indicated with italics.

reading & writing

Dutch is written with the Latin alphabet, which is exactly the same as in English. For spelling purposes (eg if you need to spell your name out to book into a hotel) the pronunciation of each letter is given in the box below.

alphabet					
A a	aa	*J j*	yey	*S s*	es
B b	bey	*K k*	kaa	*T t*	tey
C c	sey	*L l*	el	*U u*	ew
D d	dey	*M m*	em	*V v*	vey
E e	ey	*N n*	en	*W w*	wey
F f	ef	*O o*	oh	*X x*	iks
G g	khey	*P p*	pey	*Y y*	ey/*eep*·see·lon
H h	haa	*Q q*	kew	*Z z*	zet
I i	ee	*R r*	er		

a–z phrasebuilder
grammatica – bouwblokken

contents

The list below shows which grammatical structures you can use to say what you want. Look under each function – listed in alphabetical order – for information on how to build your own sentences. For example, to tell the taxi driver where your hotel is, look for **giving instructions** and you'll be directed to information on **demonstratives**, etc. A **glossary** of grammatical terms is included at the end of this chapter to help you.

diminutives

Dutch speakers love a diminutive or two, so much so that it has become a feature of the language. They don't only use them to indicate the smallness of something, like in *autootje* aw·toh·chuh (little car), but also to express endearment when talking with or about children (*kindjes kin·*chus 'small/cute children'), lovers (*schatje skhat·*yuh, *liefje leef·*yuh, both meaning 'darling') or pets (*hondje hon·*chuh 'doggy') – or anything else kind or cute. They'll even add it to your first name! Similarly, anything that's considered cosy will have a diminutive ending whacked onto it – a seven-course dinner with friends is an *etentje ey·*tuhn·chuh (cosy meal) with a *glaasje wijn khlaas·*yuh weyn (a cosy glass of wine) rather than just a *glas wijn* khlas weyn. Diminutives can also indicate relativity – you'd rather wait an *uurtje ewr·*chuh (60 minutes passing quickly and pleasantly) than an *uur* ewr. And strange but true, a diminutive can be a euphemism for something big – if someone says you have a *buikje böyk·*yuh (little belly), it's not really meant as a compliment. Dutch speakers are masters at using diminutives to say 'A' when they mean 'B' or to make understatements, eg *een mondje Frans spreken* uhn mon·chuh frans sprey·kuhn (lit: to speak a little-mouthfull of French) actually means 'to speak French quite well'. Ultimately, it's often the context determining what's the real effect of the diminutive – a *nummer* nu·muhr is a 'number', but a *nummertje* nu·muhr·chuh is a 'short, lighthearted song or performance' or … 'sexual intercourse'. There's a set of rules governing the spelling of diminutive endings depending on the final sound of the base word, which you shouldn't worry about too much – if you see or hear the ending -*je* ·yuh (also often pronounced ·chuh) tucked onto the end of a word, you're looking at a *verkleinwoordje* vuhr·kleyn·wohr·chuh (ie little diminutive).

adjectives & adverbs

Dutch adjectives mostly come before the noun they describe and after the article, if one is present (see also **articles**). When they are placed before the noun, the ending -e is added to adjectives.

(the) good friend   *(de) goede vriend*   (duh) *khoo*·duh vreent
     (lit: (the) good friend)
(the) good hotel   *(het) goede hotel*   (huht) *khoo*·duh hoh·*tel*
     (lit: (the) good-neuter hotel-neuter)

The exception to this rule is when adjectives come before a neuter singular noun which has the indefinite article *een* uhn (a) in front of it. No -e ending is added in this case.

a good hotel   *een goed hotel*   uhn khoot hoh·*tel*
     (lit: a good-neuter hotel-neuter)

Adjectives can also come after the noun (eg when they're connected to the noun with 'is' or 'are'). When this is the case, no -e ending is added either.

The train is full.
   De trein is vol.   duh treyn is vol
   (lit: the train is full)

Adverbs are basically the same as adjectives in Dutch – the only difference is that you don't need to add an -e ending to adverbs. There's no equivalent to the English '-ly' ending. In Dutch, adverbs are generally placed after the verb they refer to. See also **verbs**.

The music's loud.
   De muziek is luid.   duh mew·*zeek* is löyt
   (lit: the music is loud)

He's talking loudly.
   Hij spreekt luid.   hey spreykt löyt
   (lit: he speaks loud)

articles

When you're referring to someone or something in particular, the definite article (the equivalent of 'the' in English) is used in Dutch. The definite article is *de* duh for common gender nouns and *het* huht for neuter nouns. When you're referring to plural definite nouns, the article *de* duh is used for both the common and neuter genders (see **gender** and **plurals**).

the train	*de trein*	duh treyn
the house	*het huis* n	huht höys
the trains	*de treinen*	duh trey·nuhn
the houses	*de huizen* n pl	duh höy·zuhn

The indefinite article (the same as English 'a') is *een* uhn for both genders. As in English, there's no plural form of the indefinite article – you just use the plural noun on its own.

| a train | *een trein* | uhn treyn |
| a house | *een huis* n | uhn höys |

be

describing people/things • making statements

As in many languages, the verb 'be' is quite irregular in Dutch. Here are the present and past tense forms of *zijn* zeyn (be):

zijn – present tense					
I	am	*ik*	*ben*	ik	ben
you sg inf	are	*jij*	*bent*	yey	bent
you sg pol	are	*u*	*bent*	ew	bent
he/she/it	is	*hij/zij/het*	*is*	hey/zey/huht	is
we	are	*wij*	*zijn*	wey	zeyn
you pl inf	are	*jullie*	*zijn*	yew·lee	zeyn
you pl pol	are	*u*	*bent*	ew	bent
they	are	*zij*	*zijn*	zey	zeyn

zijn – past tense					
I	was	ik	was	ik	was
you sg inf	were	jij	was	yey	was
you sg pol	were	u	was	ew	was
he/she/it	was	hij/zij/het	was	hey/zey/huht	was
we	were	wij	waren	wey	waa·ruhn
you pl inf	were	jullie	waren	yew·lee	waa·ruhn
you pl pol	were	u	was	ew	was
they	were	zij	waren	zey	waa·ruhn

demonstratives

giving instructions · indicating location · pointing things out

The Dutch words for 'this' and 'that' vary according to the gender of the noun that they precede – just like the definite articles. The plural demonstratives ('these' and 'those') are the same for both genders. See also **articles**, **gender** and **plurals**.

demonstratives			
m&f	this man/woman	*deze man/vrouw*	dey·zuh man/vraw
n	this house	*dit huis*	dit höys
pl	these houses	*deze huizen*	dey·zuh höy·zuhn
m&f	that man/woman	*die man/vrouw*	dee man/vraw
n	that house	*dat huis*	dat höys
pl	those houses	*die huizen*	dee höy·zuhn

gender

naming people/things

Dutch nouns have either masculine, feminine or neuter gender. The distinction is purely grammatical and not related to a noun's meaning. You need to learn the gender for each noun as you go, but you can recognise it by the definite article that's used with it: *de* duh for masculine and feminine gender and *het* huht for neuter gender.

The grammatical distinction between masculine and feminine is only relevant in archaic forms, so we've only indicated the neuter nouns with n in this phrasebook. Masculine and feminine nouns are known as 'common gender' and have been left unmarked in this phrasebook. There are some exceptions that have distinct masculine and feminine forms, for example for professions. Where this happens, we've marked them with m and f respectively. See also **adjectives & adverbs**, **articles** and **demonstratives**.

have

possessing

The present and past tense forms of *hebben he·buhn* (have) are given in the next two tables. The verb is used the same way as in English. For negative statements with 'have', see **negatives**.

hebben – present tense					
I	have	ik	heb	ik	hep
you sg inf	have	jij	hebt	yey	hept
you sg pol	have	u	heeft	ew	heyft
he/she/it	has	hij/zij/het	heeft	hey/zey/huht	heyft
we	have	wij	hebben	wey	he·buhn
you pl inf	have	jullie	hebben	yew·lee	he·buhn
you pl pol	have	u	heeft	ew	heyft
they	have	zij	hebben	zey	he·buhn

hebben – past tense					
I	had	ik	had	ik	hat
you sg inf	had	jij	had	yey	hat
you sg pol	had	u	had	ew	hat
he/she	had	hij/zij	had	hey/zey	hat
we	had	wij	hadden	wey	ha·duhn
you pl inf	had	jullie	hadden	yew·lee	ha·duhn
you pl pol	had	u	had	ew	hat
they	had	zij	hadden	zey	ha·duhn

negatives

In Dutch, negative statements are made by adding the word *niet* neet (not) to a sentence – note that it goes after the verb.

I understand.
Ik begrijp het.   ik buh·*khreyp* huht
(lit: I understand it)

I don't understand.
Ik begrijp het niet.   ik buh·*khreyp* huht neet
(lit: I understand it not)

The position of *niet* varies but it's often placed at the end of the phrase or just before the part of the phrase you're negating.

I'm not coming today.
Ik kom vandaag niet.   ik kom van·*daakh* neet
(lit: I come today not)

I'm not coming at four o'clock.
Ik kom niet om vier uur.   ik kom neet om veer ewr
(lit: I come not at four hour)

To make a negative expression that equates to 'I have no …' or 'There aren't any …', use *geen* kheyn (none) instead of *niet*.

I don't have any money.
Ik heb geen geld.   ik hep kheyn khelt
(lit: I have none money)

personal pronouns

Personal pronouns ('I', 'you', etc) have different forms in Dutch depending on whether they're the subject or the object in a sentence. It's the same in English, which has 'I' as the subject pronoun but 'me' as the object pronoun (eg 'I see her' and 'She sees me'). These are the Dutch subject pronouns:

subject pronouns					
I	*ik*	ik	**we**	*wij (we)*	wey (wuh)
you sg inf	*jij (je)*	yey (yuh)	**you** pl inf	*jullie*	*yew*·lee
you sg pol	*u*	ew	**you** pl pol	*u*	ew
he	*hij*	hey			
she	*zij (ze)*	zey (zuh)	**they**	*zij (ze)*	zey (zuh)
it	*het*	huht			

Often, the unemphatic forms (shown in brackets in the table above) are used. It's only when you particularly want to emphasise the subject that you use the emphatic forms.

She went to the museum.
> *Ze bezocht het*   zuh buh·*zokht* huht
> *museum.*   mew·*zey*·yum
> (lit: she-unemphatic visited the museum)

***She* went to the museum, but he didn't.**
> *Zij bezocht het*   zey buh·*zokht* huht
> *museum, maar hij niet.*   mew·*zey*·yum maar hey neet
> (lit: she-emphatic visited the museum, but he not)

The forms of the direct object pronouns are listed in the next table. The unemphatic forms are given in brackets.

direct object pronouns					
me	*mij (me)*	mey (muh)	**us**	*ons*	ons
you sg inf	*jou (je)*	yaw (yuh)	**you** pl inf	*jullie*	yew·lee
you sg pol	*u*	ew	**you** pl pol	*u*	ew
him	*hem**	hem		*hen (ze)*	hen (zuh)
her	*haar (ze)*	haar (zuh)	**them**		
it	*het**	huht			

*In spoken Dutch, you're likely to hear *hem* and *het* shortened to 'm and 't.

The indirect object pronouns are the same as the emphatic direct object pronouns in Dutch, as shown with the following examples.

I saw her.
  Ik zag haar.   ik zakh haar
  (lit: I saw her)

I gave the guidebook to her.
  Ik gaf de reisgids aan haar. ik khaf duh *reys*·khits aan haar
  (lit: I gave the guidebook to her)

I gave it to her.
  Ik gaf het haar.   ik khaf huht haar
  (lit: I gave it her)

As the previous tables show, Dutch has two forms for the English 'you'. The polite form *u* ew, which has the same form for singular and plural, is used when meeting people for the first time, people in a position of authority or people you don't know well. Note that *u* takes third-person singular verb forms. An informal 'you' is either *jij* yey for singular or *jullie* yew·lee for plural.

In this book, we've used the pronouns appropriate to the context – generally the informal 'you' – and we've indicated the alternative forms with **inf** and **pol** respectively where required. For more information, see the box **all about you** on page 109.

plurals

There are two main plural endings for nouns: *-en* (or just *-n* if the noun already ends in an *-e*) and *-s*. The *-(e)n* form is the more common one of the two. The *-s* ending is mainly used when nouns end in *-el*, *-er*, *-em* or *-en*.

	singular		**plural**	
train(s)	*trein*	treyn	*treinen*	*trey*·nuhn
hotel(s)	*hotel*	hoh·*tel*	*hotels*	hoh·*tels*

Some words of Latin origin follow the Latin pattern for plurals: eg *museum* mew·*zee*·yuhm becomes *musea* mew·*zey*·ya. Words ending in *-heid* ·heyt change that ending to *-heden* ·*hey*·duhn in the plural, eg *schoonheid* skhohn·heyt (beauty) becomes *schoonheden* skhohn·*hey*·duhn (beauties). Words ending in a long vowel written only once (with no accent on it) take the *'s* ·s in plural, eg *auto* aw·toh (car) becomes *auto's* aw·tohs.

possessives

In Dutch, possessive adjectives (words for 'my', 'your' etc) function just like their English equivalents, as shown below.

possessive adjectives					
my	*mijn (m'n)*	meyn (muhn)	**our**	*onze**	*on*·zuh
your sg inf	*jouw (je)*	yaw (yuh)	**your** pl inf	*jullie*	*yew*·lee
your sg pol	*uw*	ew	**your** pl pol	*uw*	ew
his	*zijn (z'n)*	zeyn (zuhn)	**their**	*hun*	hun
hers	*haar*	haar			

*onze becomes *ons* ons before neuter singular nouns. The unemphatic forms you might hear are given in brackets above.

That's my backpack.

Dat is mijn rugzak.   dat is meyn *rukh*·zak
(lit: that is my backpack)

To say 'mine', 'yours' etc, use the common or neuter gender forms from the following table (separated with a slash), depending on the gender of what you're referring to.

possessive pronouns					
mine	*de/het mijne*	duh/huht *mey*·nuh	**ours**	*de/het onze*	duh/huht *on*·zuh
yours sg inf	*de/het jouwe*	duh/huht *yaw*·wuh	**yours** pl inf	*die/dat van jullie*	dee/dat van *yew*·lee
yours sg pol	*de/het uwe*	duh/huht *ew*·wuh	**yours** pl pol	*de/het uwe*	duh/huht *ew*·wuh
his/ hers	*de/het zijne*	duh/huht *zey*·nuh	**theirs**	*de/het hunne*	duh/huht *hu*·nuh
hers	*de/het hare*	duh/huht *haa*·ruh			

Alternatively, you can use a demonstrative followed by the construction 'is/are' + *van* … + emphatic direct object pronoun (see **demonstratives** and **personal pronouns**).

This/That is mine.

Dit/Dat is van mij.   dit/dat is van mey
(lit: this/that is from me)

That backpack is mine.

Die rugzak is van mij.   dee *rukh*·zak is van mey
(lit: that backpack is from me)

prepositions

giving instructions • indicating location • pointing things out

Like English, Dutch uses prepositions to explain where things are in time or space. Common Dutch prepositions are listed on the next page with their approximate English equivalents.

prepositions					
after	*na*	naa	in (time)	*over*	in
before	*voor*	vohr	since	*sinds*	sins
in (place)	*in*	in	until	*tot*	tot

questions

asking questions • negating

Forming yes/no questions is quite simple in Dutch – just swap the order of the verb and the pronoun in the statement.

She took a photo.
  Zij nam een foto.   zey nam uhn *foh*·toh
  (lit: she took a photo)

Did she take a photo?
  Nam zij een foto?   nam zey uhn *foh*·toh
  (lit: took she a photo)

Note also that when the word order is reversed, the ending 't' is dropped from the singular informal 'you' form (*jij* yey). As in English, there are also question words for more specific questions. These words go at the start of the sentence.

question words					
How?	*Hoe?*	hoo	Where?	*Waar?*	waar
What?	*Wat?*	wat	Who?	*Wie?*	wee
When?	*Wanneer?*	wa·*neyr*	Why?	*Waarom?*	waa·*rom*

verbs

doing things

Dutch verbs mostly follow regular patterns. The infinitive (ie the dictionary form of a verb) usually ends in *-en* or *-n*. To form different tenses, you remove these infinitive endings to get the verb stem and then add a regular series of endings.

present tense

The present tense is formed by adding either *-t* or *-en* to the verb stem, as shown in the table below. There might be some changes in the verb stem due to Dutch spelling rules related to vowel length, but you'll still be understood even if you don't get it exactly right. Here are the present tense forms of the verb *danken* dang·kuhn (thank).

danken – present tense					
I	thank	*ik*	*dank*	ik	dangk
you sg inf	thank	*jij*	*dankt* *	yey	dangkt
you sg pol	thank	*u*	*dankt*	ew	dangkt
he/she	thanks	*hij/zij*	*dankt*	hey/zey	dangkt
we	thank	*wij*	*danken*	wey	*dang·kuhn*
you pl inf	thank	*jullie*	*danken*	yew·lee	*dang·kuhn*
you pl pol	thank	*u*	*dankt*	ew	dangkt
they	thank	*zij*	*danken*	zey	*dang·kuhn*

* When word order is reversed (eg in questions), the ending 't' is dropped from the singular informal 'you' form (*jij* yey).

past tense

Dutch verbs can be 'strong' or 'weak' and form their past tense according to which group they belong to. Unlike weak verbs, strong verbs have a vowel change in the verb stem in the past tense (like 'begin' becomes 'began/begun' in English). The past tense endings are then added to the strong verb stem, as shown in the table on the following page for the verb *vragen* vraa·khuhn (ask).

For space reasons we can't include the past tense stems of strong verbs in this chapter, but you could try getting hold of a book on Dutch verbs such as *201 Dutch verbs* by Henry Stern (Barron's Educational Series 1980) as a useful reference.

vragen – past tense					
I	asked	*ik*	*vroeg*	ik	vrookh
you sg inf	asked	*jij*	*vroeg*	yey	vrookh
you sg pol	asked	*u*	*vroeg*	ew	vrookh
he/she	asked	*hij/zij*	*vroeg*	hey/zey	vrookh
we	asked	*wij*	*vroegen*	wey	*vroo*·khuhn
you pl inf	asked	*jullie*	*vroegen*	yew·lee	*vroo*·khuhn
you pl pol	asked	*u*	*vroeg*	ew	vrookh
they	asked	*zij*	*vroegen*	zey	*vroo*·khuhn

As shown in the next table with the verb *reizen* rey·zuhn (travel), weak verbs simply add an ending to form the past tense, with no change in the verb stem (like 'jump' becomes 'jumped' in English). The ending for most verbs is *-de(n)*, but if a verb stem ends in *ch, f, k, p, s* or *t*, the endings are *-te* and *-ten* instead.

reizen – past tense					
I	travelled	*ik*	*reisde*	ik	*reys*·duh
you sg inf	travelled	*jij*	*reisde*	yey	*reys*·duh
you sg pol	travelled	*u*	*reisde*	ew	*reys*·duh
he/she	travelled	*hij/zij*	*reisde*	hey/zey	*reys*·duh
we	travelled	*wij*	*reisden*	wey	*reys*·duhn
you pl inf	travelled	*jullie*	*reisden*	yew·lee	*reys*·duhn
you pl pol	travelled	*u*	*reisde*	ew	*reys*·duh
they	travelled	*zij*	*reisden*	zey	*reys*·duhn

future tense

The future tense in Dutch is easy – it works the same as in English. To form the future tense, you simply combine the auxiliary verb *zullen* zu·luhn (will) with the infinitive of the main verb, just like you use 'will + infinitive' in English (eg 'I will go'). The forms of *zullen* are given in the table below. If it's clear you're speaking about the future or if you use an expression of time, you can just use the present tense.

I'll visit Maastricht.
   Ik zal Maastricht bezoeken.   ik zal maas·*trikht* buh·*zoo*·kuhn
   (lit: I will Maastricht to-visit)

I'll return soon.
   Ik kom gauw terug.   ik kom khaw tuh·*rukh*
   (lit: I come soon back)

zullen (will)					
I will	*ik zal*	ik zal	**we will**	*wij zullen*	wey zu·luhn
you will sg inf	*jij zult/ zal* *	yey zult/ zal	**you will** pl inf	*jullie zullen*	*yew*·lee zu·luhn
you will sg pol	*u zult*	u zult	**you will** pl pol	*u zuit*	ew zult
he will	*hij zal*	hey zal	**they will**	*zij zullen*	zey zu·luhn
she will	*zij zal*	zey zal			

* both forms are correct

word order

making statements

The word order in Dutch in simple sentences is the same as in English: subject–verb–object.

She sent an email.
   Zij stuurde een email.   zey *stewr*·duh uhn *ee*·meyl
   (lit: she sent an email)

See also **negatives** and **questions**.

glossary

adjective	a word that describes something – 'his bike had **faulty** brakes'
adverb	a word that explains how an action is done – 'the mechanic changed the wheel **quickly**'
article	the words 'a', 'an' and 'the'
auxiliary verb	a *verb* used with another verb to indicate tense – 'he **will** win'
demonstrative	a word that means 'this' or 'that'
direct object	the thing or person in the sentence that has the action directed to it – 'he won **the race**'
gender	classification of *nouns* into classes (like masculine, feminine and neuter), requiring other words (eg *adjectives*) to belong to the same class
indirect object	the person or thing in the sentence that is the recipient of the action – 'they gave **him** a drug test'
infinitive	dictionary form of a *verb* – '**to fix** a flat tyre'
noun	a thing, person or idea – 'the big **chainring**'
number	whether a word is singular or plural – 'the **peloton** caught the **breakaways**'
personal pronoun	a word that means 'I', 'you' etc
possessive adjective	a word that means 'my', 'your' etc
possessive pronoun	a word that means 'mine', 'yours' etc
preposition	a word like 'for' or 'before' in English
subject	the thing or person in the sentence that does the action – 'his **chain** snapped'
tense	form of a *verb* that tells you whether the action is in the present, past or future – eg 'ride' (present), 'rode' (past), 'will ride' (future)
verb	a word that tells you what action happened – 'he **attacked** the peloton'
verb stem	part of a *verb* that doesn't change – eg '**cycl**e' in '**cycl**ing' and '**cycl**ed'

language difficulties
taalproblemen

Do you speak (English)?
Spreekt u (Engels)? pol — spreykt ew (*eng*·uhls)

Does anyone speak (English)?
Is er hier iemand die — is uhr heer *ee*·mant dee
(Engels) spreekt? — (*eng*·uhls) spreykt

Do you understand (me)?
Begrijpt u (mij)? pol — buh·*khreypt* ew (mey)

I (don't) understand.
Ik begrijp het (niet). — ik buh·*khreyp* huht (neet)

I speak (English).
Ik spreek (Engels). — ik spreyk (*eng*·uhls)

I don't speak (Dutch).
Ik spreek geen (Nederlands). — ik spreyk kheyn (*ney*·duhr·lants)

I speak a little.
Ik spreek het een beetje. — ik spreyk huht uhn *bey*·chuh

What does (dag) mean?
Wat betekent (dag)? — wat buh·*tey*·kuhnt (dakh)

I'd like to practise (Dutch).
Ik wil graag mijn — ik wil khraakh meyn
(Nederlands) wat — (*ney*·duhr·lants) wat
oefenen. — *oo*·fuh·nuhn

Let's speak (Dutch).
Laat ons (Nederlands) — laat ons (*ney*·duhr·lants)
spreken. — *sprey*·kuhn

Could you please speak more slowly?
Kunt u alstublieft wat — kunt ew al·stew·*bleeft* wat
langzamer spreken? pol — *lang*·zaa·muhr *sprey*·kuhn

Could you
please ...? — *Kunt u dat* — kunt ew dat
— *alstublieft ...?* pol — al·stew·*bleeft* ...
  repeat that — *herhalen* — her·*haa*·luhn
  write it down — *opschrijven* — op·*skhrey*·vuhn

How do you …?	Hoe …?	hoo …
pronounce this	*spreek je dit uit*	spreyk yuh dit öyt
write	*schrijf je*	skhreyf yuh
(*dank u wel*)	(*dank u wel*)	(dangk ew wel)

tongue twisters

De knappe kapper knipt en kapt knap, maar de knappe knecht van de knappe kapper knipt en kapt nog knapper dan de knappe kapper knipt en kapt.

duh *kna·*puh *ka·*puhr knipt en kapt knap, maar duh *kna·*puh knekht van duh *kna·*puh *ka·*puhr knipt en kapt nokh *kna·*puhr dan duh *kna·*puh *ka·*puhr knipt en kapt

(The handsome hairdresser cuts and chops beautifully, but the handsome helper of the handsome hairdresser cuts and chops even more beautifully than the handsome hairdresser cuts and chops.)

Frans zei in het Frans tegen Frans dat Frans in het Frans Frans wordt geschreven, nee zei Frans in het Frans tegen Frans, Frans wordt in het Frans niet Frans geschreven, Frans wordt in het Frans François geschreven.

frans zey in huht frans *tey·*khuhn frans dat frans in huht frans frans wort khuh·*skhrey·*vuhn ney zey frans in huht frans *tey·*khun frans frans wort in huht frans neet frans khuh·*skhrey·*vuhn frans wort in huht frans fran·*swa* khuh·*skhrey·*vuhn

(Frans said to Frans in French that Frans in French is written as Frans, no said Frans in French to Frans, Frans is not written as Frans in French, Frans is written as François in French.)

Zeven Zwevegemse zotten zwommen zeven zondagen zonder zwembroek, ze zeiden, ze zijn zeker zot zonder zwembroek zwemmen.

*zey·*vuhn *zwey·*vuh·khem·suh zo·tuhn *zwo·*muhn *zey·*vuhn zon·daa·khuhn *zon·*duhr *zwem·*brook zuh *zey·*duhn zuh zeyn *zey·*kuhr zot *zon·*duhr *zwem·*brook *zwe·*muhn

(Seven fools from Zwevegem went swimming seven Sundays without bathers, they said, they must be crazy to go swimming without bathers.)

numbers & amounts

cardinal numbers

		hoofdtelwoorden
0	*nul*	nul
1	*één*	eyn
2	*twee*	twey
3	*drie*	dree
4	*vier*	veer
5	*vijf*	veyf
6	*zes*	zes
7	*zeven*	*zey*·vuhn
8	*acht*	akht
9	*negen*	*ney*·khuhn
10	*tien*	teen
11	*elf*	elf
12	*twaalf*	twaalf
13	*dertien*	*der*·teen
14	*veertien*	*veyr*·teen
15	*vijftien*	*veyf*·teen
16	*zestien*	*zes*·teen
17	*zeventien*	*zey*·vuhn·teen
18	*achttien*	*akh*·teen
19	*negentien*	*ney*·khuhn·teen
20	*twintig*	*twin*·tikh
21	*eenentwintig*	*eyn*·en·*twin*·tikh
22	*tweeëntwintig*	*twey*·en·*twin*·tikh
30	*dertig*	*der*·tikh
40	*veertig*	*feyr*·tikh
50	*vijftig*	*feyf*·tikh
60	*zestig*	*ses*·tikh
70	*zeventig*	*sey*·vuhn·tikh
80	*tachtig*	*takh*·tikh
90	*negentig*	*ney*·khuhn·tikh

100	honderd	hon·duhrt
200	tweehonderd	twey·hon·duhrt
1000	duizend	döy·zuhnt
1,000,000	een miljoen	uhn mil·yoon

ordinal numbers

To form the ordinal number, add *-de* ·duh to the cardinal number, except for *eerste/1ste* (first) and *derde/3de* (third), which are irregular. Also, *achtste/8ste* (eight) and multiples of 10 use the ending *-ste* ·stuh instead of *-de*, eg *twintigste/20ste* (twentieth) and *honderdste/100ste* (hundredth). Note that ordinal numbers can be used in dates – eg *7de/zevende april* (7 April).

1st	eerste/1ste	eyr·stuh
2nd	tweede/2de	twey·duh
3rd	derde/3de	der·duh
4th	vierde/4de	veer·duh
5th	vijfde/5de	veyf·duh

fractions & decimals

a quarter	een kwart	uhn kwart
a third	een derde	uhn der·duh
a half	een half	uhn half
(of a number)		
three and a half	drie en half	dree en half
a half	een helft	uhn helft
(of something)		
a half of the cake	een helft van de cake	uhn helft van duh keek
three-quarters	drie vierde	dree veer·duh
all	alle	a·luh
none	geen	kheyn

Decimals are written – and pronounced – with a comma, not a dot as in English.

three point fourteen (3.14)	*drie comma veertien (3,14)*	dree ko·ma veyr·teen
four point two (4.2)	*vier comma twee (4,2)*	veer ko·ma twey
five point one (5.1)	*vijf comma één (5,1)*	veyf ko·ma eyn

useful amounts

handige hoeveelheden

How much/many?	*Hoeveel?*	hoo·veyl
Please give me ...	*Ik wil graag ...*	ik wil khraakh ...
(100) grams	*(honderd) gram*	(hon·duhrt) khram
half a dozen	*een half dozijn*	uhn half do·zeyn
half a kilo	*een halve kilo*	uhn hal·vuh kee·loh
a kilo	*een kilo*	uhn kee·loh
a bottle	*een fles*	uhn fles
a jar	*een pot* ⑩	uhn pot
	een bokaal ⑬	uhn boh·kaal
a packet	*een pak*	uhn pak
a piece	*een stuk*	uhn stuk
(three) pieces	*(drie) stuks*	(dree) stuks
a slice	*een plak/snee* ⑩/⑬	uhn plak/sney
(six) slices	*(zes) plakken* ⑩	(zes) pla·kuhn
	(zes) sneetjes ⑬	(zes) sney·chuhs
a tin	*een blik*	uhn blik
a few	*enkele*	eng·kuh·luh
less	*minder*	min·duhr
(just) a little	*een (klein)*	uhn (kleyn)
	beetje	bey·chuh
a lot	*veel*	veyl
many	*vele*	vey·luh
more	*meer*	meyr
some	*enkele*	eng·kuh·luh

For more amounts, see **self-catering**, page 177.

frisian

If you thought it was only Belgium that had a complex linguistic situation – with Dutch, French and German as its three official languages – you're mistaken. The Netherlands, too, has a second language in addition to Dutch – Frisian (called *Fries* frees in Dutch and *Frysk* freesk in Frisian itself) has official status in the northern Dutch province of Friesland. In 1997 the spelling of the province's name was officially altered from the Dutch *Friesland* frees·lant to *Fryslân* frees·lan, the local version of the name. There are about 700,000 speakers of Frisian – around 400,000 live in Friesland, while the rest live mostly in Germany. The language spoken in Friesland is, more precisely, West Frisian, with closely related East Frisian and North Frisian spoken in Germany – but it's simply referred to as 'Frisian' in the Netherlands.

Frisian is a member of the West Germanic family of languages and is historically the closest relative of English (there's even an old saying that goes 'as milk is to cheese, are English and Freese'). It developed from Old Frisian, spoken in the Middle Ages along the North Sea coast from Belgium to Germany. Over the centuries, however, Old Frisian and Old English drifted apart considerably, so that a modern-day English speaker won't be able to make much sense of Frisian – just like the Dutch have difficulty understanding it. The majority of Frisians, on the other hand, are perfectly conversant in standard Dutch. You're actually more likely to hear Frisian coming from older people than the younger generation, but most of the locals know some as a sign of cultural pride. In Friesland, Frisian is used alongside Dutch in the media, public administration, in the courts and in education (either taught as a compulsory subject or used as the medium of instruction in schools). Most native speakers of Frisian live in the rural areas.

You'll usually see written examples of Frisian, such as place names and street signs. Here are the most important place names in Friesland, given in both languages:

Frisian	Dutch
Frjentsjer	*Franeker*
Harns	*Harlingen*
Hylpen	*Hindeloopen*
Ljouwert	*Leeuwarden*
Snits	*Sneek*

telling the time

In everyday language, the 12-hour clock is used. You'll only see the 24-hour clock on train and bus timetables. The terms 'am' and 'pm' are not used as such in Dutch – the time of day is specified using one of the expressions below, such as *'s avonds saa·vonts* (in the evening).

What time is it?	*Hoe laat is het?*	hoo laat is huht
It's (10) o'clock.	*Het is (tien) uur.*	huht is (teen) ewr
Five past (10).	*Vijf over (tien).*	veyf (ch·vuhr) teen
Quarter past (10).	*Kwart over (tien).*	kwart (oh·vuhr) teen
Half past (10).	*Half (elf).*	half (elf)
	(lit: half eleven)	
Quarter to (11).	*Kwart voor (elf).*	kwart vohr (elf)
Twenty to (11).	*Tien over half (elf).*	teen oh·ver half (elf)
	(lit: ten past half eleven)	
Ten to (11).	*Tien voor (elf).*	teen vohr (elf)
am (night)	*'s nachts*	snakhts
am (morning)	*'s ochtends*	sokh·tuhns
pm (afternoon)	*'s middags*	smi·dakhs
pm (evening)	*'s avonds*	saa·vonts
At what time ...?	*Hoe laat ...?*	hoo laat ...
At (five).	*Om (vijf uur).*	om (veyf ewr)

At (7.57pm). (in everyday speech)

Om (drie voor acht   om (dree vohr akht
's avonds)./Om (7.57).   saa·vonts)
(lit: at three to eight in-the-evening)

At (7.57pm). (in timetables)

Om (negentien uur   om (ney·khuhn·teen ewr
zevenenvijftig)./Om (19.57).   zey·vuhn·en·feyf·tikh)
(lit: at nineteen hour fifty-seven)

time & dates

37

the calendar

days of the week

Monday	*maandag*	*maan*·dakh
Tuesday	*dinsdag*	*dins*·dakh
Wednesday	*woensdag*	*woons*·dakh
Thursday	*donderdag*	*don*·duhr·dakh
Friday	*vrijdag*	*vrey*·dakh
Saturday	*zaterdag*	*zaa*·tuhr·dakh
Sunday	*zondag*	*zon*·dakh

months

January	*januari*	*ya*·new·waa·ree
February	*februari*	*fey*·brew·waa·ree
March	*maart*	maart
April	*april*	a·*pril*
May	*mei*	mey
June	*juni*	*yew*·nee
July	*juli*	*yew*·lee
August	*augustus*	aw·*khus*·tus
September	*september*	sep·*tem*·buhr
October	*oktober*	ok·*toh*·buhr
November	*november*	noh·*vem*·buhr
December	*december*	dey·*sem*·buhr

dates

What date is it today?
   De hoeveelste is het   duh hoo·*veyl*·stuh is huht
   vandaag?   van·*daakh*

It's (7 April).
   Het is de (zevende april).   huht is duh (*zey*·vuhn·duh a·*pril*)

seasons

spring	lente	len·tuh
summer	zomer	zoh·muhr
autumn/fall	herfst	herfst
winter	winter	win·tuhr

and the fifth season is ...

When hell freezes over. (ie never)

Als Pasen en Pinksteren als *paa*·suhn en *pink*·stuh·ruhn
op één dag vallen. op eyn dakh *va*·luhn
(lit: when Easter and Pentecost fall on the same day)

present

het heden

now	nu	new
today	vandaag	van·*daakh*
this morning	vanochtend	van·*okh*·tuhnt
this afternoon	vanmiddag	van·*mi*·dakh
tonight	vanavond	va·*naa*·vont
this week	deze week	*dey*·zuh weyk
this month	deze maand	*dey*·zuh maant
this year	dit jaar	dit yaar

past

het verleden

yesterday	gisteren	*khis*·tuh·ruhn
day before yesterday	eergisteren	eyr·*khis*·tuh·ruhn
(three days) ago	(drie dagen) geleden	(dree *daa*·khuhn) khuh·*ley*·duhn
since (May)	sinds (mei)	sins (mey)

last ...		
night	*gisteravond*	khis·tuhr·*aa*·vont
week	*vorige week*	*voh*·ri·khuh weyk
month	*vorige maand*	*voh*·ri·khuh maant
year	*vorig jaar*	*voh*·rikh yaar

yesterday ...		
morning	*gisterochtend*	khis·tuhr·*okh*·tuhnt
afternoon	*gistermiddag*	khis·tuhr·*mi*·dakh
evening	*gisteravond*	khis·tuhr·*aa*·vont

future

de toekomst

tomorrow	*morgen*	*mor*·khuhn
day after tomorrow	*overmorgen*	*oh*·vuhr·mor·khuhn
in (six days)	*over (zes dagen)*	*oh*·vuhr (zes *daa*·khuhn)
until (June)	*tot (juni)*	tot (*yew*·nee)
next year	*volgend jaar*	*vol*·khuhnt yaar

next ...	*volgende ...*	*vol*·khuhn·duh ...
week	*week*	weyk
month	*maand*	maant

tomorrow ...		
morning	*morgenochtend*	mor·khuhn·*okh*·tuhnt
afternoon	*morgenmiddag*	mor·khuhn·*mi*·dakh
evening	*morgenavond*	mor·khuhn·*aa*·vont

during the day

gedurende de dag

Note that in Flanders you may also hear *namiddag* used for 'afternoon', to distinguish it from *middag* (noon), and *morgen* as an alternative for *ochtend* (morning).

afternoon	*middag* Ⓝ	*mi·*dakh
	namiddag Ⓑ	*naa·*mi·dakh
dawn	*dageraad*	*daa·*khuh·raat
day	*dag*	dakh
evening	*avond*	*aa·*vont
midday/noon	*middag*	*mi·*dakh
midnight	*middernacht*	mi·duhr·*nakht*
morning	*ochtend* Ⓝ	*okh·*tuhnt
	morgen Ⓑ	*mor·*khuhn
night	*nacht*	nakht
sunrise	*zonsopgang*	zons·*op·*gang
sunset	*zonsondergang*	zons·*on·*duhr·gang

Festival of the Flemish Community
    Feest van de Vlaamse   feyst van duh *vlaam·*suh
    Gemeenschap Ⓑ   khuh·*meyn·*skhap

On 11 July, the Flemish commemorate the *Guldensporenslag* *khul·duhn·spoh·*ruhn·slakh (Battle of the Gilded Spurs) of 1302, when they beat their French rulers and asserted their cultural and political independence – at least for a while. They've picked that day as their 'Flemish National Day'. The Francophone Walloons celebrate on 27 September, while the small German-speaking community lets their hair down on 15 November.

National Day
    Nationale Feestdag Ⓑ   na·syoh·*naa·*luh *feys·*dakh

The Flemish and the Walloons each have their own language, culture and government, but on 21 July everyone – well, nearly everyone – considers themselves a Belgian in the first place, if only to enjoy the extra day off! A big annual *militaire optocht* mee·lee·*tey·*ruh *op·*tokht (military parade) – also commonly known as *défilé* dey·fee·*ley* – is held in Brussels in front of the Royal Palace and is overseen by the Royal Family, who is an important symbol of unity. The date goes back to 21 July 1830, when Belgium was declared independent from France after yet another uprising and when the present-day kingdom was founded.

Queen's Day

Koninginnedag Ⓝ   koh·ning·*khi*·nuh·dakh

In the Netherlands, everyone gets a holiday on the Queen's birthday (30 April). Funnily enough, 30 April isn't the current Queen's birthday – when she assumed the throne in 1980, Queen Beatrix stated that she wished to keep celebrating *Koninginnedag* on 30 April, the birthday of her mother, Queen Juliana. The day is marked by street parties and festivities all around the country and almost everyone wears *oranje* oh·*ran*·yuh (orange), the colour that stands for national pride and refers to the Royal Family's name – *Oranje-Nassau* oh·*ran*·yuh na·saw. Every year, the Queen and her family attend a few festivities in person and these visits are always broadcast on television.

Prince's Day

Prinsjesdag Ⓝ   prin·shus·dakh

Every third Tuesday in September, the opening of the Dutch parliamentary year is marked by a speech given by the Queen – but written by the Prime Minister and his cabinet – to the *Staten-Generaal staa*·tuhn khey·ney·*raal* (the Dutch parliament). The Queen travels from her residence to the Binnenhof *bi*·nuhn·hof (lit: inner courtyard) – the location of the parliament sessions – and back in the *Gouden Koets khaw*·duhn koots (Gilded Carriage), cheered on by people lining the streets. Back at the palace, she salutes the crowd from the balcony. The same day, the Minister of Finance proposes the budget, which is carried in a special suitcase marked with the words *Derde Dinsdag van September der*·duh *dins*·dakh van sep·*tem*·buhr (Third Tuesday of September).

How much is it?
Hoeveel kost het? hoo·*veyl* kost huht

Can you write down the price?
Kunt u de prijs kunt ew duh preys
opschrijven? pol *op*·skhrey·vuhn

Do I have to pay?
Moet ik betalen? moot ik buh·*taa*·luhn

I'd like to return this, please.
Ik wil dit graag ik wil dit khraakh
retourneren. re·*toor*·*ney*·ruhn

I'd like …,	*Ik wil graag …*	ik wil khraakh …
please.		
my change	*mijn wisselgeld*	meyn *wi*·suhl·khelt
a receipt	*een kwitantie*	uhn kwee·*tan*·see
a refund	*mijn geld terug*	meyn khelt tuh·*rukh*

I'd like to …	*Ik wil graag …*	ik wil khraakh …
arrange a	*een giro-*	uhn *khee*·roh·
transfer	*betaling*	buh·taa·ling
	maken Ⓝ	*maa*·kuhn
	een over-	uhn *oh*·vuhr·
	schrijving doen Ⓑ	skhrey·ving doon
cash a cheque	*een cheque innen*	uhn shek *i*·nuhn
change a	*een reischeque*	uhn *reys*·shek
travellers	*innen*	*i*·nuhn
cheque		
change money	*geld wisselen*	khelt *wi*·suh·luhn
get a cash	*een voorschot*	uhn *vohr*·skhot
advance	*bekomen*	buh·*koh*·muhn
get change	*dit biljet wisselen*	dit bil·*yet wi*·suh·luhn
for this note	*in muntstukken*	in *munt*·stu·kuhn
withdraw	*geld afhalen*	khelt *af*·haa·luhn
money		

Do you accept ...?	Accepteert u ...? pol	ak·sep·teyrt ew ...
credit cards	kredietkaarten	krey·deet·kaar·tuhn
debit cards	debetkaarten	dey·bet·kaar·tuhn
travellers cheques	reischeques	reys·sheks

Where's ...?	Waar vind ik een ...?	waar vint ik uhn ...
an automated teller machine	pin-automaat Ⓝ geldautomaat Ⓑ	pin·aw·toh·maat khelt·aw·toh·maat
a foreign exchange office	wisselkantoor	wi·suhl·kan·tohr

What's the ...?	Wat is de ...?	wat is duh ...
charge	kost hiervoor	kost heer·vohr
exchange rate	wisselkoers	wi·suhl·koors

It's ...	Het is ...	huht is ...
free	gratis	khraa·tis
(12) euros	(twaalf) euro	(twaalf) eu·roh

How much is it per ...?	Hoeveel kost het per ...?	hoo·veyl kost huht puhr ...
caravan	caravan	ke·ruh·ven Ⓝ ka·ra·van Ⓑ
day	dag	dakh
game	spel	spel
hour	uur	ewr
(five) minutes	(vijf) minuten	(veyf) mee·new·tuhn
night	nacht	nakht
page	pagina	paa·khee·na
person	persoon	puhr·sohn
tent	tent	tent
vehicle	wagen	waa·khuhn
week	week	weyk

For more money-related phrases, see **banking**, page 89.

getting around

rondreizen

Note that in Belgium, the word *premetro* is used to refer to a metro line that's still part of the tram network.

Which … goes to (Amsterdam)?	Welke … gaat naar (Amsterdam)?	wel·kuh … khaat naar (am·stuhr·dam)
boat	boot	boht
bus	bus	bus
train	trein	treyn

Is this the … to (the left bank)?	Is dit de … naar (de linkeroever)?	is dit duh … naar (duh ling·kuhr·oo·vuhr)
ferry	veerboot Ⓝ	veyr·boht
	ferry Ⓑ	fe·ree
metro	metro	mey·troh
premetro	premetro	prey·mey·troh
tram	tram	trem/tram Ⓝ/Ⓑ

When's the … (bus)?	Hoe laat gaat de … (bus)?	hoo laat khaat duh … (bus)
first	eerste	eyr·stuh
last	laatste	laat·stuh
next	volgende	vol·khun·duh

What time does it leave?
Hoe laat vertrekt het?   hoo laat vuhr·*trekt* huht

What time does it get to (Gouda)?
Hoe laat komt het aan in (Gouda)?   hoo laat komt huht aan in (*khow*·da)

How long will it be delayed?
Hoeveel vertraging is er?   hoo·*veyl* vuhr·*traa*·khing is uhr

Is this seat available?
Is deze zitplaats vrij?   is *dey*·zuh *zit*·plaats vrey

That's my seat.
Dat is mijn zitplaats.   dat is meyn *zit*·plaats

Please stop here.
Stop hier alstublieft. pol   stop heer al·stew·*bleeft*

How long do we stop here?
Hoelang houden we   hoo·*lang* haw·duhn wuh
hier halt?   heer halt

tickets

The word *kaartje* is the one that's most commonly used to indicate transport tickets, but you may also hear *ticket* (pronounced as in English, *ti*·kuht, or ti·*ket* in Belgium), *biljet* bil·*yet* and *vervoerbewijs* vuhr·*voor*·buh·weys.

Where do I buy a ticket/strip card?
Waar kan ik een kaartje/   waar kan uhn *kaar*·chuh/
strippenkaart kopen?   stri·puhn·kaart *koh*·puhn

Do I need to book (well in advance)?
Moet ik (lang op voorhand)   moot ik (lang op *vohr*·hant)
reserveren?   rey·ser·*vey*·ruhn

Can I get a sleeping berth?
Kan ik een slaapplaats   kan ik uhn *slaa*·plaats
hebben?   *he*·buhn

I'd like a ticket for my bike/dog.
Ik wil een kaartje voor   ik wil uhn *kaar*·chuh vohr
mijn fiets/hond kopen.   meyn feets/hont *koh*·puhn

I'd like a Train+Bike ticket.
Ik wil graag een   ik wil khraakh uhn
Trein+Fiets ticket. ®   treyn plus feets ti·*ket*

Can I pick up a rental bike at the (Leeuwarden) train station, please?
Kan ik een huurfiets   kan ik uhn *hewr*·feets
oppikken in het station   o·pi·kuhn in huht sta·*syon*
van (Leeuwarden)   van (*ley*·war·duhn)
alstublieft? pol   al·stew·*bleeft*

The local rail systems in the Low Countries can take you quickly to just about anywhere. A vast array of discount passes, multi-travel deals, weekend fares, seasonal specials, specific trip offers combining train travel with admission to attractions or events, and other lower-cost options are on offer. Not all options are available everywhere all the time, so always inquire about the cheapest option for your trip:

What's the cheapest way of travelling to (The Hague)?
Wat is de goedkoopste manier om naar (Den Haag) te reizen?
wat is duh khoot·kohp·stuh ma·neer om naar (duhn haakh) tuh rey·zuhn

Is there a special ticket deal for …?	Is er een speciaal kaartje voor …?	is uhr uhn spey·syaal kaar·chuh vohr …
a day trip to (the coast)	een dagtrip naar (de kust)	uhn dakh·trip naar (duh kust)
the (Van Gogh) exhibition	de (Van Gogh) tentoonstelling	duh (van khokh) tuhn·tohn·ste·ling
families	families	fa·mee·lees
groups	groepen	khroo·puhn
a weekend trip to (Brussels)	een weekendtrip naar (Brussel)	uhn wey·kent·trip naar (bru·suhl)
the zoo	de dierentuin	duh dee·ruhn·töyn
A … ticket (to Maastricht).	Een … (naar Maastricht) graag.	uhn … (naar maas·trikht) khraakh
one-way	enkele reis	eng·kuh·luh reys
return	retourtje ⓝ	ruh·toor·chuh
	heen- en terugreis ⓑ	heyn·en· tuh·rukh·reys
A … ticket (to Bruges).	Een … kaartje (naar Brugge) graag.	uhn … kaar·chuh (naar bru·khuh) khraakh
1st-class	eerste klas	eyr·stuh klas
2nd-class	tweede klas	twey·duh klas
A … ticket (to Sneek).	Een kaartje voor … (naar Sneek) graag.	uhn kaar·chuh vohr … (naar sneyk) khraakh
child's	een kind	uhn kint
seniors'	senioren	sey·nyoh·ruhn
student	een student	uhn stew·dent

I'd like a/an … seat.	Ik wil graag een zitplaats …	ik wil khraakh uhn zit·plaats …
aisle	bij het gangpad	bey huht khang·pat
nonsmoking	voor niet-rokers	vohr neet·roh·kuhrs
smoking	voor rokers	vohr roh·kuhrs
window	bij het raam	bey huht raam
Is there …?	Is er … aan boord?	is uhr … aan bohrt
air conditioning	airconditioning	eyr·kon·di·shuh·ning
a toilet	een toilet	uhn twa·let

How much is it?
Hoeveel kost het?   hoo·veyl kost huht

How long does the trip take?
Hoe lang duurt de reis?   hoo lang dewrt duh reys

Is it a direct route?
Is het een rechtstreekse verbinding?   is huht uhn rekh·streyk·suh vuhr·bin·ding

What time should I check in?
Hoe laat moet ik inchecken?   hoo laat moot ik in·she·kuhn

I'd like to … my ticket, please.	Ik wil graag mijn kaartje …	ik wil khraakh meyn kaar·chuh …
cancel	annuleren	a·new·ley·ruhn
change	wijzigen	wey·zi·khuhn
collect	afhalen	af·haa·luhn
confirm	bevestigen	buh·ves·ti·khuhn

---

listen for …

deze/die	dey·zuh/dee	this/that one
dienstregeling	deenst·rey·khuh·ling	timetable
geannuleerd	khuh·a·new·leyrt	cancelled
loket n	lo·ket	ticket window
perron n	pe·ron	platform
reisagent	reys·a·khent	travel agent
staking	staa·king	strike n
vertraagd	vuhr·traakht	delayed
vol	vol	full

luggage

bagage

Where can I find a/the ...?	*Waar vind ik ...?*	waar vint ik ...
baggage belt	*de bagage-band*	duh ba-*khaa*-zhuh-bant
baggage claim	*het bagage inleverpunt*	huht ba-*khaa*-zhuh in-ley-vuhr-punt
left-luggage office	*de bagage-depot*	duh ba-*khaa*-zhuh-dey-*poh*
luggage locker	*de bagage-kluizen*	duh ba-*khaa*-zhuh-*klöy*-zuhn
porter service	*de kruiersservice*	duh *kröy*-yuhr-seur-vis
trolley	*een bagage-wagentje*	uhn ba-*khaa*-zhuh-*waa*-khuhn-chuh
My luggage has been ...	*Mijn bagage is ...*	meyn ba-*khaa*-zhuh is ...
damaged	*beschadigd*	buh-*skhaa*-dikht
lost	*verloren*	vuhr-*loh*-ruhn
stolen	*gestolen*	khuh-*stoh*-luhn

Can I have some coins/tokens?
Ik wil graag enkele muntstukken/jetons.
ik wil khraakh *eng*-kuh-luh munt-stu-kuhn/zhuh-*tons*

backpack	*rugzak*	*rukh*-zak
bag	*tas*	tas
box	*doos*	dohs
cosmetic bag	*toiletzak*	twa-*let*-zak
dress bag	*tas voor een jurk/ kleed* ⑩/⑬	tas vohr uhn yurk/ kleyt
suit bag	*tas voor een pak/ kostuum* ⑩/⑬	tas vohr uhn pak/ kos-*tewm*
suitcase	*koffer*	*ko*-fuhr

doorreis	*dohr*·reys	transit
handbagage	hant·ba·khaa·zhuh	carry-on baggage
hersluitbare	her·*slöyt*·baa·ruh	resealable
doorzichtige	dohr·*zikh*·ti·khuh	transparent
plastic tas	*ples*·tik tas	plastic bag
instapkaart	*in*·stap·kaart	boarding pass
overvracht	*oh*·vuhr·vrakht	excess baggage
scherpe	*skher*·puh	sharp objects
voorwerpen	*vohr*·wer·puhn	
verzegelde tas	*vuhr·zey*·khul·duh tas	sealed bag
vloeistoffen	*vlooy*·sto·fuhn	liquids

plane

vliegtuig

Where does flight (KL1083) depart?
Waar vertrekt vlucht   waar vuhr·*trekt* vlukht
(KL1083)?   (kaa el teen *dree·en·takh*·tikh)

Where does flight (KL1082) arrive?
Waar komt vlucht   waar komt vlukht
(KL1082) aan?   (kaa el teen *twey·en·takh*·tikh) aan

Where's (the) ...?	*Waar is ...?*	waar is ...
airport shuttle	*de shuttledienst*	duh *shu*·tuhl·deenst
arrivals hall	*de aankomsthal*	duh *aan*·komst·hal
departures hall	*de vertrekhal*	duh vuhr·*trek*·hal
duty-free shop	*het taxfree winkelen*	huht *taks*·free *wing*·kuh·luhn
gate (12)	*gate (twaalf)*	geyt (twaalf)
transfer desk	*de transferbalie*	duh trans·*fer*·baa·lee

airport signs

Aankomst	*aan*·komst	**Arrival**
Hellingbaan	*he*·ling·baan	**Travelator**
Naar de Platforms	naar duh plat·*forms*	**To the Trains**
Roltrap	*rol*·trap	**Escalator**
Vertrek	vuhr·*trek*	**Departure**

bus & coach

Is this a bus stop?
Is dit een bushalte?   is dit uhn *bus*·hal·tuh

How often do buses come?
Hoe vaak komt de bus?   hoo vaak komt duh bus

Does it stop at (Keukenhof)?
Stopt het in (Keukenhof)?   stopt huht in (*keu*·kuhn·hof)

What's the next stop?
Welk is de volgende   welk is duh *vol*·khuhn·duh
halte?   *hal*·tuh

I'd like to get off at (Lisse).
Ik wil graag in (Lisse)   ik wil khraak in (*li*·suh)
uitstappen.   öyt·sta·puhn

bus station	*busstation* n	*bus*·sta·syon
bus stop	*bushalte*	*bus*·hal·tuh
city bus	*stadsbus*	*stats*·bus
coach	*touringcar*	*too*·ring·kar
departure bay	*vertrekplaats*	vuhr·*trek*·plaats
intercity a	*intercity*	in·tuhr·*si*·tee
local a	*plaatselijk*	*plaat*·suh·luhk
shuttle bus	*shuttle bus*	*shu*·tuhl bus
timetable	*dienstregeling*	*deenst*·rey·khuh·ling

For bus numbers, see **numbers & amounts**, page 33.

train

What's the next station?
Welk is het volgende   welk is huht *vol*·kuhn·duh
station?   sta·*syon*

Does it stop at (Berchem)?
Stopt het in (Berchem)?   stopt huht in (*ber*·chuhm)

Do I need to change?
Moet ik overstappen?   moot ik *oh*·vuhr·sta·puhn

Is it ...?	Is het een ...?	is huht uhn ...
direct	directe	dee·*rek*·tuh
	verbinding	vuhr·*bin*·ding
express	expressdienst	eks·*pres*·deenst

Which carriage is for ...?	Welke wagon is ...?	*wel*·kuh wa·*khon* is ...
1st class	eerste klas	*eyr*·stuh klas
bicycles	voor fietsen	vohr *feet*·suhn
(Roosendaal)	voor (Roosendaal)	vohr (*roh*·zuhn·daal)

Which carriage is for dining?
Welk is de welk is duh
restauratiewagen? res·toh·*raa*·see·waa·khuhn

boat

boot

What's the ... like today?	In welke conditie is ... vandaag?	in *wel*·kuh kon·*dee*·see is ... van·*daakh*
lake	het meer	huht meyr
river	de rivier	duh ree·*veer*
sea	de zee	duh zey

Are there life jackets?
Zijn er zwemvesten zeyn uhr *zwem*·ves·tuhn
aan boord? aan bohrt

What island/beach is this?
Welk eiland/strand is dit? welk *ey*·lant/strant is dit

boat	boot	boht
cabin	cabine	ka·*bee*·nuh
captain	kapitein	ka·pee·*teyn*
deck	dek n	dek
ferry	veerboot/ferry ⑩/⑪	*veyr*·boht/*fe*·ree
house boat	woonboot	*wohn*·boht
lifeboat	reddingsboot	*re*·dings·boht
life jacket	zwemvest n	*zwem*·vest
sailing boat	zeilboot	*zeyl*·boht
ship	schip n	skhip

de volgende halte is ...		
duh *vol*·khun·duh *hal*·tuh is ...	**the next stop will be ...**	
gedeelte/trein naar ...		
khuh·*deyl*·tuh/treyn naar ...	**carriage/train to ...**	
we komen aan in ...		
wuh *koh*·muhn aan in ...	**we're arriving at ...**	

taxi

taxi

I'd like a taxi ...	*Ik wil graag een taxi ...*	ik wil khraakh uhn *tak*·see ...
at (9am)	*om (negen uur 's ochtends)*	om (*ney*·khuhn ewr *sokh*·tuhns)
now	*nu*	new
tomorrow	*voor morgen*	vohr *mor*·khuhn
I'd like to book a ...	*Ik wil graag een ... reserveren.*	ik wil khraakh uhn ... rey·ser·*vey*·ruhn
shared taxi	*deeltaxi*	*aeyl*·tak·see
train taxi	*treintaxi*	*treyn*·tak·see

Where's the taxi rank?
Waar is de taxistandplaats? waar is duh *tak*·see·stant·plaats

Is this taxi available?
Is deze taxi vrij? is *dey*·zuh *tak*·see vrey

Please take me to (this address).
Breng me alstublieft naar (dit adres). pol breng muh al·stew·*bleeft* naar (dit a·*dres*)

How much is it (to Geleen)?
Hoeveel kost het naar (Geleen)? hoo·*veyl* kost huht naar (khuh·*leyn*)

How much is the flag fall/hiring charge?
Hoeveel is het vertrekbedrag? hoo·*veyl* is huht vuhr·*trek*·buh·drakh

Please come back at (10 o'clock).
Kom om (tien uur) terug alstublieft. pol kom om (teen ewr) tuh·*rukh* al·stew·*bleeft*

Please slow down.
Rijd alstublieft wat   reyt al·stew·*bleeft* wat
langzamer. pol   *lang*·zaa·muhr

Please stop/wait here.
Stop/Wacht hier   stop/wakht heer
alstublieft. pol   al·stew·*bleeft*

For other useful phrases, see **directions**, page 61 and **money**, page 43.

car & motorbike

car & motorbike hire

I'd like to hire a/an ...	*Ik wil graag een ... huren.*	ik wil khraakh uhn ... *hew*·ruhn
4WD	*fourwheeldrive*	*fohr*·weel·drayf
automatic/ manual	*auto met automatische / manuele versnellingen*	*aw*·toh met aw·toh·*maa*·tee·suh/ ma·new·*wey*·luh vuhr·*sne*·ling·uhn
car	*auto*	*aw*·toh
moped	*brommer*	*bro*·muhr
motorbike	*motorfiets*	*moh*·tor·feets

with ...	*met ...*	met ...
air conditioning	*airconditioning*	*eyr*·kon·di·shuh·ning
antifreeze	*antivries*	an·tee·*vrees*
a child safety seat	*een kinderzitje*	uhn *kin*·duhr·zi·chuh
a driver	*chauffeur*	shoh·*feur*
snow chains	*sneeuwkettingen*	sneyw·ke·ting·uhn

How much for daily/weekly hire?
Hoeveel is het per   hoo·*veyl* is huht puhr
dag/week?   dakh/weyk

Does that include insurance?
Is verzekering   is vuhr·*zey*·kuh·ring
inbegrepen?   *in*·buh·khrey·puhn

Does that include mileage?
Is een aantal kilometer inbegrepen?
is uhn *aan*·tal *kee*·lo·mey·tuhr in·buh·khrey·puhn

Do you have a road map?
Heeft u een wegenkaart? pol
heyft ew uhn *wey*·khuhn·kaart

on the road

What's the speed limit?
Wat is de snelheids-beperking?
wat is duh *snel*·heyts·buh·*per*·king

Is this the road to (Middelburg)?
Gaat deze weg naar (Middelburg)?
khaat *dey*·zuh wekh naar (*mi*·duhl·burkh)

Where's a petrol/gas station?
Waar is er een benzinestation?
waar is uhr uhn ben·*zee*·nuh·sta·syon

Can you check the ...?	*Kunt u alstublieft ... checken?* pol	kunt ew al·stew·*bleeft* ... che·kuhn
oil	*de olie*	duh *oh*·lee
tyre pressure	*de druk in de banden*	duh druk in duh *ban*·duhn
water	*het water*	huht *waa*·tuhr

(How long) Can I park here?
(Hoe lang) Kan ik hier parkeren?
(hoo lang) kan ik heer par·*key*·ruhn

Do I have to pay?
Moet ik betalen?
moot ik buh·*taa*·luhn

problems

I need a mechanic.
Ik heb een monteur/ mecanicien nodig. ⓝ/ⓑ
ik hep uhn mon·*teur*/ mey·ka·nee·*sye* noh·dikh

I've had an accident.
Ik heb een ongeluk gehad.
ik hep uhn *on*·khuh·luk khuh·*hat*

The car/motorbike has broken down (at the traffic lights).
De auto/motorfiets staat met panne (bij de verkeerslichten).
de *aw*·toh/*moh*·tor·feets staat met *pa*·nuh (bey duh vuhr·*keyrs*·likh·tuhn)

The car/motorbike won't start.
De auto/motorfiets start niet.
duh *aw*·toh/*moh*·tor·feets start neet

I have a flat tyre.
Ik heb een lekke band.
ik hep uhn *le*·kuh bant

I've lost my car keys.
Ik ben de sleutels van mijn auto kwijt.
ik ben duh *sleu*·tuhls van meyn *aw*·toh kweyt

I've locked the keys inside.
Ik heb de sleutels in de gesloten auto laten zitten.
ik hep duh *sleu*·tuhls in duh khuh·*sloh*·tuhn *aw*·toh *laa*·tuhn *zi*·tuhn

I've run out of petrol.
Ik zit zonder benzine.
ik zit *zon*·duhr ben·*zee*·nuh

Can you fix it (today)?
   Kunt u het (vandaag)   kunt ew huht (van·*daakh*)
   herstellen? **pol**   her·*ste*·luhn

How long will it take?
   Hoe lang duurt het?   hoo lang dewrt huht

bicycle

I'd like ...	*Ik wil graag ...*	ik wil khraakh ...
my bicycle repaired	*mijn fiets laten herstellen*	meyn feets *laa*·tuhn her·*ste*·luhn
to buy a bicycle	*een fiets kopen*	uhn feets *koh*·puhn
to buy a bike lock	*een fietsslot kopen*	uhn *feet*·slot *koh*·puhn
to hire a bicycle	*een fiets huren*	uhn feets *hew*·ruhn

seat
zadel n
zaa·duhl

luggage rack
bagagerekje n
ba·*khaa*·zhuh·rek·yuh

chain
ketting
ke·ting

spoke
spaak
spaak

stand
staander
staan·duhr

frame
frame n
freym

pedal
pedaal
pey·daal

bell
bel
bel

handlebars
stuur n
stewr

wheel
wiel n
weel

tyre
band
bant

I'd like a ... bike.	Ik wil graag een ...	ik wil khraakh uhn ...
children's	kinderfiets	kin·duhr·feets
mountain	mountain bike	maw·tuhn baayk
racing	racefiets	reys·feets
second-hand	tweedehands fiets	twey·duh·hants feets

I'd like to hire a ...	Ik wil graag een ... huren.	ik wil khraakh uhn ... hew·ruhn
basket	mandje	man·chuh
child seat	kinderzitje	kin·duhr·zi·chuh
helmet	helm	helm

How much is it per day/hour?
Hoeveel is het per dag/uur? hoo·veyl is huht puhr dakh/ewr

Do I need a helmet?
Heb ik een helm nodig? hep ik uhn helm noh·dikh

Are there bicycle paths?
Zijn er fietspaden? zeyn uhr feets·paa·duhn

Is there a bicycle-path map?
Bestaat er een kaart met de fietspaden? buh·staat uhr uhn kaart met duh feets·paa·duhn

Can we get there by bike?
Kunnen we er met de fiets heen? ku·nuhn wuh uhr met duh feets heyn

Do you have bicycle parking?
Heeft u parking voor fietsen? pol heyft ew par·king vohr feet·suhn

I have a puncture.
Ik heb een lekke band. ik hep uhn le·kuh bant

My bike's been stolen.
Mijn fiets is gestolen. meyn feets is khuh·stoh·luhn

bicycle pump	fietspomp	feets·pomp
bicycle repairman	fietsenmaker	feet·suhn·maa·kuhr
bicycle shed	fietsenhok n	feet·suhn·hok
bicycle stand	fietsenrek n	feet·suhn·rek
bicycle storage	fietsenstalling	feet·suhn·sta·ling
cycle accessories	fietsbenodigd-heden	feets·buh·noh·dikht·hey·duhn

border crossing

immigratie

I'm ...	Ik ben ...	ik ben ...
in transit	op doorreis	op *doh*·reys
on business	op zakenreis	op *zaa*·kuhn·reys
on holiday	met vakantie	met va·*kan*·see

I'm here for ...	Ik ben hier voor ...	ik ben heer vohr ...
(10) days	(tien) dagen	(teen) *daa*·khuhn
(3) weeks	(drie) weken	(dree) *wey*·kuhn
(2) months	(twee) maanden	(twey) *maan*·duhn

I'm going to (Groningen).
*Ik ben op weg naar
(Groningen).*
ik ben op wekh naar
(*khroh*·ning·uhn)

I'm staying at the (Hotel Industrie).
*Ik logeer in
(Hotel Industrie).*
ik loh·*zheyr* in
(hoh·*tel* in·du·*stree*)

The children are on this passport.
*De kinderen staan
op dit paspoort.*
duh *kin*·duh·ruhn staan
op dit *pas*·pohrt

at customs

I have nothing to declare.
Ik heb niets aan te geven.   ik hep neets aan tuh *khey*·vuhn

I have something to declare.
Ik heb iets aan te geven.   ik hep eets aan tuh *khey*·vuhn

Do I have to declare this?
Moet ik dit aangeven?   moot ik dit *aan*·khey·vuhn

That's (not) mine.
Dat is (niet) van mij.   dat is (neet) van mey

I didn't know I had to declare it.
Ik wist niet dat ik het   ik wist neet dat ik huht
moest aangeven.   moost *aan*·khey·vuhn

Could I please have an (English) interpreter?
Mag ik alstublieft   makh ik al·stew·*bleeft*
een (Engelstalige)   uhn (*eng*·uhls·taa·li·khuh)
tolk? pol   tolk

Do you have this form in (English)?
Heeft u dit formulier   heyft ew dit for·mew·*leer*
in het (Engels)? pol   in huht (*eng*·uhls)

For phrases on payments and receipts, see **money**, page 43.

signs		
BTW teruggave	bey·tey·*wey* tuh·*rukh*·khaa·vuh	**VAT refunds**
Douane	doo·*waa*·nuh	**Customs**
Immigratie	ee·mee·*graa*·see	**Immigration**
Niets aan te Geven	neets aan tuh *khey*·vuhn	**Nothing to Declare**
Paspoortcontrole	*pas*·pohrt·kon·troh·luh	**Passport Control**
Quarantaine	ka·ron·*tey*·nuh	**Quarantine**
Taxfree	taks·free	**Duty-Free**

Where's the ...?	*Waar is ...?*	waar is ...
bank	*de bank*	duh bangk
market	*de markt*	duh markt
How do I get there?	*Hoe kom ik er?*	hoo kom ik uhr
How far is it?	*Hoe ver is het?*	hoo ver is huht
Can you show me (on the map)?	*Kunt u het mij tonen (op de kaart)?* **pol**	kunt ew huht mey *toh*·nuhn (op duh kaart)

It's ...	*Het is ...*	huht is ...
behind ...	*achter ...*	*akh*·tuhr ...
close	*dichtbij*	dikht·*bey*
far	*ver*	ver
here	*hier*	heer
in front of ...	*voor ...*	vohr ...
near ...	*dicht bij ...*	dikht bey ...
next to ...	*naast ...*	naast ...
on the corner	*op de hoek*	op duh hook
opposite ...	*tegenover ...*	tey·khuhn·*oh*·vuhr ...
straight ahead	*rechtdoor*	rekh·*dohr*
there	*daar*	daar

---

what's in a name?

Dutch words in street names and on signs are often combined into a single long place name which can be tricky for a foreigner to decipher (eg *Derde Leliedwarsstraat* means 'third lily-cross-street'). In bilingual Brussels, you might see something like *Rue du Marché-Aux-Herbes Graanmarkt Straat,* which is actually the French version of the street name (*Rue du Marché-Aux-Herbes*) followed by the Dutch version (*Graanmarkt Straat*), both meaning 'wheat-market street'. Note that the French *Rue* goes first and that the Dutch *Straat* is tucked onto the end (both mean 'street').

directions

Turn left/ right ...	*Sla linksaf/ rechtsaf ...*	slaa *lingks·*af/ *rekhs·*af ...
at the corner	*op de hoek*	op duh hook
at the traffic lights	*bij de verkeerslichten*	bey duh vuhr·*keyrs·*likh·tuhn
by bicycle	*met de fiets*	met duh feets
by bus	*met de bus*	met duh bus
by train	*met de trein*	met duh treyn
on foot	*te voet*	tuh voot
north	*noord*	nohrt
south	*zuid*	zöyt
east	*oost*	ohst
west	*west*	west
What ... is this?	*Welke ... is dit?*	*wel·*kuh ... is dit
canal	*gracht*	khrakht
council	*gemeente*	khuh·*meyn·*tuh
road	*weg*	wekh
street	*straat*	straat

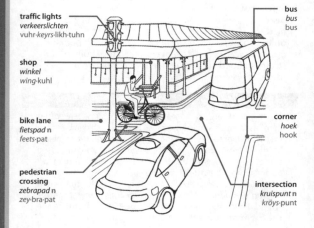

traffic lights
verkeerslichten
vuhr·*keyrs·*likh·tuhn

shop
winkel
*wing·*kuhl

bike lane
fietspad n
*feets·*pat

pedestrian crossing
zebrapad n
*zey·*bra·pat

bus
bus
bus

corner
hoek
hook

intersection
kruispunt n
*kröys·*punt

finding accommodation

Where's a ...?	*Waar vind ik een ...?*	waar vint ik uhn ...
bed and breakfast	*gastenkamer*	khas·tuhn·kaa·muhr
camping ground	*camping*	kem·ping ⓝ kam·ping ⓑ
guesthouse	*pension*	pen·syon
hikers' hut	*trekkershut*	tre·kuhrs·hut
holiday resort	*vakantiecentrum*	va·kan·see·sen·trum
hotel	*hotel*	hoh·tel
motel	*motel*	moh·tel
nature campground	*natuurcamping*	na·tewr·kem·ping ⓝ na·tewr·kam·ping ⓑ
youth hostel	*jeugdherberg*	yeukht·her·berkh

Can you recommend somewhere ...?	*Kunt u iets ... aanbevelen?* pol	kunt ew eets ... aan·buh·vey·luhn
cheap	*goedkoops*	khoot·kohps
good	*goeds*	khoots
luxurious	*luxueus*	luk·sew·weus
nearby	*dichtbij*	dikht·bey
romantic	*romantisch*	roh·man·tees
safe for women travellers	*dat veilig is voor vrouwelijke reizigers*	dat vey·likh is vohr vraw·wuh·luh·kuh rey·zi·khuhrs

I want something	*Ik wil iets*	ik wil eets
near the ...	*dicht bij ...*	dikht bey ...
beach	*het strand*	huht strant
city centre	*het stadscentrum*	huht stat·sen·trum
night life	*de*	duh
	uitgaansbuurt	öyt·gaans·bewrt
shops	*de winkels*	duh *wing*·kuhls
train station	*het station*	huht sta·*syon*

What's the address?
Wat is het adres?   wat is huht a·*dres*

For responses, see **directions**, page 61.

booking ahead & checking in

I'd like to book a room, please.
Ik wil graag een   ik wil khraakh uhn
kamer reserveren.   kaa·muhr rey·ser·*vey*·ruhn

I have a reservation.
Ik heb een reservatie.   ik hep uhn rey·ser·*vaa*·see

My name's ...
Mijn naam is ...   meyn naam is ...

For (three) nights/weeks.
Voor (drie) nachten/   vohr (dree) *nakh*·tuhn/
weken.   *wey*·kuhn

From (2 July) to (6 July).
Van (de tweede juli)   van (duh *twey*·duh *yew*·lee)
tot (de zesde juli).   tot (duh *zes*·duh *yew*·lee)

local talk		
dive n	*krot*	krot
messy place	*stal* (lit: stable) ®	stal
top spot	*klassehotel*	kla·suh·hoh·tel
very neat	*prima in orde*	*pree*·ma in *or*·duh
	(lit: excellent in order)	

Hoeveel nachten?	hoo·*veyl* nakh·tuhn	**How many nights?**
identiteits-	ee·den·tee·*teyts·*	**identification**
bewijs	buh·weys	
receptie	rey·*sep*·see	**reception**
sleutel	*sleu*·tuhl	**key**
vol	vol	**full**

Do I need to pay upfront?
Moet ik vooraf betalen?   moot ik *voh*·raf buh·*taa*·luhn

How much is it per ...?	*Hoeveel kost het per ...?*	hoo·*veyl* kost huht puhr ...
night	*nacht*	nakht
person	*persoon*	puhr·*sohn*
week	*week*	weyk

Can I pay by ...?	*Kan ik met een ... betalen?*	kan ik met uhn ... buh·*taa*·luhn
credit card	*kredietkaart*	krey·*deet*·kaart
travellers cheque	*reischeque*	*reys*·shek

Do you have a ... room?	*Heeft u een ...?* pol	heyft ew uhn ...
single	*éénpersoons-kamer*	*eyn*·puhr·sohns·*kaa*·muhr
double	*tweepersoons-kamer met een dubbel bed*	*twey*·puhr·sohns·*kaa*·muhr met uhn *du*·buhl bet
twin	*tweepersoons-kamer met lits jumeaux*	*twey*·puhr·sohns·*kaa*·muhr met lee zhew·*moh*

Can I see it?
Kan ik een kijkje nemen?   kan ik uhn *keyk*·yuh *ney*·muhn

I'll take it.
Ik neem het.   ik neym huht

For other methods of payment, see **money**, page 43, and **banking**, page 89.

Badkamer	*bat*·kaa·muhr	**Bathroom**
Kamers vrij	*kaa*·muhrs vrey	**Vacancy**
Vol/Volzet ⑩/⑱	vol/vol·*zet*	**No Vacancy**
Wasinrichting	*was*·in·rikh·ting	**Laundry**

requests & queries

verzoeken & vragen

Is breakfast included?
Is het ontbijt   is huht ont·*beyt*
inbegrepen?   *in*·buh·khrey·puhn

When's breakfast served?
Hoe laat wordt het   hoo laat wort huht
ontbijt geserveerd?   ont·*beyt* khuh·ser·*veyrt*

Where's breakfast served?
Waar wordt het ontbijt   waar wort huht ont·*beyt*
geserveerd?   khuh·ser·*veyrt*

Is there hot water all day?
Is er de hele dag   is uhr duh *hey*·luh dakh
warm water?   warm *waa*·tuhr

Please wake me at (seven).
Maak mij wakker om   maak mey *wa*·kuhr om
(zeven) uur alstublieft. **pol**   (*zey*·vuhn) ewr al·stew·*bleeft*

Can I use the ...?	*Kan ik de ...*	kan ik duh ...
	gebruiken?	khuh·*bröy*·kuhn
bicycle	*fiets*	feets
kitchen	*keuken*	*keu*·kuhn
laundry	*wasinrichting*	*was*·in·rikh·ting
telephone	*telefoon*	tey·ley·*fohn*

Do you have a/an …?	Heeft u een …? pol	heyft ew uhn …
elevator/lift	*lift*	lift
laundry service	*wasdienst*	*was*·deenst
message board	*berichtenbord*	buh·*rikh*·tuhn·bort
safe	*kluis*	klöys
sauna	*sauna*	*saw*·na
swimming pool	*zwembad*	*zwem*·bat

Could I have a …, please?	Kan ik een …	kan ik uhn …
	hebben	*he*·buhn
	alstublieft? pol	al·stew·*bleeft*
bicycle	*fiets*	feets
fan	*ventilator*	ven·tee·*laa*·tor
hairdryer	*haardroger*	*haar*·droh·khuhr
receipt	*kwitantie*	kwee·*tan*·see

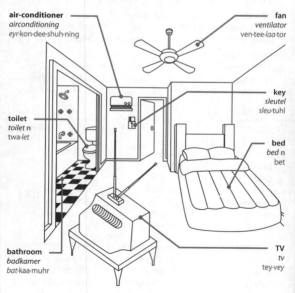

air-conditioner
airconditioning
eyr·kon·dee·shuh·ning

fan
ventilator
ven·tee·*laa*·tor

key
sleutel
sleu·tuhl

toilet
toilet n
twa·*let*

bed
bed n
bet

bathroom
badkamer
bat·kaa·muhr

TV
tv
tey·*vey*

accommodation

67

Could I have my key, please?
    Kan ik mijn sleutel hebben   kan ik meyn *sleu*·tuhl *he*·buhn
    alstublieft? pol   al·stew·*bleeft*

Do you have a car park?
    Heeft u parking? pol   heyft ew *par*·king

Do you rent out bicycles?
    Verhuurt u fietsen? pol   vuhr·*hewrt* ew *feet*·suhn

Do you arrange tours/trips here?
    Organiseert u   or·kha·nee·*zeyrt* ew
    rondleidingen/tochten? pol   *ront*·ley·ding·uhn/*tokh*·tuhn

Do you change money here?
    Wisselt u geld hier? pol   *wi*·suhlt ew khelt heer

Is there a message for me?
    Is er een bericht voor mij?   is uhr uhn buh·*rikht* vohr mey

Can I leave a message for someone?
    Kan ik een bericht voor   kan ik uhn buh·*rikht* vohr
    iemand achterlaten?   ee·mant *akh*·tuhr·laa·tuhn

I'm locked out of my room.
    Ik heb mezelf   ik hep muh·*zelf*
    buitengesloten.   *böy*·tuhn·khuh·sloh·tuhn

complaints

klachten

It's too …	*Het is te …*	huht is tuh …
bright	*licht*	likht
cold	*koud*	kawt
dark	*donker*	*dong*·kuhr
expensive	*duur*	dewr
noisy	*lawaaierig*	la·*waa*·yuh·rikh
small	*klein*	kleyn

This … isn't clean.	*… is niet schoon.*	… is neet skhohn
pillow	*Dit kussen*	dit *ku*·suhn
sheet	*Dit laken*	dit *laa*·kuhn
towel	*Deze handdoek*	*dey*·zuh han·dook

The ... doesn't work.	De ... is stuk.	duh ... is stuk
air conditioner	aircon-ditioning	eyr·kon·dee·shuh·ning
fan	ventilator	ven·tee·*laa*·tor
heater	verwarming	vuhr·*war*·ming

The toilet doesn't work.
Het toilet is stuk. — huht twa·*let* is stuk

There's no hot water.
Er is geen warm water. — uhr is kheyn warm *waa*·tuhr

Can I get another (blanket)?
Kan ik nog een (deken) — kan ik nokh uhn (*dey*·kuhn)
hebben alstublieft? pol — he·buhn al·stew·*bleeft*

a knock at the door ...

Who is it?	Wie is daar?	wee is daar
Just a moment, please.	Een momentje alstublieft. pol	uhn moh·*men*·chuh al·stew·*bleeft*
Come in.	Kom binnen.	kom *bi*·nuhn
Come back later, please.	Kom later terug alstublieft. pol	kom *laa*·tuhr tuh·*rukh* al·stew·*bleeft*

checking out

What time is checkout?
Hoe laat is het uitchecken? — hoo laat is huht öyt·che·kuhn

Can I have a late checkout?
Kan ik later uitchecken? — kan ik *laa*·tuhr öyt·che·kuhn

Can you call a taxi for me (for 11 o'clock)?
Kunt u een taxi — kunt ew uhn tak·see
(voor elf uur) voor mij — (vohr elf ewr) vohr mey
regelen alstublieft? pol — *rey*·khuh·luhn al·stew·*bleeft*

I'm leaving now.
Ik vertrek nu. — ik vuhr·*trek* new

Can I leave my bags here?
Kan ik mijn bagage   kan ik meyn ba·*khaa*·zhuh
hier laten?   heer *laa*·tuhn

There's a mistake in the bill/check.
Er zit een fout in de   uhr zit uhn fawt in duh
rekening.   *rey*·kuh·ning

Could I have	*Kan ik mijn …*	kan ik meyn …
my …, please?	*hebben*	*he*·buhn
	alstublieft? pol	al·stew·*bleeft*
deposit	*borg*	borkh
passport	*paspoort*	*pas*·pohrt
valuables	*waardevolle*	*waar*·duh·vo·luh
	bezittingen	buh·*zi*·ting·uhn

I had a great stay, thanks.
Ik heb een aangenaam   ik hep uhn *aan*·khuh·naam
verblijf gehad, dank u. pol   vuhr·*bleyf* khuh·hat dangk ew

I'll recommend it to my friends.
Ik zal het aan mijn   ik zal huht aan meyn
vrienden aanbevelen.   *vreen*·duhn *aan*·buh·vey·luhn

I'll be back in (three) days.
Ik kom terug binnen   ik kom tuh·*rukh bi*·nuhn
(drie) dagen.   (dree) *daa*·khuhn

I'll be back on (Tuesday).
Ik kom (dinsdag) terug.   ik kom (*dins*·dakh) tuh·*rukh*

camping

kamperen

Do you have …?	*Heeft u …?* pol	heyft ew …
electricity	*elektriciteit*	ey·lek·tree·see·*teyt*
a laundry	*een*	uhn
	wasinrichting	*was*·in·rikh·ting
shower facilities	*douches*	*doo*·shuhs
a site	*een*	uhn
	kampeerplaats	kam·*peyr*·plaats
tents for hire	*tenten te huur*	ten·tuhn tuh hewr

Who do I ask to stay here?
Aan wie kan ik vragen of ik   aan wee kan ik *vraa*·khuhn of ik
hier mag overnachten?   heer makh oh·vuhr·*nakh*·tuhn

Is it coin-operated?
Werkt het met   werkt huht met
muntstukken?   *munt*·stu·kuhn

Is the water drinkable?
Is het drinkbaar water?   is huht *dringk*·baar *waa*·tuhr

Could I borrow …? *Kan ik … lenen?*   kan ik … *ley*·nuhn

How much is	*Hoeveel is*	hoo·*veyl* is
it per …?	*het per …?*	huht puhr …
person	*persoon*	puhr·*sohn*
vehicle	*auto*	*aw*·toh

Can I …?	*Mag ik …?*	makh ik …
camp here	*hier kamperen*	heer kam·*pey*·ruhn
park next to	*naast mijn*	naast meyn
my tent	*tent parkeren*	tent par·*key*·ruhn

renting

huren

Do you have	*Heeft u een …*	heyft ew uhn …
a/an … for rent?	*te huur?* pol	tuh hewr
apartment	*flat* Ⓝ	flet
	appartement Ⓑ	a·par·tuh·*ment*
cabin	*hut*	hut
house	*huis*	höys
room	*kamer*	*kaa*·muhr

Is there a bond?
Is er een borg te   is uhr uhn borkh tuh
betalen?   buh·*taa*·luhn

Are bills extra?
Zijn onkosten extra?   zeyn *on*·kos·tuhn *ek*·straa

Are pets permitted?
Zijn huisdieren   zeyn *höys*·dee·ruhn
toegelaten?   *too*·khu·laa·tuhn

furnished	gemeubileerd	khuh·meu·bee·*leyrt*
housing permit	woonvergunning	*wohn*·vuhr·khu·ning
partly furnished	gedeeltelijk	khuh·*deyl*·tuh·luhk
	gemeubileerd	khuh·meu·bee·*leyrt*
unfurnished	onge-	*on*·khuh·
	meubileerd	meu·bee·leyrt

staying with locals

logeren

Can I stay at your place?
Kan ik bij jou thuis   kan ik bey jaw töys
overnachten?   oh·vuhr·*nakh*·tuhn

Is there anything I can do to help?
Kan ik ergens mee helpen?   kan ik *er*·khuhns mey *hel*·puhn

Thanks for your hospitality.
Bedankt voor uw/je   buh·*dangkt* vohr ew/yuh
gastvrijheid. pol/inf   khast·*vrey*·heyt

I have my own ...	Ik heb mijn eigen ...	ik hep meyn *ey*·khuhn ...
mattress	matras	ma·*tras*
sleeping bag	slaapzak	*slaap*·zak

Can I ...?	Kan ik ...?	kan ik ...
bring anything for the meal	iets om te eten meebrengen	eets om tuh *ey*·tuhn *mey*·breng·uhn
do the dishes	de afwas doen	duh *af*·was doon
set/clear the table	de tafel dekken/ afruimen	duh *taa*·fuhl *de*·kuhn/ *af*·röy·muhn
take out the rubbish	het afval buitenzetten	huht *af*·val *böy*·tuhn·ze·tuhn

To compliment your hosts' cooking, see **eating out**, page 171.

looking for ...

Are shops open on (Queen's Day)?
Zijn de winkels open   zeyn duh *wing*·kuhls oh·puhn
op (Koninginnedag)?   op (koh·ning·*khi*·nuh·dakh)

What hours are shops open?
Wat zijn de   wat zeyn de
openingsuren   *oh*·puh·nings·*ew*·ruhn
voor de winkels?   vohr duh *wing*·kuhls

Where can I buy (a padlock)?
Waar kan ik (een   waar kan ik (uhn
hangslot) kopen?   *hang*·slot) *koh*·puhn

Where's a ...?	*Waar vind ik een ...?*	waar vint ik uhn ...
chocolate shop	*chocoladewinkel*	sho·koh·*laa*·duh·*wing*·kuhl
department store	*warenhuis* ⓝ	*waa*·ruhn·höys *khroht*·
	grootwarenhuis ⓑ	waa·ruhn·höys
grocery shop	*kruidenierszaak*	kröy·duh·*neers*·zaak
nightshop	*nachtwinkel*	*nakht*·wing·kuhl
supermarket	*supermarkt*	*sew*·puhr·markt

For more items and shopping locations, see the **dictionary**.

---

glorious chocolate

Chocolate shops are generally known as *chocoladewinkels*,
but you might also come across these terms:

bonbonzaak ⓝ   bon·*bon*·zaak
chocolaterie   shoh·koh·la·*tree*
pralinewinkel ⓑ   pra·*lee*·nuh·wing·kuhl

making a purchase

I'm just looking.
Ik kijk alleen maar. — ik keyk a·*leyn* maar

I'd like to buy (an adaptor plug).
Ik wil graag een (adapter) kopen. — ik wil khraakh uhn (a·*dap*·tuhr) *koh*·puhn

The quality isn't good.
Het is geen goede kwaliteit. — huht is kheyn *khoo*·duh kwa·lee·*teyt*

How much is it?
Hoeveel kost het? — hoo·*veyl* kost huht

Can you write down the price?
Kunt u de prijs opschrijven alstublieft? **pol** — kunt ew duh preys *op*·skhrey·vuhn al·stew·*bleeft*

Do you have any others?
Heeft u nog andere? **pol** — heyft ew nokh *an*·duh·ruh

Can I look at it?
Kan ik het even zien? — kan ik huht *ey*·vuhn zeen

Is this (240) volts?
Is het (tweehonderd veertig) volt? — is huht (twey·*hon*·duhrt *feyr*·tikh) volt

Do you accept …?	*Accepteert u …?* **pol**	ak·sep·*teyrt* ew …
credit cards	*kredietkaarten*	krey·*deet*·kaar·tuhn
debit cards	*debetkaarten*	*dey*·bet·kaar·tuhn
travellers cheques	*reischeques*	*reys*·sheks

I'd like … please.	*Ik wil graag …*	ik wil khraakh …
my change	*mijn wisselgeld*	meyn *wi*·suhl·khelt
a receipt	*een kwitantie*	uhn kwee·*tan*·see
a refund	*mijn geld terug*	meyn khelt tuh·*rukh*

Could I have a bag, please?
Kan ik alstublieft een draagtasje hebben? pol
kan ik al·stew·*bleeft* uhn *draakh*·ta·shuh he·buhn

I don't need a bag, thanks.
Ik heb geen draagtasje nodig, dank u pol
ik hep kheyn *draakh*·ta·shuh *noh*·dikh dangk ew

Could I have it wrapped?
Kunt u het inpakken? pol
kunt ew huht *in*·pa·kuhn

Does it have a guarantee?
Komt het met garantie?
komt huht met ga·*ran*·see

Can I have it sent abroad?
Kan ik het naar het buitenland sturen?
kan ik huht naar huht *böy*·tuhn·lant *stew*·ruhn

Can you order it for me?
Kunt u het voor mij bestellen? pol
kunt ew huht vohr mey be·*ste*·luhn

Can I pick it up later?
Kan ik het later oppikken?
kan ik huht *laa*·tuhr o·pi·kuhn

I'd like to return this, please.
Ik wil dit graag retourneren.
ik wil dit khraakh ruh·toor·*ney*·ruhn

---

faulty things

There are two main ways to say that something is faulty in Dutch. For anything that needs to function, whether it's mechanical or electronic, say:

Het is kapot.   huht is ka·*pot*   **It's faulty.**
   (meaning: it's broken)

For any defects that don't necessarily impact functioning, eg a fault in fabric or in clothes, or a crack in the paint or porcelain of an object, use the expression:

Er zit een fout in.   uhr zit uhn fawt in   **It's faulty.**
   (meaning: there's a mistake in it)

bargain	*koopje* n	*kohp*·yuh
bargain hunter	*koopjesjager*	*kohp*·yuhs·yaa·khur
closing-down sale	*uitverkoop*	öyt·vuhr·kohp
discount	*korting*	*kor*·ting
end-of-season sale	*seizoens-opruiming*	sey·*zoons*·op·röy·ming
sale (general) n	*verkoop*	vuhr·*kohp*
special offer	*aanbieding*	*aan*·bee·ding
specials	*koopjes* n pl Ⓝ	*kohp*·yuhs
	solden Ⓑ	*sol*·duhn
super bargain	*spotkoopje* n	spot·kohp·yuh

bargaining

afdingen

That's too expensive.
  Dat is te duur.   dat is tuh dewr

Can you lower the price?
  Kunt u wat van de   kunt ew wat van duh
  prijs afdoen? pol   preys *af*·doon

Do you have something cheaper?
  Heeft u iets   heyft ew eets
  goedkopers? pol   khoot·*koh*·puhrs

What's your final price?
  Wat is uw beste prijs? pol   wat is ew *bes*·tuh preys

I'll give you (five) euros.
  Ik wil er (vijf) euro voor   ik wil uhr (veyf) *eu*·roh vohr
  betalen.   buh·*taa*·luhn

books & reading

Do you have …?	Heeft u …? pol	heyft ew …
a book by	een boek van	uhn book van
(Hugo Claus)	(Hugo Claus)	(hew·khoh klaws)
an entertainment	een uitgaans-	uhn öyt·khaans·
guide	gids	khits

Is there an	Is er een	is uhr uhn
(English)-	(Engels)-	(eng·uhls)·
language …?	talige …?	taa·li·khuh …
bookshop	boekhandel	book·han·duhl
section	afdeling	af·dey·ling

I'd like a/an …	Ik wil graag een …	ik wil khraakh uhn …
dictionary	woordenboek	wohr·duhn·book
newspaper	(Engels-	(eng·uhls·
(in English)	talige) krant	taa·li·khuh) krant
notepad	notitieblok	noh·tee·see·blok

Can you recommend a book for me?
Kunt u mij een boek   kunt ew mey uhn book
aanbevelen? pol   aan·buh·vey·luhn

Do you have Lonely Planet guidebooks/phrasebooks?
Heeft u reisgidsen/   heyft ew reys·khit·suhn/
taalgidsen van   taal·khit·suhn van
Lonely Planet? pol   lohn·lee ple·nuht

---

listen for …

Kan ik u helpen? pol
   kan ik ew hel·puhn   **Can I help you?**

Kan ik u nog ergens anders mee helpen? pol
   kan ik ew nokh er·khuns   **Anything else?**
   an·duhrs mey hel·puhn

Nee, we hebben er geen.
   ney wuh he·buhn uhr kheyn   **No, we don't have any.**

clothes

My size is (40).	*Ik heb maat (veertig).*	ik hep maat (feyr·tikh)
Can I try it on?	*Kan ik het passen?*	kan ik huht pa·suhn
It doesn't fit.	*Het past niet.*	huht past neet
small	*small*	smal
medium	*medium*	mey·dyum
large	*large*	larsh

For different types of clothing see the **dictionary**, and for sizes see **numbers & amounts**, page 33.

hairdressing

I'd like (a) ...	*Ik wil graag ...*	ik wil khraakh ...
colour	*een kleuring*	uhn kleu·ring
foils/streaks/ highlights (with foils)	*highlights (met folies)*	haay·laayts (met foh·lees)
haircut	*mijn haar laten knippen*	meyn haar laa·tuhn kni·puhn
my beard trimmed	*mijn baard laten bijknippen*	meyn baart laa·tuhn bey·kni·puhn
my hair washed/ blow-dried	*mijn haar laten wassen/ föhnen*	meyn haar laa·tuhn wa·suhn/ feu·nuhn
shave (beard)	*een scheerbeurt*	uhn skheyr·beurt
shave (head)	*mijn hoofd laten kaal scheren*	meyn hohft laa·tuhn kaal skhey·ruhn

I'd like a trim.
  *Ik wil het laten
  bijknippen.*
  ik wil huht *laa*·tuhn
  bey·kni·puhn

Don't cut it too short.
  *Knip het niet te kort
  alstublieft. pol*
  knip huht neet tuh kort
  al·stew·*bleeft*

Please use a new blade.
  *Gebruik een nieuw
  mesje alstublieft. pol*
  khuh·*bröyk* uhn neew
  me·shuh al·stew·*bleeft*

Shave it all off! (beard)
  Scheer het allemaal af!
  skheyr huht *a*·luh·maal af

Shave it all off! (head)
  Scheer me kaal!
  skheyr muh kaal

I don't like this.
  Ik vind dit niet goed!
  ik vint dit neet khoot

I should never have let you near me!
  *Ik had jou nooit in
  mijn buurt mogen
  laten komen!*
  ik hat jaw noyt in
  meyn bewrt *moh*·khuhn
  laa·tuhn ko·muhn

music & DVD

I'd like a ...   *Ik wil graag een ...*   ik wil khraakh uhn ...
  blank tape   *lege cassette*   *ley*·khuh ka·*se*·tuh
  CD   *cd*   sey·*dey*
  DVD   *dvd*   dey·vey·*dey*
  video   *video*   vee·dey·yoh

I'm looking for something by (Deus).
  *Ik ben op zoek naar
  iets van (Deus).*
  ik ben op zook naar
  eets van (*dey*·yus)

What's their best recording?
  Wat is hun beste album?
  wat is hun *bes*·tuh *al*·bum

Can I listen to this?
  *Kan ik hier naar dit
  luisteren?*
  kan ik heer naar dit
  löy·stuh·ruhn

Will this work on any DVD player?
Werkt dit op elke
dvd-speler?
werkt dit op *el*·kuh
dey·vey·*dey*·*spey*·luhr

Is this for a (PAL/NTSC) system?
Is dit voor een (PAL/
NTSC) systeem?
is dit vohr uhn (pal/
en·tey·es·*sey*) sees·*teym*

video & photography

Can you …?	*Kunt u …?* pol	kunt ew …
print digital	*digitale*	dee·khee·*taa*·luh
photos	*foto's*	*foh*·tohs
	afdrukken	*af*·dru·kuhn
develop this	*deze film*	*dey*·zuh film
film	*ontwikkelen*	ont·*wi*·kuh·luhn
load my film	*mijn film*	meyn film
	laden	*laa*·duhn
recharge the	*de batterij*	duh ba·tuh·*rey*
battery for	*voor mijn*	vohr meyn
my digital	*digitale*	dee·khee·*taa*·luh
camera	*fototoestel*	*foh*·toh·too·stel
	opladen	*op*·laa·duhn
transfer my	*mijn foto's*	meyn *foh*·tohs
photos to CD	*op cd zetten*	op sey·*dey* ze·tuhn
Do you have (a)	*Heeft u … voor*	heyft ew … vohr
… for this camera?	*dit fototoestel?* pol	dit *foh*·toh·too·stel
batteries	*batterijen*	ba·tuh·*rey*·yuhn
flash(bulb)	*een flits(lamp)*	uhn (*flits*·)lamp
(zoom) lens	*een (zoom)lens*	uhn (*zoom*·)lens
light meter	*een lichtmeter*	uhn *likht*·mey·tuhr
memory cards	*geheugen-*	khuh·*heu*·khun·
	kaarten	kaar·tuhn

I need ... film for this camera.	Ik heb ... voor dit fototoestel nodig.	ik hep ... vohr dit foh·toh·too·stel noh·dikh
APS	APS film	aa·pey·es film
B&W	zwart-wit film	zwart·wit film
colour	kleurenfilm	kleu·ruhn·film
slide	diafilm	dee·ya·film
(200) speed	een film van (tweehonderd) ASA	uhn film van (twey·hon·duhrt) aa·sa
... camera		
digital	digitaal fototoestel	dee·khee·taal foh·toh·too·stel
disposable	wegwerp-camera	wekh·werp·kaa·mey·ra
underwater	onderwater-camera	on·duhr·waa·tuhr·kaa·mey·ra
video	video-camera	vee·dey·yoh·kaa·mey·ra

I need a cable to connect my camera to a computer.
Ik heb een kabel nodig om mijn fototoestel met een computer te verbinden.
ik hep uhn *kaa*·buhl noh·dikh om meyn *foh*·toh·too·stel met uhn kom·*pyew*·tuhr tuh vuhr·*bin*·duhn

I need a cable to recharge this battery.
Ik heb een kabel nodig om deze batterij op te laden.
ik hep uhn *kaa*·buhl noh·dikh om *dey*·zuh ba·tuh·*rey* op tuh *laa*·duhn

I need a video cassette for this camera.
Ik heb een video-cassette voor deze camera nodig.
ik hep uhn *vee*·dey·yoh·ka·*se*·tuh vohr *dey*·zuh *kaa*·mey·ra noh·dikh

When will it be ready?
Wanneer is het klaar?
wa·*neyr* is huht klaar

How much is it?
Hoeveel kost het?
hoo·*veyl* kost huht

I need a passport photo taken.
Ik heb paspoortfoto's nodig.
ik hep *pas*·pohrt·foh·tohs noh·dikh

I'm not happy with these photos.
Ik ben niet tevreden   ik ben neet tuh·*vrey*·duhn
met deze foto's.   met *dey*·zuh foh·tohs

I don't want to pay the full price.
Ik wil de volle prijs niet   ik wil duh *vo*·luh preys neet
betalen.   buh·*taa*·luhn

repairs

reparaties

Can I have my	*Kan ik mijn ... hier*	kan ik meyn ... heer
... repaired here?	*laten herstellen?*	*laa*·tuhn her·*ste*·luhn
When will my ...	*Wanneer is mijn*	wa·*neyr* is meyn
be ready?	*... klaar?*	... klaar
backpack	*rugzak*	*rukh*·zak
bag	*tas*	tas
(video)camera	*(video)-camera*	*(vee*·dey·yoh)·*kaa*·mey·ra
(sun)glasses	*(zonne)bril*	*(zo*·nuh·)bril

souvenirs		
beer	*bier* n	beer
beer glasses	*bierglazen* n pl	*beer*·khlaa·zuhn
carpets	*tapijten* n pl	ta·*pey*·tuhn
cartoons	*stripverhalen* n pl	*strip*·vuhr·haa·luhn
cheese	*kaas*	kaas
chocolate	*chocolade*	shoh·koh·*laa*·duh
chocolates	*bonbons* Ⓝ	bon·*bons*
	pralines ®	pra·*lee*·nuh
(wooden) clogs	*klompen*	*klom*·puhn
delftware	*Delfts blauw* n	delfts blaw
diamonds	*diamanten*	dee·ya·*man*·tuhn
gin	*jenever*	yuh·*ney*·vuhr Ⓝ
		zhuh·*ney*·vuhr ®
lace	*kant*	kant
mural tapestries	*muurtapijten* n pl	*mewr*·ta·pey·tuhn
tapestry	*tappiserie*	ta·pee·suh·*ree*
Tintin	*Kuifje*	*köyf*·yuh
souvenirs	*souvenirs* n pl	soo·vuh·*neers*

communications

the internet

het internet

Where's the local internet café?
Waar is het plaatselijk   waar is huht *plaat*·suh·luhk
internetcafé?   in·tuhr·net·ka·*fey*

I'd like to …	*Ik wil graag …*	ik wil khraakh …
burn a CD	*iets op cd zetten*	eets op sey·*dey* ze·tuhn
check my email	*mijn e-mails checken*	meyn *ee*·meyls *che*·kuhn
download my photos	*mijn foto's downloaden*	meyn *foh*·tohs *dawn*·loh·duhn
get internet access	*op het internet gaan*	op huht *in*·tuhr·net khaan
use a printer	*een printer gebruiken*	uhn *prin*·tuhr khuh·*bröy*·kuhn
use a scanner	*een scanner gebruiken*	uhn *ske*·nuhr khuh·*bröy*·kuhn

Do you have …?	*Heeft u …?* pol	heyft ew …
Macs	*Apple computers*	e·puhl kom·*pyoo*·tuhrs
PCs	*pc's*	pey·*seys*
a Zip drive	*een zipdrive*	uhn *zip*·draayf

How much per …?	*Hoeveel kost het per …?*	hoo·*veyl* kost huht puhr …
hour	*uur*	ewr
(five) minutes	*(vijf) minuten*	(veyf) mee·*new*·tuhn
page	*pagina*	*paa*·khee·na

Can I connect my ... to this computer?	Kan ik mijn ... met deze computer verbinden?	kan ik meyn ... met *dey*·zuh kom·*pyoo*·tuhr vuhr·*bin*·duhn
camera	fototoestel	*foh*·toh·too·stel
iPod	iPod	*aay*·pot
media player (MP3)	MP3speler	em·pey·*tree*·spey·luhr
portable hard drive	draagbare harde schijf	*draakh*·baa·ruh *har*·duh skheyf
PSP	psp	pey·es·*pey*
USB flash drive (memory stick)	USB memory stick	ew·es·*bey* me·*moh*·ree stik

How do I log on?	Hoe log ik in?	hoo lokh ik in
Stupid internet!	Stom internet!	stom *in*·tuhr·net
It's crashed.	Het is geblokkeerd.	huht is khuh·blo·*keyrt*
I've finished.	Ik ben klaar.	ik ben klaar

mobile/cell phone

mobiele telefoons

I'd like a ...	Ik wil graag een ...	ik wil khraakh uhn ...
charger for my phone	lader voor mijn telefoon	*laa*·duhr vohr meyn tey·ley·*fohn*
mobile/cell phone for hire	mobiele telefoon huren ⓝ GSM huren ⓑ	moh·*bee*·luh tey·ley·*fohn* hew·ruhn khey·es·*em* hew·ruhn
prepaid mobile/cell phone	mobiele telefoon met beltegoed ⓝ GSM met beltegoed ⓑ	moh·*bee*·luh tey·ley·*fohn* met bel·tuh·khoot khey·es·*em* met bel·tuh·khoot
SIM card for your network	sim-kaart voor uw netwerk pol	sim·kaart vohr ew *net*·werk

What are the call rates?
Wat zijn de tarieven?   wat zeyn duh ta·*ree*·vuhn

(30c) per (30) seconds.
(Dertig cent) voor   *(der*·tikh sent) vohr
(dertig) seconden.   *(der*·tikh) suh·*kon*·duhn

phone

telefoon

What's your phone number?
Wat is uw/jouw   wat is ew/yaw
telefoonnummer? pol/inf   tey·ley·*fohn*·nu·muhr

Where's the nearest public phone?
Waar is de   waar is duh
dichtsbijzijnde   dikhts·bey·*zeyn*·duh
openbare telefoon?   oh·puhn·baa·ruh tey·ley·*fohn*

Can I look at a phone book?
Mag ik het telefoonboek   makh ik huht tey·ley·*fohn*·book
even inkijken?   *ey*·vuhn *in*·key·kuhn

Can I have some coins?
Kan ik enkele   kan ik *eng*·kuh·luh
muntstukken hebben?   *munt*·stu·kuhn *he*·buhn

I want to ...	*Ik wil graag ...*	ik wil khraakh ...
buy a phonecard	*een telefoon-kaart kopen*	uhn tey·ley·*fohn*·kaart *koh*·puhn
call (Ireland)	*(Ierland) bellen*	(*eer*·lant) *be*·luhn
make a (local) call	*een (lokaal) telefoon-gesprek maken*	uhn (loh·*kaal*) tey·ley·*fohn*·khuh·sprek *maa*·kuhn
reverse the charges	*dat de ontvanger betaalt*	dat duh ont·*vang*·uhr buh·*taalt*
speak for (three) minutes	*(drie) minuten spreken*	(dree) mee·*new*·tuhn *sprey*·kuhn

How much does ... cost?	*Hoeveel kost ...?*	hoo·*veyl* kost ...
a (three)-minute call	*een gesprek van (drie) minuten*	uhn khuh·*sprek* van (dree) mee·*new*·tuhn
each extra minute	*het per extra minuut*	huht puhr *ek*·stra mee·*newt*

What's the country code for (Australia)?
Wat is de prefix voor (Australië)?
wat is duh prey·*fiks* vohr (aw·*straa*·lee·yuh)

What's the area code for (Brussels)?
Wat is de prefix voor de zone (Brussel)?
wat is duh prey·*fiks* vohr duh *zoh*·nuh (*bru*·suhl)

The number is ...
Het nummer is ...
huht *nu*·muhr is ...

It's engaged.
Het is bezet.
huht is buh·*zet*

I've been cut off.
De verbinding is verbroken.
duh vuhr·*bin*·ding is vuhr·*broh*·kuhn

The connection's bad.
Het is een slechte verbinding.
huht is uhn *slekh*·tuh vuhr·*bin*·ding

---

listen for ...

Fout/Verkeerd nummer. ⓃⒷ fawt/vuhr·*keyrt* nu·muhr	**Wrong number.**
Met wie spreek ik? met wee spreyk ik	**Who's calling?**
Met wie wilt u spreken? pol met wee wilt ew *sprey*·kuhn	**Who do you want to speak to?**
Een momentje. uhn moh·*men*·chuh	**One moment.**
Hij/Zij is er niet. hey/zey is uhr neet	**He/She isn't here.**

Hello.
Hallo.   ha·*loh*

It's …
Het is …   huht is …

Can I please speak to (Piet)?
Kan ik met (Piet) spreken   kan ik met (peet) *sprey*·kuhn
alstublieft? pol   al·stew·*bleeft*

Please tell him/her I called.
Zeg hem/haar alstublieft   zekh hem/haar al·stew·*bleeft*
dat ik gebeld heb. pol   dat ik khuh·*belt* hep

Can I leave a message?
Kan ik een boodschap laten?   kan ik uhn *boht*·skhap *laa*·tuhn

My number is …
Mijn nummer is …   meyn *nu*·muhr is …

I don't have a contact number.
Ik heb geen contact-   ik hep kheyn kon·*takt*·
nummer.   nu·muhr

I'll call back later.
Ik bel later terug.   ik bel *laa*·tuhr tuh·*rukh*

What time should I call?
Hoe laat kan ik best bellen?   hoo laat kan ik best *be*·luhn

For telephone numbers, see also **numbers & amounts**, page 33.

post office

postkantoor

I want to send a …	*Ik wil een … sturen.*	ik wil uhn … *stew*·ruhn
letter	*brief*	breef
parcel	*pakje*	*pak*·yuh
postcard	*ansichtkaart* Ⓝ	*an*·sikht·kaart
	postkaart Ⓑ	*post*·kaart

I want to buy	Ik wil een …	ik wil uhn …
a/an …	kopen.	koh·puhn
aerogram	aerogram	aay·roh·gram
(padded)	(gewatteerde)	(khuh·wa·teyr·duh)
envelope	envelop	en·vuh·lop
stamp	postzegel	post·zey·khul

customs	douane-	doo·waa·nuh·
declaration	verklaring	vuhr·klaa·ring
mail n	post	post
PO box	postbus	post·bus
postal address	postadres n	post·a·dres
postcode	postcode	post·koh·duh

Please send it by airmail to (Australia).
Stuur het alstublieft
per luchtpost naar
(Australië). pol

stewr huht al·stew·bleeft
puhr lukht·post naar
(aw·straa·lee·yuh)

It contains (souvenirs).
Het bevat (souveniers). huht buh·vat (soo·vuh·neers)

Where's the poste restante section?
Waar is de poste restante
afdeling?

waar is duh post res·tan·tuh
af·dey·ling

Is there any mail for me?
Is er post voor mij? is uhr post vohr mey

Do you have public internet access here?
Heeft u hier een
openbare
internetaansluiting? pol

heyft ew heer uhn
oh·puhn·baa·ruh
in·tuhr·net·aan·slöy·ting

snail mail		
airmail	luchtpost	lukht·post
express mail	exprespost/	eks·pres·post/
	prioritair	pree·yoh·ree·teyr
registered mail	aangetekende	aan·khuh·tey·kuhn·duh
	post	post
surface mail	gewone post	khuh·woh·nuh post

What days is the bank open?
Welke dagen is de
bank open?
wel·kuh *daa*·khuhn is duh
bangk *oh*·puhn

What times is the bank open?
Wat zijn de openings-
uren van de bank?
wat zeyn duh *oh*·puh·nings·
ew·ruhn van duh bangk

Where can I ...?	*Waar kan ik ...?*	waar kan ik ...
I'd like to ...	*Ik wil graag ...*	ik wil khraakh ...
arrange a transfer	*een giro-betaling maken* ⓝ	uhn *khee*·roh·buh·taa·ling *maa*·kuhn
	een over-schrijving doen ⓑ	uhn *oh*·vuhr·skhrey·ving doon
cash a cheque	*een cheque innen*	uhn shek *i*·nuhn
change a travellers cheque	*een reischeque innen*	uhn *reys*·shek *i*·nuhn
change money	*geld wisselen*	khelt *wi*·suh·luhn
get a cash advance	*een voorschot bekomen*	uhn *vohr*·skhot buh·*koh*·muhn
get change for this note	*dit biljet wisselen in muntstukken*	dit bil·*yet* *wi*·suh·luhn in *munt*·stu·kuhn
withdraw money	*geld afhalen*	khelt *af*·haa·luhn
Where's ...?	*Waar vind ik een ...?*	waar vint ik uhn ...
an automated teller machine	*pin-automaat* ⓝ	*pin*·aw·toh·maat
	geldautomaat ⓑ	khelt·aw·toh·maat
a foreign exchange office	*wisselkantoor*	*wi*·suhl·kan·tohr

The automated teller machine took my card.

De pin-automaat/   duh *pin*·aw·toh·maat/
geldautomaat heeft   *khelt*·aw·toh·maat heyft
mijn kaart ingeslikt. Ⓝ/Ⓑ   meyn kaart *in*·khuh·slikt

I've forgotten my PIN.

Ik ben mijn pin vergeten. Ⓝ   ik ben meyn pin vuhr·*khey*·tuhn
Ik ben mijn geheime   ik ben meyn khuh·*hey*·muh
code vergeten. Ⓑ   koh·duh vuhr·*khey*·tuhn

Can I use my credit card to withdraw money?

Kan ik geld afhalen met   kan ik khelt *af*·haa·luhn met
mijn kredietkaart?   meyn krey·*deet*·kaart

Has my money arrived yet?

Is mijn geld al   is mijn khelt al
aangekomen?   *aan*·khuh·koh·muhn

How long will it take to arrive?

Hoe lang duurt het tot   hoo lang dewrt huht tot
mijn geld aankomt?   meyn khelt *aan*·komt

What's the …?   *Wat is de …?*   wat is duh …
  charge for that   *kost hiervoor*   kost heer·*vohr*
  exchange rate   *wisselkoers*   *wi*·suhl·koors

For other useful phrases, see **money**, page 43.

---

listen for…

Er is een probleem.
   uhr is uhn proh·*bleym*   **There's a problem.**

Er staat geen geld meer op de rekening.
   uhr staat kheyn khelt meyr   **You have no funds left.**
   op duh *rey*·kuh·ning

We kunnen dat niet doen.
   wuh *ku*·nuhn dat neet doon   **We can't do that.**

Teken hier.
   tey·kuhn heer   **Sign here.**

identiteitsbewijs   ee·den·tee·*teyts*·   **identification**
   buh·weys

paspoort   *pas*·pohrt   **passport**

I'd like a/an ... *Ik wil graag een ...* ik wil khraakh uhn ...
- **audio set** *audiogids* aw·dee·yoh·khits
- **catalogue** *catalogus* ka·taa·loh·khus
- **guide (in English)** *gids (in het Engels)* khits (in huht eng·uhls)
- **map (building)** *plattegrond* pla·tuh·khront
- **map (town)** *kaart* kaart

Do you have information on ... sights? *Heeft u informatie over bezienswaardigheden van ... belang?* pol heyft ew in·for·maa·see oh·vuhr buh·zeens· waar·dikh·hey·duhn van ... buh·lang

- **architectural** *architecturaal* ar·khee·tek·tew·raal
- **cultural** *cultureel* kul·tew·reyl
- **historical** *historisch* his·toh·ris
- **religious** *religieus* ruh·lee·khyeus

I'd like to see ...
Ik wil graag ... zien. ik wil khraakh ... zeen

What's that?
Wat is dat? wat is dat

How old is it?
Hoe oud is het? hoo awt is huht

Who built/made/painted it?
Wie heeft het gebouwd/ gemaakt/geschilderd? wee heyft huht khuh·bawt/ khuh·maakt/khuh·skhil·duhrt

Could you take a photo of me/us?
Kunt u een foto van mij/ons nemen alstublieft? pol kunt ew uhn foh·toh van mey/ons ney·muhn al·stew·bleeft

Can I take a photo (of you)?
Mag ik een foto (van u) nemen? pol makh ik uhn foh·toh (van ew) ney·muhn

I'll send you the photo.
Ik stuur de foto op. ik stewr duh foh·toh op

getting in

What time does it open/close?
Hoe laat gaat het open/dicht?
hoo laat khaat huht *oh*·puhn/dikht

What's the admission charge?
Wat is de toegangsprijs?
wat is duh *too*·khangs·preys

Is there a discount for …?	*Is er korting voor …?*	is uhr *kor*·ting vohr …
children	*kinderen*	*kin*·duh·ruhn
families	*families*	fa·*mee*·lees
groups	*groepen*	*khroo*·puhn
older people	*senioren*	sey·*nyoh*·ruhn
pensioners	*gepensio-neerden*	khuh·pen·syoh·*neyr*·duhn
students	*studenten*	stew·*den*·tuhn

signs

Bezet	buh·*zet*	**Occupied**
Dames/Heren	*daa*·muhs/*hey*·ruhn	**Women/Men**
Geen Toegang	kheen *too*·khang	**No Entry**
Ingang/Uitgang	*in*·khang/*öyt*·khang	**Entrance/Exit**
Inlichtingen	*in*·likh·ting·uhn	**Information**
Niet Aanraken Alstublieft	neet *aan*·raa·kuhn al·stew·*bleeft*	**No Touching**
Open/ Gesloten	*oh*·puhn/ khuh·*sloh*·tuhn	**Open/ Closed**
Toiletten	twa·*le*·tuhn	**Toilets/WC**
Verboden	vuhr·*boh*·duhn	**Prohibited**
Verboden te Fotograferen	vuhr·*boh*·duhn tuh foh·toh·khra·*fey*·ruhn	**No Photography**
Verboden te Roken	vuhr·*boh*·duhn tuh *roh*·kuhn	**No Smoking**
Warm/Koud	warm/kawt	**Hot/Cold**

tours

rondleidingen

Can you recommend a …?	*Kunt u een … aanbevelen?* pol	kunt ew uhn … *aan*·buh·vey·luhn
When's the next …?	*Wanneer is de volgende …?*	wa·*neyr* is duh *vol*·khuhn·duh …
boat trip	*boottocht*	*boh*·tokht
canal cruise	*kanaaltocht*	ka·*naal*·tokht
cycle tour	*fietstocht*	*feets*·tokht
day trip	*daguitstap*	*dakh*·öyt·stap
harbour cruise	*haven- rondvaart*	*haa*·vuhn· ront·vaart
tour	*rondleiding*	*ront*·ley·ding
Is … included?	*Is … inbegrepen?*	is … *in*·buh·khrey·puhn
accommodation	*accommodatie*	a·koh·moh·*daa*·see
transport	*transport*	trans·*port*

must-sees of the low countries

abbey	*abdij*	ap·*dey*
almshouse	*hofje* Ⓝ	*hof*·yuh
	godshuis n Ⓑ	*khots*·höys
battlefields	*slagvelden* n pl	*slakh*·vel·duhn
béguinage	*begijnhof* n	buh·*kheyn*·hof
belfry	*belfort* n	*bel*·fort
brewery	*brouwerij*	braw·wuh·*rey*
bulb fields	*bollenvelden* n pl	*bo*·luh·vel·duhn
carillon	*beiaard*	*bey*·yaart
city gate	*(stads)poort*	*(stats·)*pohrt
cloister	*klooster* n	*kloh*·stuhr
courtyard	*hofje* n	*hof*·yuh
covered market	*hallen*	*ha*·luhn
distillery	*jenever-*stokerij*	zhuh·*ney*·vuhr·stoh·kuh·*rey*
drained land	*polder*	*pol*·duhr
façade	*gevel*	*khey*·vuhl
flea market	*rommelmarkt*	*ro*·muhl·markt
fortress	*burcht/slot*	burkht/slot
gable	*geveltop*	*khey*·vuhl·top
lighthouse	*vuurtoren*	vewr·toh·ruhn
(wind)mill	*(wind)molen*	*(wint·)moh*·luhn
trenches	*loopgraven* n pl	*lohp*·khraa·vuhn
war graves	*oorlogsgraven* n pl	*ohr*·lokhs·khraa·vuhn

Is food included?
Zijn maaltijden inbegrepen?
zeyn *maal*·tey·duhn *in*·buh·khrey·puhn

How long is the (tour)?
Hoe lang duurt de (rondleiding)?
hoo lang dewrt duh *(ront·ley·ding)*

What time should we be back?
Hoe laat moeten we terug zijn?
hoo laat *moo*·tuhn wuh tuh·*rukh* zeyn

I'm with them.
Ik ben met hen.
ik ben met hen

I've lost my group.
Ik ben mijn groep kwijt.
ik ben meyn khroop kweyt

I'm attending a ...	Ik ben hier voor een ...	ik ben heer vohr uhn ...
conference	conferentie	kon·fey·ren·see
course	cursus	kur·sus
meeting	vergadering	vuhr·khaa·duh·ring
trade fair	beurs	beurs

I'm with ...	Ik ben hier met ...	ik ben heer met ...
(InBev)	(InBev)	(in·bef)
my colleague(s)	mijn collega('s)	meyn ko·ley·kha(s)
(two) others	(twee) anderen	(twey) an·duh·ruhn

I'm alone.
Ik ben hier op mijn eentje. ik ben heer op meyn *eyn*·chuh

I have an appointment with ...
Ik heb een afspraak met ... ik hep uhn *af*·spraak met ...

I'm staying at the (Hotel Industrie), room (205).
Ik logeer in (Hotel ik loh·*zheyr* in (hoh·*tel*
Industrie), kamer in·dus·*tree*) *kaa*·muhr
(tweehonderd en vijf). (twey·*hon*·duhrt en veyf)

I'm here for (two) days/weeks.
Ik ben hier voor (twee) ik ben heer voor (twey)
dagen/weken. *daa*·khuhn/*wey*·kuhn

Can I please have your business card?
Mag ik een makh ik uhn
visitekaartje van u? pol vee·*zee*·tuh·kaar·chuh van ew

Here's my ...	*Hier is mijn ...*	heer is meyn ...
What's your ...?	*Wat is uw/*	wat is ew/
	jouw ...? pol/inf	yaw ...
address	*adres*	a·*dres*
cell/mobile	*mobiel*	moh·*beel*
number	*telefoon-*	tey·ley·*fohn·*
	nummer ⓝ	nu·muhr
	GSM-nummer ⓑ	khey·es·*em*·nu·muhr
email address	*e-mailadres*	ee·meyl·a·dres
fax number	*faxnummer*	*faks*·nu·muhr
pager number	*beepernummer*	*bee*·puhr·nu·muhr
work number	*telefoon-*	tey·ley·*fohn·*
	nummer	nu·muhr
	van het werk	van huht werk
Where's the ...?	*Waar is ...?*	waar is ...
business	*het business-*	huht *bis*·nis·
centre	*centre*	sen·tuhr
business	*het*	huht
district	*zakencentrum*	*zaa*·kuhn·sen·trum
conference	*de conferentie*	duh kon·fey·*ren*·see
industrial	*de industrie-*	duh in·dus·*tree*·
estate	*zone*	zoh·nuh
meeting	*de vergade-*	duh vuhr·*khaa*·duh·
	ring	ring
I need ...	*Ik heb ... nodig.*	ik hep ... *noh*·dikh
a computer	*een computer*	uhn kom·*pyoo*·tuhr
an internet	*een internet-*	uhn *in*·tuhr·net·
connection	*aansluiting*	aan·*slöy*·ting
an interpreter	*een tolk*	uhn tolk
who speaks	*(die Engels*	(dee *eng*·uhls
(English)	*spreekt)*	spreykt)
more business	*meer visite-*	meyr vee·*zee*·tuh·
cards	*kaartjes*	kaar·chus

I need space to set up.
Ik heb plaats nodig ik hep plaats *noh*·dikh
om mij op te stellen. om mey op tuh *ste*·luhn

I need to send a fax.
Ik moet een fax sturen. ik moot uhn faks *stew*·ruhn

That went very well.
Dat ging vlotjes.   dat khing *vlo*·chus

Thank you for your interest.
Bedankt voor uw   be·*dangkt* vohr ew
interesse. **pol**   in·tuh·*re*·suh

Shall we go for a drink/meal?
Zullen we iets gaan   *zu*·luhn wuh eets khaan
drinken/eten?   *dring*·kuhn/*ey*·tuhn

It's on me.
Ik betaal.   ik buh·*taal*

---

cards on the table

Dutch businesspeople tend to be big on academic titles, at least on their business cards (rather than as a form of address). There's a vast (and often confusing) nomenclature and an even greater number of abbreviations to choose from to indicate your academic degree(s) in front of your name; there are rules and regulations, and much debate … but in the end everyone agrees it's not all that important.

On Dutch *visitekaartjes* vee·*zee*·tuh·*kaar*·chus (business cards) you might see abbreviations like these in front of someone's name:

bc.	baccalaureus	**hbo degree (tertiary education outside university)**
dr.	doctor (PhD)	**university degree with a PhD**
drs.	doctorandus	**university degree**
ing.	ingenieur	**engineer**
ir.	ingenieur	**engineer (with a university degree)**
mr.	meester	**lawyer**

If you're the proud owner of more than one title, these will be combined following specific rules such as: *drs. + dr. = dr.* and *ing. + dr. = dr. ing.* which could lead to combinations such as *mr. ir. drs. ing.* Note that there's no specific title for a medical doctor – usually their card will read something like *Jaap Steen, arts* (*arts* arts meaning 'doctor').

business

97

loan words

Over the centuries, English has borrowed many words from Dutch – or via Dutch from other languages. Many of them are nautical terms, but there are also painting terms, food terms and so on. Here are some examples.

loanword:	origin:
booze	Middle Dutch *būsen*
boss	*baas* (master)
brandy	*brandewijn* (burnt wine)
bundle	probably Middle Dutch *bundel*
coleslaw	*koolsla* (cabbage salad)
cookie	*koekje*, diminutive of *koek* (cake)
cruise	*kruisen* (to cross)
deck	Middle Dutch *dec* (covering)
dock (nautical)	Middle Dutch *docke*
duffel	cloth named after *Duffel*, a Belgian town
easel	*ezel* (donkey)
freight	Middle Dutch *vrecht* – *vracht* (load) in present-day Dutch
landscape	from *landskip* (Dutch painting term), based on Middle Dutch *landscap* (region)
mannequin	*manneken* (little man), diminutive of *man* (man)
pickle	possibly Middle Dutch *pekel*
pump	Middle Dutch *pumpe* (pipe)
sketch	Dutch *schets*
skipper	Middle Dutch *schipper* (shipper)
slurp	Middle Dutch *slorpen* (to sip)
smuggle	*smokkelen*
snoop	*snoepen* (to eat furtively)
splinter	Middle Dutch *splinter/splinte* (splint)
split	Middle Dutch *splitten* (to cleave)
spook	*spook* (ghost)
tub	Middle Dutch *tubbe*
waffle	*wafel* (earlier *wæfel*)
wagon	*wagen* (wain, or these days, car)

The Low Countries have done a lot lately to make public venues wheelchair-accessible, and all new buildings have ramps and/or lifts. More wheelchair-accessible buses are also popping up. Arrangements for assistance on trains can be made if you ring up the station or, in the Netherlands, the *Bureau Assistentieverlening Gehandicapten* (Bureau for assistance to disabled people), the day before your trip. In Belgium, there's also the railways' brochure *Gids voor de Reiziger met Beperkte Mobiliteit* (Guide for Travellers with Limited Mobility).

I have a disability.
Ik heb een handicap.
ik hep uhn *hen*·dee·kep/*han*·dee·kap ⑩/⑧

I need assistance.
Ik heb hulp nodig.
ik hep hulp *noh*·dikh

I'm deaf/hard of hearing.
Ik ben doof/hardhorend.
ik ben dohf/hart·*hoh*·ruhnt

I have a hearing aid.
Ik heb een hoorapparaat.
ik hep uhn *hohr*·a·pa·raat

My companion's blind.
Mijn metgezel is blind.
meyn *met*·khuh·zel is blint

What services do you have for people with a disability?
Welke voorzieningen heeft u voor personen met een handicap? pol
wel·kuh vohr·*zee*·ning·uhn heyft ew vohr puhr·*soh*·nuhn met uhn *hen*·dee·kep/*han*·dee·kap ⑩/⑧

Are there disabled parking spaces?
Zijn er parkeerplaatsen voor gehandicapten?
zeyn uhr par·*keyr*·plaat·suhn vohr khuh·*hen*·dee·kep·tuhn/khuh·*han*·dee·kap·tuhn ⑩/⑧

Is there wheelchair access?
Is het toegankelijk voor rolstoelgebruikers?
is huht too·*khang*·kuh·luhk vohr *rol*·stool·khuh·*bröy*·kuhrs

How wide is the entrance?
Hoe breed is de ingang?
hoo breyt is duh *in*·khang

Are guide dogs permitted?
Zijn geleidehonden toegelaten?
zeyn khuh·*ley*·duh·hon·duhn too·khuh·laa·tuhn

How many steps are there?
Hoeveel treden zijn er?
hoo·*veyl* trey·duhn zeyn uhr

Is there an elevator/lift?
Is er een lift?
is uhr uhn lift

Are there disabled toilets?
Zijn er toiletten voor gehandicapten?
zeyn uhr twa·*le*·tuhn vohr khuh·*hen*·dee·kep·tuhn/ khuh·*han*·dee·kap·tuhn Ⓝ/Ⓑ

Are there rails in the bathroom?
Is er een reling in de badkamer?
is uhr uhn *rey*·ling in duh *bat*·kaa·muhr

Is there somewhere I can sit down?
Kan ik hier ergens neerzitten?
kan ik heer *er*·khuhns *neyr*·zi·tuhn

Could you call me a disabled taxi?
Kunt u een taxi voor gehandicapten voor me bestellen alstublieft? pol
kunt ew uhn *tak*·see vohr khuh·*hen*·dee·kep·tuhn/ khuh·*han*·dee·kap·tuhn vohr muh buh·*ste*·luhn al·stew·*bleeft* Ⓝ/Ⓑ

Could you help me cross the street safely?
Kunt u me helpen de straat veilig over te steken? pol
kunt ew muh *hel*·puhn duh straat *vey*·likh *oh*·vuhr tuh *stey*·kuhn

guide dog (assistance dog)	*geleidehond*	khuh·*ley*·duh·hont
guide dog (seeing-eye dog)	*blinde-geleidehond*	*blin*·duh·khuh·*ley*·duh·hont
person with a disability	*persoon met een handicap*	puhr·*sohn* met uhn *hen*·dee·kep/ *han*·dee·kap Ⓝ/Ⓑ
ramp	*helling*	*he*·ling
senior person	*oudere persoon*	*aw*·duh·ruh puhr·*sohn*
walking frame	*looprek* n	*lohp*·rek
walking stick	*wandelstok*	*wan*·duhl·stok
wheelchair	*rolstoel*	*rol*·stool

travelling with children

op reis met kinderen

Where's the nearest …?	*Waar is de dichtsbijzijnde …?*	waar is duh dikhts·bey·zeyn·duh …
drinking fountain	*drinkwaterfontein*	dringk·waa·tuhr·fon·teyn
playground	*speeltuin*	speyl·töyn
Where's the nearest …?	*Waar is het dichtsbijzijnde …?*	waar is huht dikhts·bey·zeyn·duh …
park	*park*	park
swimming pool	*zwembad*	zwem·bat
tap	*kraantje*	kraan·chuh
theme park	*pretpark*	pret·park
Do you sell …?	*Verkoopt u …?* pol	vuhr·kohpt ew …
baby wipes	*babydoekjes*	bey·bee·dook·yuhs
disposable nappies	*wegwerpluiers*	wekh·werp·löy·yuhrs
painkillers for infants	*pijnstillers voor babies*	peyn·sti·luhrs vohr bey·bees
Is there a …?	*Is er een …?*	is uhr uhn …
baby change room	*kamer om babies te verschonen*	kaa·muhr om bey·bees tuh vuhr·skhoh·nuhn
child discount	*korting voor kinderen*	kor·ting vohr kin·duh·ruhn
child-minding service	*oppasdienst*	o·pas·deenst
children's menu	*kindermenu*	kin·duhr·muh·new
child's portion	*portie voor kinderen*	por·see vohr kin·duh·ruhn
crèche	*crèche*	kresh
family ticket	*familieticket*	fa·mee·lee·ti·kuht

I need a/an ...	*Ik heb een ...*	ik hep uhn ...
	nodig.	noh·dikh
baby (car) seat	*baby-*	bey·bee·
	autostoel	aw·toh·stool
(English-	*babysit*	bey·bee·sit
speaking)	*(die Engels*	(dee eng·uhls
babysitter	*spreekt)*	spreykt)
booster seat	*zitting-*	zi·ting·
	verhoger	vuhr·hoh·khuhr
	voor de auto	vohr duh aw·toh
child (bicycle)	*kinderzitje*	kin·duhr·zi·chuh
seat	*voor de fiets*	vohr de feets
child (car) seat	*kinder-*	kin·duhr·
	autostoel	aw·toh·stool
cot	*wieg*	weekh
highchair	*kinderstoel*	kin·duhr·stool
plastic bag	*plastic/*	ples·tik/
	plastieken tas Ⓝ/Ⓑ	plas·tee·kuhn tas
plastic sheet	*stuk plastic/*	stuk ples·tik/
	plastiek Ⓝ/Ⓑ	plas·teek
potty	*potje*	po·chuh
pram	*kinderwagen*	kin·duhr·waa·khun
pushchair/	*wandel-*	wan·duhl·
stroller	*wagen*	waa·khun
sick bag	*papieren zak*	pa·pee·ruhn zak

Are there any good places to take children around here?
Zijn er hier in de buurt   zeyn uhr heer in duh bewrt
goede plekken om   khoo·duh ple·kuhn om
kinderen mee naar toe   kin·duh·ruhn mey naar too
te nemen?   tuh ney·muhn

Is there space for a pram?
Is er plaats voor een   is uhr plaats vohr uhn
kinderwagen?   kin·duhr·waa·khuhn

Are children allowed?
Zijn kinderen   zeyn kin·duh·ruhn
toegelaten?   too·khuh·laa·tuhn

Where can I change a nappy?
Waar kan ik een luier   waar kan ik uhn löy·yuhr
verschonen?   vuhr·shoh·nuhn

Is it OK if I breast-feed here?

| *Kan ik hier de borst* | kan ik heer duh borst |
| *geven?* | *khey*·vuhn |

Could I have some paper and pencils, please?

Zou ik wat papier en	zaw ik wat pa·*peer* en
enkele potloden kunnen	*eng*·kuh·luh *pot*·loh·duhn
hebben alstublieft? pol	ku·nuhn *he*·buhn al·stew·*bleeft*

Is this suitable for (six)-year-old children?

| *Is dit geschikt voor* | is dit khuh·*skhikt* vohr |
| *kinderen van (zes) jaar?* | *kin*·duh·ruhn van (zes) yaar |

Do you know a dentist/doctor who is good with children?

Kent u een tandarts/	kent ew een *tan*·darts/
dokter die goed is met	*dok*·tuhr dee khoot is met
kinderen? pol	*kin*·duh·ruhn

If your child is sick, see **health**, page 199.

talking with children

In this section, phrases are in the informal *je* yuh (you) form only. For more details, see the box **all about you** on page 109.

What's your name?
Hoe heet je? · hoo heyt yuh

How old are you?
Hoe oud ben je? · hoo awt ben yuh

When's your birthday?
Wanneer is je verjaardag? · wa·*neyr* is yuh vuhr·*yaar*·dakh

Do you have a brother/sister?
Heb jij een broer/zus? · hep yey uhn broor/zus

Do you go to kindergarten?
Ga je naar de kleuterschool? · khaa yuh naar duh *klöy*·tuhr·skhohl

Do you go to school?
Ga je naar school? · khaa yuh naar skhohl

What grade are you in?
In welk jaar zit je? · in welk yaar zit yuh

Do you like …?

school	*Ga je graag naar school?*	khaa yuh khraakh naar skhohl
sport	*Hou je van sport?*	haw yuh van sport
your teacher	*Vind je je juf/ meester leuk?* m/f	vint yuh yuh yuf/ *meys*·tuhr leuk

Do you learn (English)?
Leer je (Engels)? · leyr yuh (*eng*·uhls)

What do you do after school?
Wat doe je na school? · wat doo yuh naa skhohl

Who's your favourite sportsperson?
Wie is jouw favoriete sportman/sportvrouw? m/f · wee is yaw fa·voh·*ree*·tuh *sport*·man/*sport*·vraw

Are you lost?
Ben je de weg kwijt? · ben yuh duh wekh kweyt

talking about children

In this section, phrases are in the informal *je* yuh (you) form only. For more details, see the box **all about you** on page 109.

When's the baby due?
Wanneer wordt de baby verwacht?
wa·*neyr* wort duh *bey*·bee vuhr·*wakht*

What are you going to call the baby?
Welke naam heb je gekozen voor de baby?
wel·kuh naam hep yuh khuh·*koh*·zuhn vohr duh *bey*·bee

Is this your first child?
Is dit je eerste kindje?
is dit yuh *eyr*·stuh *kin*·chuh

How many children do you have?
Hoeveel kinderen heb je?
hoo·*veyl* *kin*·duh·ruhn hep yuh

What a beautiful child!
Wat een mooi kind!
wat uhn moy kint

Is it a boy or a girl?
Is het een jongen of een meisje?
is huht uhn *yong*·uhn of uhn *mey*·shuh

What's his/her name?
Hoe heet hij/zij?
hoo heyt hey/zey

How old is he/she?
Hoe oud is hij/zij?
hoo awt is hey/zey

Does he/she go to school?
Gaat hij/zij naar school?
khaat hey/zey naar skhoh

He/She has your eyes.
Hij/Zij heeft jouw ogen.
hey/zey heyft yaw *oh*·khuhn

He/She looks like you.
Hij/Zij lijkt op jou.
hey/zey leykt op yaw

You're all grown up now, so it's about time you heard the truth about Santa Claus. Did you know that the origin of this much-loved figure is *Sinterklaas* sin·tuhr·*klaas* (the word is a corruption of *St Nikolaas* sint·*nee*·koh·laas – the Dutch name for St Nicholas), patron saint of all children? Or that it was the Dutch settlers in New Amsterdam (present-day New York) who brought the tradition of Santa Claus to America?

The festival of St Nicholas is celebrated in the Low Countries on 5 and 6 December. The Catholic church officially recognises 6 December as the name day of this canonised saint, who was a historical figure – the bishop of Myra in Asia Minor in the 4th century. In the Middle Ages, St Nicholas was famous as the patron saint of *zeelieden* zey·lee·duhn (sailors) and *handelaars* han·duh·laars (merchants), and acquired high status in the Low Countries due to their maritime and trade history. Over the centuries, however, St Nicholas' other role – that of the children's patron – became more prominent.

The legend of Sinterklaas in the Low Countries paints him as an old man who lives in Spain, where during the year he takes notes on all children's behaviour. Come November, Sinterklaas, his helper *Zwarte Piet* zwar·tuh peet (Black Pete) – or various Black Petes – and his *witte paard* wi·tuh paart (white horse) arrive by boat in a Dutch port. They're welcomed by the town mayor and their parade through the town is broadcast live on TV.

During his stay, Sinterklaas visits schools, hospitals, offices and homes, leaving presents for the children. To cope with this workload, Sinterklaas relies on an army of *hulpsinterklazen* hulp·sin·tuhr·klaa·zuhn (Sinterklaas helpers) who dress up as Sinterklaas and appear all over the country. Grown-ups and children alike make or buy *cadeautjes* ka·*doh*·tyuhs (presents), hide and disguise them and write *brieven* bree·vuhn (letters) to Sinterklaas or *gedichten* khuh·*dikh*·tuhn (poems) that go with the presents and can gently mock the recipient. The presents are opened and the poems read on St Nicholas' Eve, 5 December – aka *pakjesavond* pak·yuhs·aa·vont (evening of presents) – with *chocolade* shoh·koh·*laa*·duh (chocolate) and *pepernoten* pey·puhr·noh·tuhn (ginger-bread) on the table. In Flanders, the presents are dropped off during the night by Sinterklaas via the *schoorsteen* skhohr·steyn (chimney) and opened by children on the morning of 6 December.

SOCIAL > meeting people

basics

essentiële uitdrukkingen

Yes.	*Ja.*	yaa
No.	*Nee.*	ney
Please.	*Alstublieft.* **pol**	al·stew·*bleeft*
	Alsjeblieft. **inf**	a·shuh·*bleeft*
Thank you	*Dank u (wel).* **pol**	dangk ew (wel)
(very much).	*Dank je (wel).* **inf**	dangk yuh (wel)
You're welcome.	*Graag gedaan.*	khraakh khuh·*daar*
Excuse me.	*Excuseer mij.*	eks·kew·*zeyr* mey
(to get attention)		
Excuse me.	*Pardon.*	par·*don*
(to get past)		
Sorry.	*Sorry.*	*so*·ree

greetings & goodbyes

groeten & afscheid nemen

It's customary to greet people with a firm handshake and often a double cheek kiss or even a triple one – except on business occasions, when you'd do away with the kissing, of course. Young people tend to greet each other with a single quick kiss on one cheek when meeting up. Both men and women can initiate the greeting and kissing.

It's good manners to say *goedendag* (good day) or *dag* (hello) upon entering a shop, and *dag* (bye) or *tot ziens* (see you later) when leaving.

Hello.	*Dag./Hallo.*	dakh/ha·*loh*
Hi. (colloquial)	*Hoi.*	hoy

Good …

morning	*Goedemorgen.*	khoo·duh·*mor*·khuhn
day	*Goedendag.*	khoo·duh·*dakh*
afternoon	*Goedemiddag.*	khoo·duh·*mi*·dakh
evening	*Goedenavond.*	khoo·duh·*naa*·vont
night	*Goedenacht.*	khoo·duh·*nakht*

How are you?
Hoe gaat het   hoo khaat huht
met u/jou? pol/inf   met ew/yaw

Fine. And you?
Goed.   khoot
En met u/jou? pol/inf   en met ew/yaw

What's your name?
Hoe heet u/je? pol/inf   hoo heyt ew/yuh

My name is …
Ik heet …   ik heyt …

I'd like to introduce you to (Wannes).
Laat me u/je aan   laat muh ew/yuh aan
(Wannes) voorstellen. pol/inf   (*wa*·nuhs) *vohr*·ste·luhn

I'm pleased to meet you.
Aangenaam.   *aan*·khuh·naam

This is my …	*Dit is mijn …*	dit is meyn …
child	*kind*	kint
colleague	*collega*	ko·*ley*·kha
friend	*vriend* m	vreent
	vriendin f	vreen·*din*
husband	*man*	man
partner (intimate)	*partner*	*part*·nuhr
wife	*vrouw*	vraw

See you later.	*Tot ziens.*	tot zeens
Bye./Goodbye.	*Dag.*	dakh
Bye! (colloquial)	*Doei!*	dooy
Good night.	*Goedenacht.*	khoo·duh·*nakht*
Bon voyage!	*Goede reis!*	*khoo*·duh reys

addressing people

Forms of address in Dutch are simple. The three terms below are appropriate on all formal occasions and when meeting people for the first time, unless they're young. Always use these titles until the person indicates that it's OK for you to address them with their first name by saying *Je mag mij … noemen.* yuh makh mey … *noo*·muhn (You can call me …). Note that *Juffrouw* is rarely used these days: use it only if you want to be polite to a teenage girl – in all other cases it's old-fashioned.

Mr/Sir	*Meneer (Mr)*	muh·*neyr*
Ms/Mrs/Madam	*Mevrouw (Mevr)*	muh·*vraw*
Miss	*Juffrouw (Mej)*	*yu*·fraw

See also the box **cards on the table** on page 97.

all about you

Dutch has two forms for the English 'you' – *jij* yey and *u* ew. The polite form *u* is used when meeting people for the first time (unless they're young), with older people, people in a position of authority and for everyone you don't know well, unless they indicate that you can address them with *jij* by saying *Zeg maar jij.* zekh maar yey (meaning 'You can use the informal *jij*'). You use the informal *jij* with family, friends and anyone you know well, with children younger than you and with people of more or less your own age in informal settings (such as in pubs or when playing sport). Note that the informal *jij* (emphatic) can also appear as *je* yuh (nonemphatic). The English possessive 'your' also has two variants in Dutch: *jouw* yaw (informal) and *uw* ew (polite). For more on pronouns, see the **phrasebuilder**, page 22.

making conversation

What a beautiful day!
Wat een prachtige dag! — wat uhn *prakh*·ti·khuh dakh

Nice/Awful weather, isn't it?
Mooi/Afschuwelijk weer, niet waar? — moy/af·*skhew*·wuh·luhk weyr neet waar

Do you live here?
Woont u hier? pol — wohnt ew heer
Woon je hier? inf — wohn yuh heer

Where are you going?
Waar gaat u heen? pol — waar khaat ew heyn
Waar ga je heen? inf — waar khaa yuh heyn

Do you like it here?
Vind u/je het hier leuk? pol/inf — vint ew/yuh huht heer leuk

I love it here.
Ik vind het hier erg leuk. — ik vint huht heer erkh leuk

What's this called?
Hoe noem je dit? — hoo noom yuh dit

Can I take a photo (of you)?
Mag ik een foto (van u/je) nemen? pol/inf — makh ik uhn *foh*·toh (van ew/yuh) *ney*·muhn

I'll send you the photo.
Ik stuur de foto op. — ik stewr duh *foh*·toh op

That's (beautiful), isn't it!
Dat is (mooi), niet waar? — dat is (moy) neet waar

Are you here on holiday?
Bent u hier met vakantie? pol — bent ew heer met va·*kan*·see
Ben je hier met vakantie? inf — ben yuh heer met va·*kan*·see

---

etiquette tips

- It's OK to be a little late on social occasions (up to 15 minutes), but be punctual for all official engagements.
- Never forget someone's birthday.
- Don't inquire about a person's salary.

I'm here ...	*Ik ben hier ...*	ik ben heer ...
for a holiday	*met vakantie*	met va·*kan*·see
on business	*op zakenreis*	op *zaa*·kuhn·reys
to study	*om te studeren*	om tuh stew·*dey*·ruhn

How long are you here for?
| *Hoelang blijft u hier?* pol | hoo·*lang* bleyft ew heer |
| *Hoelang blijf je hier?* inf | hoo·*lang* bleyf yuh heer |

I'm here for (four) weeks/days.
| *Ik blijf hier (vier) dagen/ weken.* | ik bleyf heer (veer) *daa*·khuhn/ *wey*·kuhn |

nationalities

nationaliteiten

Where are you from?
| *Waar komt u vandaan?* pol | waar komt ew van·*daan* |
| *Waar kom je vandaan?* inf | waar kom yuh van·*daan* |

I'm from ...	*Ik kom uit ...*	ik kom öyt ...
Australia	*Australië*	aw·*straa*·lee·yuh
Canada	*Canada*	*ka*·na·da
England	*Engeland*	*eng*·uh·lant
South Africa	*Zuid-Afrika*	zöyt·*aa*·free·ka
the USA	*Amerika*	a·*mey*·ree·ka

age

leeftijd

How old ...?	*Hoe oud ...*	hoo awt ...
are you	*bent u* pol	bent ew
	ben je inf	ben yuh
is your	*is uw/jouw*	is ew/yaw
daughter	*dochter* pol/inf	*dokh*·tuhr
is your son	*is uw/jouw*	is ew/yaw
	zoon pol/inf	zohn

I'm ... years old.
  Ik ben ... jaar.   ik ben ... yaar

He/She is ... years old.
  Hij/Zij is ... jaar.   hey/zey is ... yaar

Too old!
  Te oud!   tuh awt

Older/Younger than you think.
  Ouder/Jonger dan   aw·duhr/yong·uhr dan
  u/je denkt. pol/inf   ew/yuh dengkt

I'm younger than I look.
  Ik ben jonger dan ik   ik ben yong·uhr dan ik
  er uitzie.   uhr öyt·zee

For your age, see **numbers & amounts**, page 33.

occupations & studies

beroepen & studies

What's your occupation?
  Wat is uw/jouw beroep? pol/inf   wat is ew/yaw buh·roop

I'm a ...	*Ik ben ...*	ik ben ...
businessperson	*zakenman* m	zaa·kuhn·man
	zakenvrouw f	zaa·kuhn·vraw
chef	*kok*	kok
chocolate maker	*chocolatier*	shoh·koh·la·tye
civil servant	*openbaar*	oh·puhn·baar
	ambtenaar	amp·tuh·naar
farmer	*boer/boerin* m/f	boor/boo·rin
interpreter	*tolk*	tolk
journalist	*journalist*	zhoor·na·list
lawyer	*advocaat*	at·voh·kaat
manual worker	*arbeider* m	ar·bey·duhr
	arbeidster f	ar·beyt·stuhr
student	*student*	stew·dent
teacher (general)	*leraar* m	ley·raar
	lerares f	ley·raa·res
translator	*vertaler*	vuhr·taa·luhr

I work for the European Community.
Ik werk voor de   ik werk vohr duh
Europese Gemeenschap.   eu·roh·*pey*·suh khuh·*meyn*·skhap

I work in the Red Light District.
Ik werk in de rosse buurt.   ik werk in duh *ro*·suh bewrt

I'm self-employed.
Ik werk voor mezelf.   ik werk vohr muh·*zelf*

I work in ...	*Ik werk in ...*	ik werk in ...
administration	*administratie*	at·mee·nee·*straa*·see
health	*de gezondheids-*	duh khuh·*zont*·heyts·
	zorg	zorkh
hospitality	*de horeca-*	duh *hoh*·rey·ka·
	sector	sek·tor

I'm ...	*Ik ben ...*	ik ben ...
retired	*met pensioen*	met pen·*syoon*
unemployed	*werkloos*	*werk*·lohs

What are you studying?	*Wat studeert u?* pol	wat stew·*deyrt* ew
	Wat studeer jij? inf	wat stew·*deyr* yey

I'm studying ...	*Ik studeer ...*	ik stew·*deyr* ...
Dutch	*Nederlands*	*ney*·duhr·lants
humanities	*humane*	hew·*maa*·nuh
	wetenschappen	*wey*·tuhn·skha·puhn
science	*wetenschappen*	*wey*·tuhn·skha·puhn

local talk

Hey!	*He daar!*	hey daar
Great!	*Fantastisch!*	fan·*tas*·tis
Sure.	*Natuurlijk.*	na·*tewr*·luhk
Maybe.	*Misschien.*	mi·*skheen*
No way!	*Geen sprake van!*	kheyn *spraa*·kuh van
Go ahead!	*Doe maar!* Ⓝ	doo maar
	Vooruit! Ⓑ	voh·*röyt*
Just a minute.	*Een minuutje.*	uhn mee·*new*·chuh
Just joking!	*Grapje!*	*khrap*·yuh
It's OK.	*In orde.*	in *or*·duh
No problem.	*Geen probleem.*	kheyn proh·*bleym*
All's OK!	*Alles kits!*	*a*·luhs kits

family

Do you have a …?	*Heeft u een …?* pol	heyft ew uhn …
	Heb jij een …? inf	hep yey uhn …
I have a …	*Ik heb een …*	ik hep uhn …
I don't have a …	*Ik heb geen …*	ik hep kheyn …
brother	*broer*	broor
daughter	*dochter*	*dokh*·tuhr
granddaughter	*kleindochter*	*kleyn*·dokh·tuhr
grandson	*kleinzoon*	*kleyn*·zohn
husband	*man*	man
partner (intimate)	*partner*	*part*·nuhr
sister	*zus*	zus
son	*zoon*	zohn
wife	*vrouw*	vraw

Are you married?
Bent u getrouwd? pol   bent ew khuh·*trawt*
Ben je getrouwd? inf   ben yuh khuh·*trawt*

I live with someone.
Ik woon samen.   ik wohn *saa*·muhn

I'm …	*Ik ben …*	ik ben …
married	*getrouwd*	khuh·*trawt*
separated	*gescheiden*	khuh·*skhey*·duhn
single	*vrijgezel*	*vrey*·khuh·zel

farewells

Tomorrow is my last day here.
Morgen is het mijn   *mor*·khuhn is huht meyn
laatste dag hier.   *laat*·stuh dakh heer

If you come to (Scotland), you can stay with me.
Als je naar (Schotland)   als yuh naar (*skhot*·lant)
komt, dan kan je bij mij   komt dan kan yuh bey mey
logeren. inf   lo·*zhey*·ruhn

Keep in touch!
Laat iets van je horen!   laat eets van yuh *hoh*-ruhn

It's been great meeting you.
Het was leuk u/jou te   huht was leuk ew/yaw tuh
leren kennen. **pol/inf**   *ley*-ruhn ke-nuhn

Here's my ...	*Hier is mijn ...*	heer is meyn ...
What's your ...?	*Wat is uw/*	wat is ew/
	jouw ...? **pol/inf**	yaw ...
address	*adres*	a-dres
email address	*e-mailadres*	ee-meyl-a-dres
phone number	*telefoonnummer*	tey-ley-*fohn*-nu-muhr

---

well-wishing

Bless you! (for sneezing)	*Gezondheid!*	khuh-*zont*-heyt
Cheers! (toast)	*Proost!*	prohst
Congratulations!	*Gefeliciteerd!*	khuh-fey-lee-see-*teyrt*
Good luck!	*Veel geluk!*	veyl khuh-*luk*
Happy birthday!	*Gefeliciteerd met je verjaardag!*	khuh-fey-lee-see-*teyrt* met yuh vuhr-*yaar*-dakh
Happy carnival!	*Prettige carnaval!*	pre-ti-khuh kar-na-*val*
Happy Easter!	*Zalig Pasen!*	zaa-likh *paa*-suhn
Happy festive season!	*Prettige einde-jaarsfeesten!*	pre-ti-khuh eyn-duh-*yaars*-feys-tuhn
Happy holidays!	*Een fijne vakantie!*	uhn *fey*-nuh va-*kan*-see
Happy New Year!	*Gelukkig nieuwjaar!*	khuh-*lu*-kikh neew-yaar
Happy travels!	*Goede reis!*	*khoo*-duh reys
Have a great Sinterklaas!	*Een fijn sinterklaasfeest!*	uhn feyn sin-tuhr-*klaas*-feyst
Merry Christmas!	*Zalig Kerstmis!*	zaa-likh *kerst*-mis

clowning around

They sure know how to turn it on for the *carnaval* kar·na·*val* in the Low Countries. Whatever its origin, the carnival (with Shrove Tuesday) – celebrated in February, just before Lent – was a rite of passage marking the end of winter and the rebirth of nature for the pagans, or contrasting exuberance with abstinence during fasting for Catholics. The carnival heartland lies in the south of the Netherlands and in Flanders – it's said that those north of the rivers Maas and Waal don't know how to handle this feast that's an escape from normal (ie organised) everyday life.

At carnival time, a fever grips the country and everyone lets their hair down. Revellers wear *maskers* mas·kuhrs (masks) and *verkleden zich* vuhr·*kley*·duhn zikh (wear fancy dress), and drink, dance and celebrate with friends and complete strangers alike for days and nights on end. It's OK to act silly and nothing is to be taken seriously – if you venture outside, revellers will drag you into pubs, and you might not emerge for days. Many towns put on a *carnavalstoet* kar·na·*val*·stoot (procession with floats) that carnival groups have worked on for a whole year. Every year, new carnival songs are being composed – and are commercially successful.

It's the ultimate party of nonsense, and one of the best places to witness (and take part in) this debauchery has got to be Maastricht. It's irresistible fun!

In this chapter, phrases are in the informal *je* yuh (you) form only. For more details, see the box **all about you** on page 109.

common interests

algemene interesses

What do you do in your spare time?
Wat doe je in je vrije tijd? wat doo yuh in yuh *vrey*·yuh teyt

Do you like ...?	*Hou je van ...*	haw yuh van ...
I (don't) like ...	*ik hou (niet) van ...*	ik haw (neet) van ...
comics	*stripverhalen*	*strip*·vuhr·haa·luhn
computer games	*computer-spelletjes*	kom·*pyoo*·tuhr·spe·luh·chus
cooking	*koken*	*koh*·kuhn
cycling	*fietsen*	*feet*·suhn
dancing	*dansen*	*dan*·suhn
doing terraces	*terrasjes doen*	tuh·*ra*·shuhs doon
drawing	*tekenen*	*tey*·kuh·nuhn
gardening	*tuinieren*	töy·*nee*·ruhn
going out	*uitgaan*	*öyt*·khaan
hiking	*wandelen*	*wan*·duh·luhn
ice-skating	*schaatsen*	*skhaat*·suhn
music	*muziek*	mew·*zeek*
painting	*schilderen*	*skhil*·duh·ruhn
photography	*fotografie*	foh·toh·khra·*fee*
reading	*lezen*	*ley*·zuhn
shopping	*winkelen*	*wing*·kuh·luhn
surfing the internet	*op het internet surfen*	op huht *in*·tuhr·net *sur*·fuhn
travelling	*reizen*	*rey*·zuhn
watching TV	*TV kijken*	tey·*vey key*·kuhn

For types of sports, see **sport**, page 143, and the **dictionary**.

music

Do you dance?	*Dans je?*	dans yuh
Do you play an instrument?	*Bespeel je een muziek-instrument?*	buh·*speyl* yuh uhn mew·*zeek*·in·strew·ment
Do you sing?	*Zing je?*	zing yuh
What ... do you like?	*Welke ... vind je leuk?*	*wel*·kuh ... vint yuh leuk
bands	*bands* ⓝ	bents
	groepen ⓑ	*khroo*·puhn
music	*muziek*	mew·*zeek*
singers	*zangers*	*zang*·uhrs
Belgian pop music	*Belgische popmuziek*	*bel*·khi·suh *pop*·mew·zeek
classical music	*klassieke muziek*	kla·*see*·kuh mew·*zeek*
Dutch pop music	*Nederpop*	*ney*·duhr·pop
electronic music	*elektronische muziek*	ey·lek·*troh*·ni·suh mew·*zeek*
traditional music	*traditionele muziek*	tra·dee·syoh·*ney*·luh mew·*zeek*
West Flemish rap	*West-Vlaamse rapmuziek*	west·*vlaam*·suh *rep*·mew·zeek
world music	*wereldmuziek*	*wey*·ruhlt·mew·zeek

Off to a concert? See **tickets**, page 46, and **going out**, page 127.

cinema & theatre

I feel like going to a/an ...	*Ik heb zin om naar een ... te gaan.*	ik hep zin om naar uhn ... tuh khaan
ballet	*ballet*	ba·*let*
film	*film*	film
opera	*opera*	*oh*·pey·ra
play	*toneelstuk*	to·*neyl*·stuk

Did you like (the film)?
Vond je (de film) leuk?   vont yuh (duh film) leuk

What's showing at the cinema tonight?
Welke films draaien   wel·kuh films draa·yuhn
vanavond?   va·naa·vont

What's showing at the theatre tonight?
Wat staat er op het   wat staat uhr op huht
theaterprogramma   tey·yaa·tuhr·proh·khra·ma
voor vanavond?   vohr va·naa·vont

Is it in (English)?
Is het in het (Engels)?   is huht in huht (eng·uhls)

Does it have (English) subtitles?
Is het met (Engelse)   is huht met (eng·uhl·suh)
ondertitels?   on·duhr·tee·tuhls

Is this seat taken?
Is deze plaats bezet?   is dey·zuh plaats buh·zet

Have you got tickets for …?
Heb jij kaartjes voor …?   hep yey kaar·chus vohr …

Are there any extra tickets?
Zijn er nog meer kaartjes?   zeyn uhr nokh meyr kaar·chus

I'd like cheap/the best tickets.
Ik wil graag de   ik wil khraakh duh
goedkoopste/beste   khoot·kohp·stuh/bes·tuh
kaartjes.   kaar·chus

Is there a matinee show?
Is er een matinee-   is uhr uhn ma·tee·ney·
voorstelling?   vohr·ste·ling

Have you seen (Antonia's Line)?
Heb jij (Antonia) gezien?   heb yey (an·toh·nya) khuh·zeen

Who's in it?
Wie speelt er in mee?   wee speylt uhr in mey

It stars (Jan Decleir).
Het is met (Jan Decleir).   huht is met (yan duh·kleyr)

I thought it was …	Ik vond het …	ik vont huht …
boring	saai Ⓝ	saay
	vervelend Ⓑ	vuhr·vey·luhnt
excellent	uitstekend	öyt·stey·kuhnt
funny	grappig	khra·pikh
interesting	interessant	in·tey·re·sant
nothing special	niks speciaals	niks spey·syaals
sad	droevig	droo·vikh

I (don't) like …	Ik hou (niet) van …	ik haw (neet) van …
action movies	actiefilms	ak·see·films
animated films	tekenfilms	tey·kuhn·films
(Dutch/	(Nederlandse/	(ney·duhr·lant·suh/
Flemish)	Vlaamse)	vlaam·suh)
cinema	cinema	see·ney·ma
comedies	komedies	koh·mey·dees
horror movies	griezelfilms	khree·zuhl·films
short films	kortfilms	kort·films
war movies	oorlogsfilms	ohr·lokhs·films

The Dutch equivalent of the French *cabaret* is *kleinkunst* *kleyn*·kunst (lit: small-art), with the *luisterlied* *löy*·stuhr·leet (lit: listening-song) the equivalent of the French *chanson*. The term *kleinkunst* is said to refer to the intimate character of the art form. The *Amsterdamse Academie voor Kleinkunst* was founded in 1960. Wim Kan (1911–1983), Toon Hermans (1916–2000), Wim Sonneveld (1917–1974) and Jules de Corte (1924–1996) are much-loved legends. Other successful *kleinkunstenaars* *kleyn*·kuns·tuh·naars (*kleinkunst* artists) are Paul van Vliet, Liesbeth List, Ramses Shaffy, Boudewijn de Groot, Bram Vermeulen and Stef Bos. Pop artists such as Rob de Nijs and Thé Lau are also counted among the best in the genre.

In Flanders, the term *kleinkunst* refers to artists who perform in Dutch, accompanied by a few (usually acoustic) instruments. For a taste of Flemish *kleinkunst*, check out Wannes Van de Velde, Raymond van het Groenewoud or the band Laïs. *Kleinkunstenaars* also make part of the line-up at the annual *Dranouter Folkfestival* dra·noo·tuhr folk·fes·ti·val in August.

feelings

gevoelens

Are you ...?	*Bent u ...?* pol	bent ew ...
	Ben jij ...? inf	ben yey ...
I'm (not) ...	*Ik ben (niet) ...*	ik ben (neet) ...
annoyed	*geërgerd*	khuh·*erkh*·uhrt
disappointed	*teleurgesteld*	tuh·*leur*·khuh·stelt
embarrassed	*gegeneerd*	khuh·zhuh·*neyrt*
happy	*gelukkig*	khuh·*lu*·kikh
in a hurry	*gehaast*	khuh·*haast*
sad	*droevig*	*droo*·vikh
surprised	*verrast*	vuh·*rast*
tired	*moe*	moo
worried	*ongerust*	on·khuh·*rust*

Are you ...?	*Heeft u ...?* pol	heyft ew ...
	Heb jij ...? inf	hep yey ...
I'm (not) ...	*ik heb (geen) ...*	ik hep (kheyn) ...
homesick	*heimwee*	*heym*·wey
hungry	*honger*	*hong*·uhr
thirsty	*dorst*	dorst

Are you hot/cold?
Heeft u het warm/koud? pol   heyft ew huht warm/kawt
Heb jij het warm/koud? inf   hep yey huht warm/kawt

I'm (not) hot/cold.
Ik heb het (niet) warm/koud.   ik hep huht (neet) warm/kawt

Are you well?
Voelt u zich goed? pol   voolt ew zikh khoot
Voel je je goed? inf   vool ye ye khoot

I'm (not) well.
Ik voel me (niet) goed.   ik vool muh (neet) khoot

If you're not feeling well, see **health**, page 199.

mixed feelings

not at all	*helemaal niet*	hey·luh·*maal* neet
I don't care at all.	*Ik geef er helemaal niet om.*	ik kheyf uhr hey·luh·*maal* neet om
a little	*een beetje*	uhn *bey*·chuh
I'm a little sad.	*Ik ben een beetje droevig.*	ik ben uhn *bey*·chuh *droo*·vikh
very	*heel*	heyl
I'm very tired.	*Ik ben heel moe.*	ik ben heyl moo
extremely	*ontzettend*	ont·*ze*·tuhnt
I'm extremely worried.	*Ik ben ontzettend ongerust.*	ik ben ont·*ze*·tuhnt on·khuh·*rust*

opinions

opinies

Did you like it?
Vond u/je het leuk? pol/inf vont ew/yuh huht leuk

What do you think of it?
Wat vond u/je er van? pol/inf wat vont ew/yuh uhr van

I thought it was …	*Ik vond het …*	ik vont huht …
It's …	*Het is …*	huht is …
awful	*afschuwelijk*	af·*skhew*·wuh·luhk
beautiful	*prachtig*	*prakh*·tikh
boring	*saai* ⓝ	saay
	vervelend ⓑ	vuhr·*vey*·luhnt
(too) expensive	*(te) duur*	(tuh) dewr
great	*geweldig*	khuh·*wel*·dikh
interesting	*interessant*	in·tey·re·*sant*
strange	*raar*	raar

politics & social issues

Who do you vote for?
Voor wie stemt u? pol — vohr wee stemt ew
Voor wie stem je? inf — vohr wee stem yuh

I'm (Australian), but I didn't vote for …
Ik ben (Australiër/ — ik ben (aw·straa·lee·yuhr/
Australische), maar ik — aw·straa·li·suh) maar ik
heb niet op … gestemd. m/f — hep neet op … khuh·stemt

I support the … party.	*Ik steun de … partij.*	ik steun duh … par·tey
communist	*communistische*	ko·mew·nis·ti·suh
conservative	*conservatieve*	kon·ser·va·tee·vuh
democratic	*democratische*	dey·moh·kraa·ti·suh
green	*groene*	khroo·nuh
liberal	*liberale*	lee·bey·raa·luh
social	*sociaal-*	soh·syaal·
democratic	*democratische*	dey·moh·kraa·ti·shuh
socialist	*socialistische*	soh·sya·lis·ti·suh

Did you hear about …?
Heeft u gehoord over …? pol — heyft ew khuh·hohrt oh·vuhr …
Heb je gehoord over …? inf — hep yuh khuh·hohrt oh·vuhr …

Do you agree with it?
Gaat u er mee akkoord? pol — khaat ew uhr mey a·kohrt
Ga je er mee akkoord? inf — khaa yuh uhr mey a·kohrt

I (don't) agree with …
Ik ga (niet) akkoord met … — ik khaa (neet) a·kohrt met …

How do people feel about …?
Wat denkt men hier — wat dengkt men heer
over …? — oh·vuhr …

How can we protest against …?
Hoe kunnen we — hoo ku·nuhn wuh
protesteren tegen …? — proh·tes·tey·ruhn tey·khuhn …

How can we support …?
Hoe kunnen we … steunen? — hoo ku·nuhn wuh … steu·nuhn

abortion	*abortus*	a·*bor*·tus
corruption	*corruptie*	ko·*rup*·see
crime	*misdaad*	*mis*·daad
drugs	*drugs*	drukhs
the economy	*de economie*	duh ey·koh·noh·*mee*
education	*onderwijs* n	on·duhr·*weys*
euthanasia	*euthanasie*	eu·ta·na·*zee*
federalism	*federalisme* n	fey·dey·ra·*lis*·muh
foreign aid	*ontwikkelingshulp*	ont·*wi*·kuh·lings·hulp
globalisation	*globalisering*	khloh·ba·lee·*zey*·ring
human rights	*mensenrechten* n pl	*men*·suh·rekh·tuhn
immigration	*immigratie*	ee·mee·graa·see
language frontier	*taalgrens*	*taal*·khrens
nationalism	*nationalisme* n	na·syoh·na·*lis*·muh
party politics	*partijpolitiek*	par·*tey*·poh·lee·teek
poverty	*armoede*	*ar*·moo·duh
privatisation	*privatisering*	pree·va·tee·*zey*·ring
prostitution	*prostitutie*	pros·tee·*tew*·see
racism	*racisme* n	ra·*sis*·muh
security	*veiligheid*	*vey*·likh·heyt
sexism	*seksisme* n	*sek*·sis·muh
social welfare	*sociale*	soh·*syaa*·luh
	zekerheid	*zey*·kuhr·heyt
taxes	*belastingen*	buh·*las*·ting·uhn
terrorism	*terrorisme* n	te·roh·*ris*·muh
unemployment	*werkloosheid*	*werk*·lohs·heyt
war in (Iraq)	*oorlog in (Irak)*	*ohr*·lokh in (ee·*rak*)

Is there help for (the) …?	*Is er hulp voor …?*	is uhr hulp vohr …
aged	*bejaarden*	buh·*yaar*·duhn
beggars	*bedelaars*	*bey*·duh·laars
homeless	*daklozen*	*dak*·loh·zuhn
street kids	*straatkinderen*	*straat*·kin·duh·ruhn

A hot topic for discussion is the so-called *gedoogbeleid* khu·*dohkh*·buh·leyt (lit: leeway-policy) – the government policy of 'condoning to a certain degree' activities prohibited by law. The notorious example of this in the Netherlands is the use of soft drugs – an illegal activity, *gedoogd* khu·*dohkht* (condoned) in a few circumstances only.

Another concept that has its origin in the Dutch desire to live independently but in harmony with each other is *verzuiling* vuhr·*zöy*·ling (pillarisation) – the practice of organising the social order according to religious and ideological lines. Although this practice is passé now, you'll still find traces of it everywhere. For instance, the various Dutch broadcasters are still linked to religious or social groups, eg AVRO (general), BNN (youth), EO (Protestant), KRO (Catholic), NCRV (Protestant), TROS (general), VARA (social-democratic) and VPRO (progressive programmes). It fits the typical Dutch way of ensuring freedom of expression, pluralism and independence – or, as the Dutch say, *leven en laten leven* ley·vuhn en *laa*·tuhn ley·vuhn (live and let live).

the environment

het milieu

Is this a protected ...?	*Is dit een ...?*	is dit uhn ...
forest	*beschermd bos*	be·*skhermt* bos
park	*beschermd park*	be·*skhermt* park
species	*beschermde soort*	be·*skherm*·duh sohrt

Is there a ... problem here?
Is er hier een probleem met ...?
is uhr heer uhn proh·*bleym* met ...

What should be done about ...?
Wat moet er gebeuren met ...?
wat moot uhr khuh·*beu*·ruhn met ...

animal rights	dierenwelzijn n	dee·ruhn·wel·zeyn
carbon dioxide emissions	koolstofdioxide-emissie	kohl·stof·dee·yok·see·duh·ey·mee·see
climate change	klimaat-verandering	klee·maat·vuhr·an·duh·ring
deforestation	ontbossing	ont·bo·sing
drought	droogte	drohkh·tuh
endangered species	bedreigde diersoort	buh·dreykh·duh deer·sohrt
energy savings	energie-besparing	ey·ner·khee·buh·spaa·ring
the environment	het milieu n	huht mil·yeu
flood risk	overstromings-gevaar n	oh·vuhr·stroh·mings·khuh·vaar
genetically modified food	genetisch gemodificeerd voedsel n	khey·ney·tis khuh·moh·dee·fee·seyrt voot·suhl
global warming	broeikaseffect n	brooy·kas·e·fekt
hydroelectricity	waterkracht-centrales	waa·tuhr·krakht·sen·traa·luhs
intensive farming	intensieve landbouw	in·ten·see·vuh lant·baw
irrigation	irrigatie	ee·ree·khaa·see
nuclear energy	atoomenergie	a·tohm·ey·ner·khee
nuclear testing	atoomtesten	a·tohm·tes·tuhn
nuclear waste	nucleair afval n	new·kley·yer af·val
overfertilisation	overbemesting	oh·vuhr·buh·mes·ting
ozone layer	ozonlaag	oh·zon·laakh
pesticides	pesticides	pes·tee·see·duhs
pollution	vervuiling	vuhr·vöy·ling
protected species	beschermde diersoort	buh·skherm·duh deer·sohrt
rising sea levels	stijgend zeeniveau n	stey·khuhnt zey·nee·voh
solar power	zonne-energie	zo·nuh·ey·ner·khee
sustainable energy	duurzame energie	dewr·zaa·muh ey·ner·khee
toxic waste	giftig afval n	khif·tikh af·val
water shortage	watertekort n	waa·tuhr·tuh·kort
water supply	watertoevoer	waa·tuhr·too·voor
wind power	windenergie	wint·ey·ner·khee

where to go

What's there to do in the evenings?
Wat is er 's avonds   wat is uhr *saa*·vonts
te doen?   tuh doon

What's on …?	*Wat is er …*	wat is uhr …
	te doen?	tuh doon
locally	*hier*	heer
today	*vandaag*	van·*daakh*
tonight	*vanavond*	va·*naa*·vont
this weekend	*dit weekend*	dit *wey*·kent

Where can I	*Waar vind ik*	waar vint ik
find …?	*de …?*	duh …
(night)clubs	*(nacht)clubs*	(*nakht*·)klups
gay/lesbian	*homotenten*	hoh·moh·ten·tuhn
venues		
places to eat	*eetgelegen-*	*eyt*·khuh·ley·khuhn·
	heden	hey·duhn
pubs	*cafés*	ka·*feys*
	kroegen	*kroo*·khuhn

Is there a local	*Is er een …?*	is uhr uhn …
… guide?		
entertainment	*plaatselijke*	*plaat*·suh·luh·kuh
	uitgaansgids	*öyt*·khaans·khits
film	*plaatselijk*	*plaat*·suh·luhk
	filmprogramma	*film*·proh·khra·ma
gay/lesbian	*plaatselijke*	*plaat*·suh·luh·kuh
	homogids	*hoh*·moh·khits
music	*plaatselijke*	*plaat*·suh·luh·kuh
	muziekgids	mew·*zeek*·khits

I feel like going to a ...	Ik heb zin om naar een ... te gaan.	ik hep zin om naar uhn ... tuh khaan
ballet	balletvoorstelling	ba·let·vohr·ste·ling
bar	bar	bar
café	koffiehuisje Ⓝ	ko·fee·höy·shuh
	brasserie Ⓑ	bra·suh·ree
concert	concert	kon·sert
dance performance	dansvoorstelling	dans·vohr·ste·ling
film	film	film
karaoke bar	karaoke	ka·ra·oh·key
nightclub	nachtclub	nakht·klup
party	feestje/fuif Ⓝ/Ⓑ	fey·shuh/föyf
performance	voorstelling	vohr·ste·ling
play	toneel-voorstelling	to·neyl·vohr·ste·ling
pub	café/kroeg	ka·fey/krookh
restaurant	restaurant	res·toh·rant

For more on types of places to drink and eat, see the box **places to eat & drink**, page 164.

to be or to have – that's the question

Some common expressions that require the verb 'be' in English use *hebben* he·buhn (have) in Dutch:

to be hungry	honger hebben	hong·uhr he·buhn
to be in a hurry	haast hebben	haast he·buhn
to be on leave	vakantie hebben	va·kan·see he·buhn
to be right	gelijk hebben	khu·leyk he·buhn
to be sleepy	slaap hebben	slaap he·buhn
to be thirsty	dorst hebben	dorst he·buhn
to be unlucky	pech hebben	pekh he·buhn
to be wrong	ongelijk hebben	on·khuh·leyk he·buhn

invitations

What are you doing …?	Wat zijn je plannen voor …?	wat zeyn yuh pla·nuhn vohr …
now	nu	new
tonight	vanavond	va·naa·vont
this weekend	dit weekend	dit wey·kent

Would you like to go for a …?	Heb je zin in een …?	hep yuh zin in uhn …
I feel like going for a …	Ik heb zin in een …	ik hep zin in uhn …
beer	biertje	beer·chuh
coffee	koffie	ko·fee
drink	drankje	drangk·yuh
meal	maaltijd	maal·teyt
walk	wandeling	wan·duh·ling

Would you like to go …?	Heb je zin om …?	hep yuh zin om …
I feel like going …	Ik heb zin om …	ik hep zin om …
dancing	te gaan dansen	tuh khaan dan·suhn
out somewhere	uit te gaan	öyt tuh khaan

My round.
Mijn rondje.   meyn ron·chuh

Do you know a good restaurant?
Ken je een goed restaurant?   ken yuh uhn khoot res·toh·rant

Do you want to come to the concert with me?
Zou je met mij naar het concert willen gaan?   zaw yuh met mey naar huht kon·sert wi·luhn khaan

We're having a party.
We houden een feestje/fuif. ⑧/⑤   wuh haw·duhn uhn fey·shuh/föyf

You should come.
Ik hoop dat je komt.   ik hohp dat yuh komt

responding to invitations

Sure!	*Natuurlijk!*	na·tewr·luhk
Yes, I'd love to.	*Ja, graag.*	yaa khraakh

That's very kind of you.
Dat is erg vriendelijk
van u/je. **pol/inf**
dat is erkh *vreen*·duh·luhk
van ew/yuh

Where shall we go?
Waar zullen we naar
toe gaan?
waar *zu*·luhn wuh naar
too khaan

No, I'm afraid I can't.
Nee, ik vrees dat ik niet kan.
ney ik vreys dat ik neet kan

Sorry, I can't sing/dance.
Sorry, maar ik kan niet
zingen/dansen.
so·ree maar ik kan neet
zing·uhn/*dan*·suhn

What about tomorrow?
Misschien morgen?
mi·*skheen* mor·khuhn

orange origins

Ever wondered why the supporters of Dutch national teams at sports matches invariably dress up in *oranje* oh·*ran*·yuh (orange), when the colour doesn't even appear on the Dutch flag? The answer's simple: orange is the national colour of the Netherlands because it refers to the Royal Family's name – *Oranje-Nassau* oh·*ran*·yuh na·saw. The family is known by this name because it used to own the principality of Orange in the south of France. As for the national flag, the orange colour was indeed present on it in earlier times, but it has been replaced with red. On royal birthdays, however, an orange banner is also displayed alongside the standard tricolour as a sign of people's allegiance to the Royal Family. For more on the celebration of national pride on Queen's Day – when the whole country goes orange for the festivities – see the box **party on in the netherlands** on page 42.

arranging to meet

What time will we meet?
Hoe laat spreken we af?   hoo laat *sprey*·kuhn wuh af

Where will we meet?
Waar spreken we af?   waar *sprey*·kuhn wuh af

Let's meet at ... *We zien elkaar ...* wuh zeen el·*kaar* ...
  (eight) o'clock   *om (acht) uur*   om (akht) ewr
  the (entrance)   *bij de (ingang)*   bey duh (*in*·khang)

I'll pick you up.   *Ik pik je op.*   ik pik yuh op
Are you ready?   *Ben je klaar?*   ben yuh klaar
I'm ready.   *Ik ben klaar.*   ik ben klaar
I'll be coming later.   *Ik kom later.*   ik kom *laa*·tuhr
Where will you be?   *Waar vind ik je?*   waar vint ik yuh

If I'm not there by (nine), don't wait for me.
Wacht niet op mij als ik er   wakht neet op mey als ik uhr
om (negen) uur niet ben.   om (*ney*·khuhn) ewr neet ben

I'll see you then!
Tot dan!   tot dan

See you later/tomorrow.
Tot later/morgen.   tot *laa*·tuhr/*mor*·khuhn

I'm looking forward to it.
Ik kijk er echt naar uit.   ik keyk uhr ekht naar öyt

Sorry I'm late.
Sorry dat ik laat ben.   *so*·ree dat ik laat ben

Never mind.
Geen probleem.   kheyn proh·*bleym*

drugs

I don't take drugs.
Ik gebruik geen drugs.   ik khuh·*bröyk* kheyn drukhs

I take … occasionally.
Ik gebruik af en toe …   ik khuh·*bröyk* af en too …

Do you want to have a smoke?
Wil je roken?   wil yuh *roh*·kuhn

Do you have a light?
Heb je een vuurtje?   hep yuh uhn *vewr*·chuh

I'm high.
Ik ben high.   ik ben haay

If the police are talking to you about drugs, see **police**, page 196, for useful phrases.

---

safe swearing

Dutch has many colourful – and often strong – swear words. This said, swearing in public is a definite no-no and will, at the least, be frowned upon and reflect badly on the perpetrator (even if English is their language of choice). Problems are expected to be dealt with in a calm, rational and constructive manner. When something really goes wrong, you can express your frustration in public with a number of safe and acceptable 'swear' options as long as you don't overuse them … and continue to solve the problem without antics. The following expressions are corruptions of more heavy-handed or blasphemous swearing words.

Potverdorie!   *pot*·vuhr·doh·ree
Verdorie!   vuhr·*doh*·ree
Verdomme!   vuhr·*do*·muh

romance

In this chapter, phrases are in the informal *je* yuh (you) form only. For more details, see the box **all about you** on page 109.

asking someone out

iemand uit vragen

Where would you like to go (tonight)?
Waar wil je (vanavond)   waar wil yuh (va·*naa*·vont)
graag heen?   khraakh heyn?

Would you like to do something (tomorrow)?
Wil je (morgen)   wil yuh (*mor*·khuhn)
iets gaan doen?   eets khaan doon

Yes, I'd love to.
Ja, graag.   yaa khraakh

Sorry, I can't.
Sorry, maar ik kan niet.   *so*·ree maar ik kan neet

local talk

He's a babe.	*Hij is een mooierd.*	hey is uhn *moh*·yuhrt
She's a babe.	*Zij is een schoonheid.*	zey is uhn *skhohn*·heyt
He/She is hot.	*Hij/Zij is een lekker stuk.*	hey/zey is uhn *le*·kuhr stuk
He's a bastard.	*Hij is een eikel.* (lit: he is a dickhead)	hey is uhn *ey*·kuhl
	Hij is een zak. (lit: he is a bag)	hey is uhn zak
She's a bitch.	*Zij is een teef.* (lit: she is a bitch)	zey is uhn teyf
	Zij is een heks. (lit: she is a witch)	zey is uhn heks
He/She gets around.	*Hij/Zij slaapt met iedereen.*	hey/zey slaapt met ee·duh·*reyn*

romance

pick-up lines

Would you like a drink?
Wil je iets drinken?   wil yuh eets *dring*·kuhn

You look like someone I know.
Jij lijkt op iemand die ik ken.   yey leykt op *ee*·mant dee ik ken

You're a fantastic dancer.
Jij danst fantastisch.   yey danst fan·*tas*·tees

Do you have a light?
Mag ik een vuurtje?   makh ik uhn *vewr*·chuh

Do you hate pick-up lines too?
Heb jij ook zo'n hekel   hep yey ohk zohn *hey*·kuhl
aan versiertrucs?   aan vuhr·*seer*·truks

I'm attracted to your phone number.
Ik voel me aangetrokken   ik vool muh *aan*·khuh·tro·kuhn
tot jouw telefoonnummer.   tot yaw tey·ley·*fohn*·nu·muhr

If you think you can pick me up, then you're right.
Als je denkt mij te   als yuh dengkt mey tuh
kunnen versieren, dan   ku·nuhn vuhr·*see*·ruhn dan
heb je het goed.   hep yuh huht khoot

Those clothes would look great in a pile next to my bed.
Die kleding zou   dee *kley*·ding zaw
geweldig staan op een   khuh·*wel*·dikh staan op uhn
hoopje naast mijn bed.   *hohp*·yuh naast meyn bet

Can I ...?	*Mag ik ...?*	makh ik ...
dance with you	*met je dansen*	met yuh *dan*·suhn
sit here	*hier zitten*	heer *zi*·tuhn
take you home	*je naar huis*	yuh naar höys
	vergezellen	vuhr·khuh·*ze*·luhn

rejections

I'm here with my girlfriend/boyfriend.
Ik ben hier met mijn   ik ben heer met meyn
vriendin/vriend.   vreen·din/vreent

Excuse me, I have to go now.
Sorry maar ik moet   so·ree maar ik moot
er vandoor.   uhr van·dohr

I'd rather not.   *Liever niet.*   lee·vuhr neet
No, thank you.   *Nee, dank je wel.*   ney dangk yuh wel

hard talk

The language below is very firm and only to be used if you're being badly hassled.

Donder op!	don·duhr op	Piss off!
Hoepel op!	hoo·puhl op	Piss off!
Hou je mond!	haw yuh mont	Shut up!
Laat me met rust!	laat met rust	Leave me alone!
Val dood!	val doht	Drop dead!

getting closer

I really like you.   *Ik vind je echt leuk.*   ik vint yuh ekht leuk
You're great.   *Jij bent fantastisch.*   yey bent fan·tas·tees
Can I kiss you?   *Mag ik je kussen?*   makh ik yuh ku·suhn

Do you want to come inside for a while?
Wil je eventjes   wil yuh ey·vuhn·chuhs
binnen komen?   bi·nuhn koh·muhn

Would you like to stay over?
Wil je blijven slapen?   wil yuh bley·vuhn slaa·puhn

Can I stay over?
Kan ik blijven slapen?   kan ik bley·vuhn slaa·puhn

seks

Kiss me.
Kus me.   kus muh

I want you.
Ik wil je.   ik wil yuh

Let's go to bed.
Laten we naar bed gaan.   laa·tuhn wuh naar bet khaan

Touch me here.
Raak me hier aan.   raak muh heer aan

Do you like this?
Vind je dit fijn?   vint yuh dit feyn

I (don't) like that.
Ik vind dat (niet) fijn.   ik vint dat (neet) feyn

I think we should stop now.
Ik denk dat we er hier mee   ik denk dat wuh uhr heer mey
moeten stoppen.   moo·tuhn sto·puhn

Do you have a (condom)?
Heb jij een (condoom)?   hep yey uhn (kon·dohm)

Let's use a (condom).
Laten we een (condoom)   laa·tuhn wuh uhn (kon·dohm)
gebruiken.   khuh·bröy·kuhn

I won't do it without protection.
Ik doe het niet zonder   ik doo huht neet zon·duhr
voorbehoedmiddel.   voor·buh·hoot·mi·duhl

It's my first time.
Het is mijn eerste keer.   huht is meyn eyr·stuh keyr

Don't worry, I'll do it myself.
Geen probleem, ik doe   kheyn proh·bleym ik doo
het zelf wel.   huht zelf wel

It helps to have a sense of humour.
Het helpt als je een goed   huht helpt als yuh uhn khoot
gevoel voor humor hebt.   khuh·vool vohr hew·mor hept

Is that why you're single?
Is dat waarom je   is dat waa·rom yuh
vrijgezel bent?   vrey·khuh·zel bent

Oh my god!	Hemeltje!	hey·muhl·chuh
That's great.	Dat is fantastisch!	dat is fan·tas·tees
Easy tiger!	Zachtjesaan	zakh·yuhs·aan
	lekker stuk!	le·kuhr stuk

faster	sneller	sne·luhr
harder	harder	har·duhr
slower	trager	traa·khuhr
softer	zachter	zakh·tuhr

That was ...	Dat was ...	dat was ...
heavenly	hemels	hey·muhls
incredible	ongelofelijk	on·khuh·loh·fuh·luhk
romantic	romantisch	roh·man·tees
wild	wild	wilt

sweet nothings

engeltje	eng·uhl·chuh	little angel
gekkie	khe·kee	little fool
liefje	leef·yuh	little darling
mooierd	moh·yuhrt	beauty m
schatje	skha·chuh	little treasure
schoonheid	skhohn·heyt	beauty f
tijgertje	tey·khuhr·chuh	little tiger
troetelbeertje	troo·tuhl·beyr·chuh	little cuddly bear

love

I think we're good together.
Ik vind dat we goed bij
elkaar passen.
ik vint dat wuh khoot bey
el·kaar pa·suhn

| I love you. | Ik hou van je. | ik haw van yuh |

Will you ...?	Wil je met ...?	wil yuh met ...
go out with me	me uitgaan	muh öyt·khaan
marry me	me trouwen	muh traw·wuhn
meet my	mijn ouders	meyn aw·duhrs
parents	kennismaken	ke·nis maa·kuhn

problems

I don't think it's working out.
Ik denk dat het niet lukt
tussen ons tweetjes.
ik dengk dat huht neet lukt
tu·suhn ons *twey*·chus

Are you seeing someone else?
Heb je iemand anders?
hep yuh *ee*·mant *an*·duhrs

He/She is just a friend.
Hij/Zij is alleen maar
een vriend/vriendin. m/f
hey/zey is a·*leyn* maar
uhn vreent/vreen·*din*

You're just using me for sex.
Je gebruikt me alleen
maar voor de seks.
yuh khuh·*bröykt* muh a·*leyn*
maar vohr duh seks

I want to call it off.
Ik wil het uitmaken.
ik wil huht öyt·maa·kuhn

I never want to see you again.
Ik wil je nooit meer zien.
ik wil yuh noyt meyr zeen

We'll work it out.
We lossen het wel op.
wuh *lo*·suhn huht wel op

leaving

I have to leave (tomorrow).
Ik moet (morgen)
vertrekken.
ik moot (*mor*·khuhn)
vuhr·*tre*·kuhn

I'll …	*Ik zal …*	ik zal …
keep in touch	*contact houden*	kon·*takt haw*·duhn
miss you	*je missen*	yuh *mi*·suhn
visit you	*je opzoeken*	yuh *op*·zoo·kuhn

beliefs & cultural differences
principes & culturele verschillen

religion

godsdienst

What's your religion?
Wat is uw/jouw   wat is ew/yaw
godsdienst? pol/inf   khots·deenst

I'm not religious.
Ik ben niet gelovig.   · ik ben neet khuh·loh·vikh

I'm …	*Ik ben …*	ik ben …
agnostic	*agnostisch*	akh·nos·tees
Buddhist	*boeddhist*	boo·dist
Catholic	*katholiek*	ka·toh·leek
Christian	*christelijk*	kris·tuh·luhk
Hindu	*hindoe*	hin·doo
Jewish	*joods*	yohts
Lutheran	*luthers*	lew·tuhrs
Muslim	*moslim*	mos·lim
Protestant	*protestants*	proh·tes·tans

I (don't) believe in …	*Ik geloof (niet) in …*	ik khuh·lohf (neet) in …
astrology	*astrologie*	a·stroh·loh·khee
fate	*het lot*	huht lot
God	*God*	khot

Can I … here?	*Kan ik hier …?*	kan ik heer …
Where can I …?	*Waar kan ik …?*	waar kan ik …
attend a service	*een dienst bijwonen*	uhn deenst bey·woh·nuhn
attend mass	*een mis bijwonen*	uhn mis bey·woh·nuhn
pray/worship	*bidden*	bi·duhn

beliefs & cultural differences

cultural differences

I didn't mean to do/say anything wrong.
Het was niet mijn — huht was neet meyn
bedoeling iets verkeerds — buh·*doo*·ling eets vuhr·*keyrts*
te doen/zeggen. — tuh doon/*ze*·khuhn

Is this a local or national custom?
Is dit een plaatselijk of — is dit uhn *plaat*·suh·luhk of
een algemeen gebruik? — uhn al·khuh·*meyn* khuh·*bröyk*

I don't want to offend you.
Ik wil u/je niet — ik wil ew/yuh neet
beledigen. **pol/inf** — buh·*ley*·di·khuhn

I'm not used to this.
Ik ben dit niet gewend. — ik ben dit neet khuh·*went*

I'd rather not join in.
Ik doe liever niet mee. — ik doo *lee*·vuhr neet mey

I'll try it.
Ik probeer het. — ik proh·*beyr* huht

I'm sorry, it's against my ...	*Sorry, maar het druist in tegen ...*	*so*·ree maar huht dröyst in *tey*·khuhn ...
beliefs	*hetgeen*	huht·*kheyn*
	waarin ik geloof	waa·*rin* ik khuh·*lohf*
principles	*mijn principes*	meyn prin·*see*·puhs
religion	*mijn*	meyn
	godsdienst	*khots*·deenst

This is ...	*Dit is ...*	dit is ...
different	*anders*	*an*·duhrs
fun	*leuk*	leuk
interesting	*interessant*	in·*tey*·re·*sant*

When's the gallery open?
Wanneer is de
kunstgalerie open?
wa·*neyr* is duh
kunst·kha·luh·*ree oh*·puhn

When's the museum open?
Wanneer is het museum
open?
wa·*neyr* is huht mew·*zey*·yum
oh·puhn

What kind of art are you interested in?
In welke soort kunst ben je
geïnteresseerd?
in *wel*·kuh sohrt kunst ben yuh
khuh·in·tey·re·*seyrt*

What's in the collection?
Waaruit bestaat de
collectie?
waa·*röyt* buh·*staat* duh
koh·*lek*·see

What do you think of …?
Wat vind je van …?
wat vint yuh van …

It's an exhibition of …
Het is een
tentoonstelling van …
huht is uhn
tuhn·*tohn*·ste·ling van …

I'm interested in …
Ik ben geïnteresseerd in …
ik ben khuh·in·tey·re·*seyrt* in …

I like the works of …
Ik hou van het werk van …
ik haw van huht werk van …

It reminds me of …
Het doet me
denken aan …
huht doot muh
deng·kuhn aan …

architecture	architectuur	ar·khee·tek·tewr
art	kunst	kunst
artwork	kunstwerk n	kunst·werk
curator	curator	kew·raa·tor
design (artwork) n	ontwerp n	ont·werp
etching	etsen	et·suhn
exhibit n	voorwerp n	vohr·werp
exhibition hall	zaal	zaal
graphic a	grafisch	khraa·fis
installation	installatie	in·sta·laa·see
opening (exhibition)	opening	oh·puh·ning
opening (theatre)	première	pruh·myey·ruh
painter	schilder	skhil·duhr
painting (artwork)	schilderij n	skhil·duh·rey
painting (technique)	schilderkunst	skhil·duhr·kunst
performance	voorstelling	vohr·ste·ling
period	periode	pey·ryoh·duh
permanent	permanente	per·ma·nen·tuh
collection	tentoonstelling	tuhn·tohn·ste·ling
print n	druk	druk
sculptor	beeldhouwer	beylt·haw·wuhr
sculpture	beeldhouwwerk n	beylt·haw·werk
statue	standbeeld n	stant·beylt
style n	stijl	steyl
technique	techniek	tekh·neek
varnishing day	vernissage	ver·nee·saa·zhuh

art through the ages

Amsterdamse School   am·stuhr·dam·suh skhohl
Amsterdam School – an architectural movement from the first half of the 20th century

de CoBrA groep   duh koh·bra khroop
the CoBrA group – a 1940s avant-garde group of artists from Copenhagen, Brussels and Amsterdam

De Stijl   duh steyl
De Stijl (lit: the style) – a group of artists, architects and designers in the Netherlands during the 1920s and 1930s

Vlaamse Primitieven   vlaam·suh pree·mee·tee·vuhn
Flemish Primitives – a group of painters from the 15th century

142

sporting interests

sportieve interesses

What sport do you follow/play?
Welke sport volg/ beoefen je? — wel·kuh sport volkh/ buh·oo·fuhn yuh

I follow …	*Ik volg het …*	ik volkh huht …
I play …	*Ik speel …*	ik speyl …
basketball	*basketball*	*bas*·ket·bal
football (soccer)	*voetbal*	*voot*·bal
hockey	*hockey*	*ho*·kee
tennis	*tennis*	*te*·nis
volleyball	*volleybal*	*vo*·lee·bal

I follow …	*Ik volg …*	ik volkh …
athletics	*de atletiek*	duh at·ley·*teek*
cycling	*het wielrennen*	huht *weel*·re·nuhn

I do …	*Ik …*	ik …
athletics	*doe aan atletiek*	doo aan at·ley·*teek*
ice-skating	*schaats*	skhaats
karate	*doe aan karate*	doo aan ka·*raa*·tey
motorcross	*doe aan motorcross*	doo aan *moh*·tor·kros
scuba diving	*duik*	döyk

I …	*Ik …*	ik …
cycle (casual)	*fiets*	feets
cycle (competitive)	*doe aan wielrennen*	doo aan *weel*·re·nuhn
run	*jog*	dzhokh
ski	*ski*	skee
swim	*zwem*	zwem
walk	*wandel*	*wan*·duhl

For more sports, see the **dictionary**.

local sports

Korfbal korf·bal (korfball) is a cross between netball, volleyball and basketball. Two (usually mixed) teams try to score goals by passing the ball through a cane basket mounted on a pole. The baskets on each end of the court have no board for the ball to rebound off. The playing field stretches beyond the baskets, so players can shoot from every angle, including from behind the baskets.

The *duivensport döy·vuhn·sport* (pigeon racing) is popular, especially in Flanders where you'll see many houses with a *duiventil döy·vuhn·til* (pigeon loft) in the backyard and people with pigeon-filled cane baskets on their bicycles, going to the pigeon-racing club on a race day. Not only older people but also youngsters take up the sport for its social dimension and for the 'love of the pigeon'.

A Frisian sport is *fierljeppen feer·lye·puhn* (pole-vaulting across canals). Unlike in pole-vaulting of the track-and-field variety (called *polsstokspringen pol·stok·spring·uhn* in Dutch), it's the distance covered that counts, not the height. Incredible distances are achieved by climbing the pole hand-over-hand while it's in motion. The current record stands at 19.40 metres.

going to a game

naar een wedstrijd gaan

Would you like to go to a game?
Wil je graag naar een   wil yuh khraakh naar uhn
wedstrijd gaan?   *wet*·streyt khaan

Who are you supporting?
Wie is je team?   wee is yuh·teem

What's the score?
Wat is de stand?   wat is duh stant

Who's ...?	Wie ...?	wee ...
playing	speelt er	speylt uhr
winning	gaat er winnen	khaat uhr *wi*·nuhn

That was a …	Dat was een …	dat was uhn …
game!	wedstrijd!	wet·streyt
bad	slechte	slekh·tuh
boring	saaie	saa·yuh
captivating	boeiende	boo·yuhn·duh
great	fantastische	fan·tas·tee·suh
nerve-wrecking	spannende	spa·nuhn·duh

cheering on

C'mon Holland!	Hup Holland hup!	hup ho·lant hup
Go (Holland)!	Kom op (Holland)!	kom op (ho·lant)
	Kom op (Oranje)!	kom op (oh·ran·yuh)
Go (Belgium)!	Allez (België)!	a·ley (bel·khee·yuh)
A goal for (the Red Devils)!	Een goal voor (de Rode Duivels)!	uhn khohl vohr (duh roh·duh döy·vuhls)

playing sport

aan sport doen

Do you want to play/join in?
Wil je spelen/meedoen?   wil yuh *spey*·luhn/*mey*·doon

Can I join in?
Kan ik meedoen?   kan ik *mey*·doon

I have an injury.
Ik heb een blessure.   ik hep uhn ble·*sew*·ruh

Your/My point.
Een punt voor jou/mij.   uhn punt vohr yaw/mey

Kick/Pass it to me!
Geef het aan mij!   kheyf huht aan mey

You're a good player.
Je bent een goede speler.   yuh bent uhn *knoo*·duh *spey*·luhr

Thanks for the game.
Bedankt voor de wedstrijd.   buh·*dangkt* vohr duh *wet*·streyt

Congratulations on the victory.
Gefeliciteerd met de overwinning.   khuh·fey·lee·see·*teyrt* met duh oh·vuhr·*wi*·ning

Where's a good place to ...?	Waar is er een goede plek om te gaan ...?	waar is uhr uhn khoo·duh plek om tuh khaan ...
fish	vissen	vi·suhn
run	joggen	dzho·khuhn
surf	surfen	sur·fuhn

Where's the nearest ...?	Waar is het dichtsbijzijnde ...?	waar is huht dikhts·bey·zeyn·duh ...
golf course	golfterrein	kholf·tuh·reyn
gym	fitnesscentrum	fit·nuhs·sen·trum
swimming pool	zwembad	zwem·bat

Do I have to be a member to attend?
Is lidmaatschap verplicht?   is lit·maat·skhap vuhr·plikht

Is there a women-only session?
Is er een tijd voor   is uhr uhn teyt vohr
vrouwen alleen?   vraw·wuhn a·leyn

Where are the changing rooms?
Waar zijn de kleedkamers?   waar zeyn duh kleyt·kaa·muhrs

What's the charge per ...?	Hoeveel kost het per ...?	hoo·veyl kost huht puhr ...
day	dag	dakh
game	spel	spel
hour	uur	ewr
visit	bezoek	buh·zook

Can I hire a ...?	Kan ik een ... huren?	kan ik uhn ... hew·ruhn
ball	bal	bal
bicycle	fiets	feets
court (basketball)	terrein	tuh·reyn
court (tennis)	(tennis)baan	(te·nis·)baan
racket	racket	re·kuht

What a . .!	*Wat een …!*	wat uhn …
goal	*goal*	gohl/khohl ⑬/⑭
hit	*slag*	slakh
kick	*trap*	trap
pass	*pas*	pas
performance	*performance*	puhr·*fohr*·muhns
shot	*schot*	skhot

cycling

wielrennen

In the Low Countries, *wielrennen* weel·re·nuhn (competitive cycling) is hugely popular and has produced many successful *kampioenen* kam·pee·*yoo*·nuhn (champions). During March and April, Belgium is in the grip of the *Belgische klassiekers* bel·khi·suh kla·*see*·kuhrs (Belgian one-day classics), which include the prestigious and spectacular *Ronde van Vlaanderen* ron·duh van *vlaan*·duh·ruhn (Tour of Flanders). The main event around the same time in Holland is the Amstel Gold Race.

Where does the race start/finish?
Waar is de start/aankomst? waar is duh start/*aan*·komst

Where does the race pass through?
Waar komt de waar komt duh
wedstrijd door? *wet*·streyt dohr

How many kilometres is today's stage/race?
Hoeveel kilometer is hoo·*veyl* kee·lo·mey·tuhr is
de rit/wedstrijd duh rit/*wet*·streyt
van vandaag? van van·*daakh*

Who's winning?
Wie leidt? wee leyt

My favourite cyclist is …
Mijn favoriete meyn fa·voh·*ree*·tuh
wielrenner is … *weel*·re·nuhr is …

Which cycling team is he in?
Voor welk team rijdt hij? vohr welk teem reyt hey

attack n	aanval	aan·val
breakaway	ontsnapping	ont·sna·ping
(mechanical) breakdown	(materiaal)pech	(ma·tey·ryaal·)pekh
chasers	achtervolgers	akh·tuhr·vol·khuhrs
climb n	klim	klim
cobblestones (pavé)	kasseien	ka·sey·yuhn
crash n	val	val
cyclist	wielrenner	weel·re·nuhr
descent	afdaling	af·daa·ling
domestique	knecht	knekht
drug test	dopingcontrole	doh·ping·kon·troh·luh
flat tyre	lekke/platte band ⊛/⊜	le·kuh/pla·tuh bant
gear	versnelling	vuhr·sne·ling
individual time trial	individuele tijdrit	in·dee·vee·dew·wey·luh teyt·rit
(yellow) jersey	(gele) trui	(khey·luh) tröy
leaders	kopgroep	kop·khroop
main rider (of a team)	kopman	kop·man
mountain stage	bergrit	berkh·rit
peloton	peloton n	puh·luh·ton
rainbow jersey (world champion)	regenboogtrui	rey·khun·bohkh·tröy
ranking	klassement n	kla·suh·ment
red lantern (last cyclist in race)	rode lantaarn	roh·duh lan·taarn
soigneur	verzorger	vuhr·zor·khuhr
spring classics	voorjaars- klassiekers	vohr·yaars· kla·see·kuhrs
sprint n	sprint	sprint
stage (in race)	rit	rit
stage winner	ritwinnaar	rit·wi·naar
team car	volgwagen	volkh·waa·khun
team time trial	ploegentijdrit	ploo·khuhn·teyt·rit
winner	winnaar	wi·naar

For phrases on getting around by bike, see **transport**, page 57.

extreme sports

I'd like to go ...
Ik wil graag gaan ...   ik wil khraakh khaan ...

I'd like to try ...
Ik wil graag ... proberen.   ik wil khraakh ... proh·*bey*·ruhn

beachsailing	*strandzeilen* n	*strant*·zey·luhn
caving	*speleologie*	spey·ley·yoh·loh·*khee*
game fishing	*sportvissen* n	*sport*·vi·suhn
hang-gliding	*deltavliegen* n	*del*·ta·vlee·khuhn
parasailing	*zeilvliegen* n	*zeyl*·vlee·khuhn
rock-climbing	*rotsklimmen* n	*rots*·kli·muhn
sailing	*zeilen* n	*zey*·luhn
skydiving	*parachute-*	pa·ra·*shew*·tuh·
	springen n	spring·uhn
white-water rafting	*wildwatervaren*	wilt·*waa*·tuhr·*vaa*·ruhn

Is the equipment secure?
Is deze uitrusting veilig?   is *dey*·zuh öyt·rus·ting *vey*·likh

Is this safe?
Is dit veilig?   is dit *vey*·likh

This is insane.
Dit is krankzinnig.   dit is krangk·*zi*·nikh

For words or phrases you might need while hiking or trekking, see **outdoors**, page 157, and **camping**, page 70.

ice-skating

How long is a session?
Hoe lang is een sessie?   hoo lang is uhn se·see

How much for a session?
Hoeveel kost een sessie?   hoo·*veyl* kost uhn se·see

Can I rent ice skates?
Kan ik schaatsen huren?   kan ik *skhaat*·suhn *hew*·ruhn

My size is (40).
Ik heb maat (veertig).   ik hep maat (*feyr*·tikh)

I need an extra pair of socks.
Ik heb een extra paar   ik hep uhn *ek*·straa paar
sokken nodig.   so·kuhn *noh*·dikh

Can I have my ice skates sharpened?
Kan ik mijn schaatsen   kan ik meyn *skhaat*·suhn
laten slijpen?   *laa*·tuhn *sley*·puhn

How thick is the ice?
Hoe dik is het ijs?   hoo dik is huht eys

Are there any cracks in the ice?
Zijn er barsten in het ijs?   zeyn uhr *bars*·tuhn in huht eys

Will it be thawing?
Gaat het dooien?   khaat huht *doh*·yuhn

Is it safe to go on this ice?
Is het veilig op dit ijs   is huht *vey*·likh op dit eys
te gaan?   tuh khaan

How deep is the water under this ice?
Hoe diep is het water   hoo deep is huht *waa*·tuhr
onder dit ijs?   *on*·duhr dit eys

Sorry, I couldn't stop.
Sorry, ik kon niet stoppen.   *so*·ree ik kon neet *sto*·puhn

Are you all right?
Gaat het?   khaat huht

Ouch, that hurts!
Au, dat doet pijn!   aw dat doot peyn

---

listen for ...

Blijf van het ijs!
  bleyf van huht eys   **Stay off the ice!**

Ga niet op dat ijs!
  khaa neet op dat eys   **Don't go on that ice!**

Dat ijs is gevaarlijk!
  dat eys is khuh·*vaar*·luhk   **That ice is dangerous!**

Het gaat dooien.
  huht khaat *doh*·yuhn   **The thaw is setting in.**

Travelling in the Low Countries during winter can be a lot of fun – not only will there be fewer tourists, but you'll be able to enjoy a vast array of typical winter activities. Over the festive season, many towns set up *kerstijsbanen kerst·eys·baa·nuhn* (temporary Christmas ice rinks) in the main square, often as part of their *kerstmarkt kerst·markt* (Christmas market). You can sip *glühwein khlew·waayn* (hot spiced wine) or *jenever yuh·ney·vuhr/zhuh·ney·vuhr* ⑩/⑱ (gin) with the locals while trying some typical hearty winter snacks to keep you warm. If you're lucky enough to get some snow, you might want to try *langlaufen lang·law·fuhn* (cross-country skiing) or go *sleetje rijden sley·chuh rey·duhn* (tobogganing). And if you're really lucky and the weather gets truly cold for an extended period, you might catch the Netherlands' legendary *Elfstedentocht elf·stey·duhn·tokht* (Eleven Cities Tour), a speed-skating competition as well as a leisure-skating tour – albeit gruelling – of nearly 200 kilometres through the province of Friesland, which has been held 15 times since 1909.

figure skating	*kunstrijden*	*kunst·rey·duhn*
	(op de schaats) n	(op duh skhaats)
gloves	*handschoenen*	*hant·skoo·nuhn*
ice	*ijs* n	eys
ice-boating	*ijszeilen* n	*eys·zey·luhn*
ice field	*ijsvlakte*	*eys·vlak·tuh*
ice hockey	*ijshockey* n	*eys·ho·kee*
(indoor) ice rink	*(overdekte)*	(oh·vuhr·*dek*·tuh)
	ijsbaan	*eys·baan*
ice skates	*schaatsen*	*skhaat·suhn*
ice-skating	*schaatsen* n	*skhaat·suhn*
ice-skating club	*ijsclub*	*eys·klup*
ice-skating competition	*schaatswedstrijd*	*skhaats·wet·streyt*
ice-skating tour	*schaatstocht*	*skhaats·tokht*
mittens	*wanten*	*wan·tuhn*
speed skating	*hardrijden*	*hard·rey·duhn*
	(op de schaats) n	(op duh skhaats)
temporary ice rink	*tijdelijke*	*tey·duh·luh·kuh*
	ijsbaan	*eys·baan*
walking on skates	*klunen*	*klew·nuhn*

sport

151

icy words

have an affair
een scheve   uhn *skhey*·vuh
schaats rijden   skhaats *rey*·duhn
(lit: skate with a bent skate)

pace up and down
ijsberen   *eys*·bey·ruhn
(lit: walk like a polar bear)

a stony stare
een ijskoude blik   uhn *eys*·kaw·duh blik
(lit: an ice-cold stare)

take no risks
niet over één nacht   neet *oh*·vuhr eyn nakht
ijs gaan   eys khaan
(lit: not walk on ice that's one night old)

tread on dangerous grounds
zich op glad ijs wagen   zikh op khlat eys *waa*·khuhn
(lit: go on very slippery ice)

soccer/football

voetbal

Who plays for (PSV Eindhoven)?
Wie speelt er voor (PSV)?   wee speylt uhr vohr (pey·es·*vey*)

He's a great (player).
Hij is een fantastische   hey is uhn fan·*tas*·tee·suh
(speler).   (*spey*·luhr)

He played brilliantly in the match against (Germany).
Hij speelde een   hey *speyl*·duh uhn
fantastische wedstrijd   fan·*tas*·tee·suh *wet*·streyt
tegen (Duitsland).   *tey*·khuhn (*döyts*·lant)

Which team is at the top of the league?
Welk team staat aan de top   welk teem staat aan duh top
van de rangschikking?   van duh *rang*·skhi·king

What a great/terrible team!
Wat een fantastisch/   wat uhn fan·*tas*·tees/
slecht team!   slekht teem

attack v	aanvallen	aan·va·luhn
attacker	aanvaller	aan·va·luhr
backward pass	terugspeelbal	tuh·rukh·speyl·bal
ball	bal	bal
centre (pass) n	voorzet	vohr·zet
coach n	trainer	trey·nuhr
corner (kick) n	hoekschop	hook·skhop
defend v	verdedigen	vuhr·dey·di·khuhn
defender	verdediger	vuhr·dey·di·khuhr
dribble v	dribbelen	dri·buh·luhn
expulsion	uitsluiting	öyt·slöy·ting
fan	supporter	sew·por·tuhr
foul n	overtreding	oh·vuhr·trey·ding
free kick	vrijschop	vrey·skhop
goal (structure)	doel n	dool
goalkeeper	doelverdediger/	dool·vuhr·dey·di·khuhr/
	keeper	kee·puhr

injury time	blessuretijd	ble·sew·ruh·teyt
manager	manager	me·ne·dzhuhr
midfield	middenveld n	mi·duhn·velt
offside	buitenspel	böy·tuhn·spel
pass n	pass	paas
penalty	strafschop	straf·skhop
player	speler	spey·luhr
red card	rode kaart	roh·duh kaart
referee	scheidsrechter	skheyts·rekh·tuhr
striker	spits	spits
throw in v	ingooien	in·khoo·yuhn
yellow card	gele kaart	khey·luh kaart
wall (of players)	muurtje n	mewr·chuh

Off to see a match? Check out **going to a game**, page 144.

tennis & table tennis

I'd like to …	Ik wil graag …	ik wil khraakh …
book a time to play	een tijd boeken	uhn teyt *boo*·kuhn
play table tennis	tafeltennissen	*taa*·fuhl·te·ni·suhn
play tennis	tennissen	*te*·ni·suhn

Can we play at night?
Kunnen we 's avonds
spelen wanneer het
donker is?

ku·nuhn wuh *saa*·vonts
spey·luhn wa·*neyr* huht
dong·kuhr is

I need my racket restrung.
Ik moet mijn racket
opnieuw laten besnaren.

ik moot meyn *re*·kuht
op·*neew laa*·tuhn buh·*snaa*·ruhn

ace	*ace*	eys
advantage	*voordeel* n	*vohr*·deyl
(table tennis) bat	*(tafeltennis)bat*	(*taa*·fuhl·te·nis·)bet
clay	*klei*	kley
fault	*overtreding*	oh·vuhr·*trey*·ding
grass	*gras* n	khras
hard court	*hard court*	haart kohrt
net	*net* n	net
ping-pong ball	*pingpongbal*	*ping*·pong·bal
play doubles v	*dubbelspel spelen*	*du*·buhl·spel *spey*·luhn
racquet	*tennisracket* n	*te*·nis·*re*·kuht
serve n	*opslag*	*op*·slakh
serve v	*opslaan*	*op*·slaan
set n	*set*	set
table-tennis table	*pingpongtafel*	*ping*·pong·taa·fuhl
tennis ball	*tennisbal*	*te*·nis·bal

water sports

watersporten

Can I book a lesson?
   Kan ik een les boeken?   kan ik uhn les *boo*·kuhn

Can I hire (a) ...	*Kan ik ... huren?*	kan ik ... *hew*·ruhn
boat	*een boot*	uhn boht
canoe	*een kano*	uhn *kaa*·noh
kayak	*een kayak*	uhn *ka*·yak
life jacket	*een reddingsvest*	uhn *re*·dings·vest
snorkelling	*materiaal om*	ma·teyr·*yaal* om
gear	*te snorkelen*	tuh *snor*·kuh·luhn
water-skis	*waterskis*	*waa*·tuhr·skees
wetsuit	*een wetsuit*	uhn *wet*·soot

Are there any ...?	*Zijn er ...?*	zeyn uhr ...
breakwaters	*golfbrekers*	*kholf*·brey·kuhrs
(water) hazards	*gevaren*	khuh·*vaa*·ruhn
reefs	*rifs*	rifs
rips	*sterke*	*ster*·kuh
	stromingen	*stroh*·ming·uhn
sandbanks	*zandbanken*	*zant*·bang·kuhn

buggy	zeilwagen	zeyl·waa·khun
(for the beach)		
canoeing	kanovaren	kaa·noh·vaa·ruhn
flying kites	vliegeren	vlee·khuh·ruhn
kayaking	kajakvaren	ka·yak·vaa·ruhn
land sailing/	strandzeilen	strant·zey·luhn
yachting		
motorboat	motorboot	moh·tor·boht
oars	roeispanen	rooy·spaa·nuhn
row v	roeien	roo·yuhn
sail v	zeilen	zey·luhn
sailboard	(wind)surfplank	(wint·)surf·plangk
sailboarding	windsurfen/	wint·sur·fuhn/
	plankzeilen	plangk·zey·luhn
sailing	zeilen	zey·luhn
sailing boat	zeilboot	zeyl·boht
surfboard	surfplank	surf·plangk
surfing	surfen	sur·fuhn
wave	golf	kholf

sea slang

The seafaring Dutch have enriched their language with many sayings inspired by all things nautical, like these:

One must cut one's coat according to one's cloth.
Men moet roeien met de   men moot *roo*·yuhn met duh
riemen die men heeft.   *ree*·muhn dee men heyft
(lit: one must row with the oars one has)

To have your cake and eat it too.
Van twee walletjes eten.   van twey *wa*·luh·chus *ey*·tuhn
(lit: eat off two quays)

The best horseman is always on his feet.
De beste stuurlui staan   duh *bes*·tuh *stewr*·löy staan
aan wal.   aan wal
(lit: the best navigators are on shore)

To keep one's eyes peeled.
Een oogje in het zeil   uhn *ohkh*·yuh in huht zeyl
houden.   *haw*·duhn
(lit: keep an eye on the sail)

In this chapter, phrases are in the informal *je* yuh (you) form only. For more details, see the box **all about you** on page 109.

hiking

wandeltochten maken

Do we need a guide?
Hebben we een gids nodig?   he·buhn wuh uhn khits *noh*·dikh

Are there guided treks?
Zijn er begeleide   zeyn uhr buh·khuh·*ley*·duh
tochten?   *tokh*·tuhn

When does it get dark?
Wanneer wordt het donker?   wa·*neyr* wort huht *dong*·kuhr

How long is the trail?
Hoe lang is het pad?   hoo lang is huht pat

How long is the hike?
Hoe lang is de tocht?   hoo lang is duh tokht

Where can I go mud-flat walking?
Waar kan ik gaan   waar kan ik khaan
wadlopen?   *wat*·loh·puhn

wad?

A *wad* wat (plural *wadden* wa·duhn) is a mud or sand bank whose level is just between the levels of *vloed* vloot (high tide) and *eb* ep (low tide), so it gets flooded twice a day. The Dutch *Waddeneilanden* wa·duhn·ey·lan·duhn (a group of islands) lie in the *Waddenzee* wa·duhn·zey, the world's largest *waddengebied* wa·duhn·khuh·beet (*wad* area), near the Dutch, German and Danish coasts. It's the perfect place to go *wadlopen* wat·loh·puhn – trekking from one *wad* to another at low tide. Inform yourself about the times of the tides before setting off and make sure you take a guide.

Where can I …?	Waar vind ik …?	waar vint ik …
find someone	iemand die	ee·mant dee
who knows this	deze plek/	dey·zuh plek/
area/region	streek kent	streyk kent
get a map	een kaart	uhn kaart

Where can I …?	Waar kan ik …?	waar kan ik …
buy supplies	inkopen doen	in·koh·puhn doon
hire camping	kampeer-	kam·peyr·
gear	materiaal	ma·teyr·yaal
	huren	hew·ruhn
hire hiking gear	een trekkers-	uhn tre·kuhrs·
	uitrusting	öyt·rus·ting
	huren	hew·ruhn

Do we need	Moeten we …	moo·tuhn wuh …
to take …?	meenemen?	mey·ney·muhn
bedding	beddegoed	be·duh·khoot
food	eten	ey·tuhn
water	water	waa·tuhr

Is the track …?	Is het pad …?	is huht pat …
(well-)marked	(goed) beweg-	(khoot) buh·wekh·
	wijzerd	wey·zuhrt
open	open	oh·puhn
scenic	schilderachtig	skhil·duhr·akh·tikh

Which is the …	Welk is de …	welk is duh …
route?	route?	roo·tuh
easiest	gemakke-	khuh·ma·kuh·
	lijkste	luhk·stuh
most	meest	meyst
interesting	interessante	in·tey·re·san·tuh
shortest	kortste	kort·stuh

Where's the …?	Waar is …?	waar is …
camping	de kamping	duh kem·ping/
ground		kam·ping ⑩/®
nearest	het dichts-	huht dikhts·
village	bijzijnde dorp	bey·zeyn·duh dorp

Where are the …?	Waar zijn de …?	waar zeyn duh …
showers	douches	doo·chus
toilets	toiletten	twa·le·tuhn

Where have you come from?
Waar kom jij vandaan?   waar kom yey van·*daan*

How long did it take?
Hoe lang heb je er   hoo lang hep yuh uhr
over gedaan?   oh·vuhr khuh·*daan*

Does this path go to (Schiermonnikoog)?
Gaat dit pad naar   khaat dit pat naar
(Schiermonnikoog)?   (skheer·mo·nik·ohk)

Can I go through here?
Kan ik langs hier gaan?   kan ik langs heer khaan

Is the water OK to drink?
Is het water drinkbaar?   is huht *waa*·tuhr *dringk*·baar

Is it safe?
Is het veilig?   is huht *vey*·likh

Is there a hut?
Is er een hut?   is uhr uhn hut

I'm lost.
Ik ben verdwaald.   ik ben vuhr·*dwaalt*

---

listen for ...

Pas op voor ...!	pas op vohr ...	**Be careful of the ...!**	
de onder-	duh *on*·duhr·	**undertow**	
stroom	strohm		
de stroming	duh *stroh*·ming	**rip**	
het getij	huht khuh·*tey*	**tide**	

Het is gevaarlijk!
huht is khuh·*vaar*·luhk   **It's dangerous!**

beach

het strand

Where's the ... beach?	*Waar is het ...?*	waar is huht ...
best	*beste strand*	*bes*·tuh strant
nearest	*dichtsbijzijnde strand*	*dikhts*·bey·zeyn·duh strant
nudist	*naaktstrand*	*naakt*·strant

How much to rent a/an ...?	Hoeveel is de huur voor een ...?	hoo·veyl is duh hewr vohr uhn ...
chair	strandstoel	strant·stool
hut	strandcabine	strant·ka·bee·nuh
umbrella (sun)	parasol	pa·ra·sol

Is it safe to dive/swim here?
Is het veilig om hier te duiken/zwemmen? — is huht vey·likh om heer tuh döy·kuhn/zwe·muhn

What time is high/low tide?
Hoe laat is het vloed/eb? — hoo laat is huht vloot/ep

Do we have to pay?
Moeten we betalen? — moo·tuhn wuh buh·taa·luhn

beach & pool signs

Verboden te Duiken	vuhr·boh·duhn tuh döy·kuhn	**No Diving**
Verboden te Zwemmen	vuhr·boh·duhn tuh zwe·muhn	**No Swimming**

weather

het weer

What's the weather like?
Hoe is het weer? — hoo is huht weyr

What will the weather be like tomorrow?
Wat voor weer wordt het morgen? — wat vohr weyr wort huht mor·khuhn

It's ...	Het is ...	huht is ...
cloudy	bewolkt	buh·wolkt
cold	koud	kawt
foggy	mistig	mis·tikh
frosty	vriesweer	vrees·weyr
hot	zeer warm	zeyr warm
icy	glad	khlat
sunny	zonnig	zo·nikh
warm	warm	warm

It's ...	Het ...	huht ...
freezing	vriest	vreest
raining	regent	*rey*·khunt
snowing	sneeuwt	sneywt
stormy	stormt	stormt
windy	waait	waayt

Where can I buy a/an .. ?	Waar kan ik een ... kopen?	waar kan ik uhn ... *koh*·puhn
rain jacket	regenjas	*rey*·khuhn·yas
umbrella (rain)	paraplu	pa·ra·*plew*

weather wonders

It's raining cats and dogs.
Het regent pijpestelen. huht *rey*·khuhnt *pey*·puh·stey·luhn
(lit: it's raining pipe stems)

It's freezing hard.
Het vriest dat het kraakt. huht vreest dat huht kraakt
(lit: it's freezing so hard that things are bursting/cracking)

flora & fauna

planten & dieren

What ... is that?	Welke ... is dat?	*wel*·kuh ... is dat
bird	vogel	*voh*·khul
flower	bloem	bloom
plant	plant	plant
tree	boom	bohm

What animal is that?
Welk dier is dat? welk deer is dat

What's it used for?
Waarvoor wordt het gebruikt? waar·*vohr* wort huht khuh·*bröykt*

Can you eat the fruit?
Is de vrucht eetbaar? is duh vrukht *eyt*·baar

Is it common?
Komt het veel voor? komt huht veyl vohr

outdoors

161

frog land

You might hear Dutch and Flemish refer to their respective countries as *kikkerlandje* ki·kuhr·lan·chuh (lit: little-frog-land). The temperate climate is often marked by cool, changeable weather, mild summers and precipitation spread evenly throughout the year – supposedly excellent breeding conditions for frogs. However, things seem to be hotting up in the Low Countries, courtesy of the *klimaatverandering* klee·*maat*·vuhr·an·duh·ring (climate change). Of course, *het weer* huht weyr (the weather), and increasingly the *broeikaseffect* brooy·kas·e·fekt (global warming, literally 'hothouse effect'), are the icebreakers par excellence.

Is it …?	*Is het …?*	is huht …
dangerous	*gevaarlijk*	khuh·*vaar*·luhk
endangered	*met uitsterven*	met öyt·ster·vuhn
	bedreigd	buh·*dreykht*
poisonous	*giftig*	khif·tikh
protected	*beschermd*	buh·*skhermt*

copse	*kreupelbosje* n	*kreu*·puhl·bo·shuh
daffodil	*narcis*	*nar*·sis
heath	*heide*	*hey*·duh
mount of mud	*terp*	terp
nature reserve	*natuurreservaat* n	na·*tew*·rey·ser·vaat
peat	*turf*	turf
pine	*den*	den
tulip	*tulp*	tulp
(pollard) willow	*(knot)wilg*	(*knot*·)wilkh

cow	*koe*	koo
fox	*vos*	vos
goose/geese	*gans/ganzen*	khans/*khan*·zuhn
migratory birds	*trekvogels*	*trek*·voh·khuls
seal	*zeehond*	*zey*·hont
sea lion	*zeekoe*	*zey*·koo
sheep	*schaap* n	skhaap

For more geographical and agricultural terms, and names of animals and plants, see the **dictionary**.

basics

essentiële uitdrukkingen

breakfast	*ontbijt* n	ont·*beyt*
lunch	*middagmaal* n/*lunch* n	mi·dakh·maal/lunsh
dinner	*avondmaal* n/*diner* n	aa·vont·maal/dee·*ney*
snack	*snack/*	snek/snak ⑨/⑧/
	tussendoortje	tu·suhn·*dohr*·chuh
today's special	*dagschotel*	dakh·skhoh·tuhl
eat v	*eten*	*ey*·tuhn
drink v	*drinken*	*dring*·kuhn
I'd like ...	*Ik wil graag ...*	ik wil khraakh ...
Please.	*Alstublieft.* pol	al·stew·*bleeft*
Thank you.	*Dank u.* pol	dangk ew

eating out

bruin café   bröyn ka·*fey*
bruine kroeg   bröy·nuh krookh
'brown café' – old-style *café/kroeg* with wooden furniture, named after the generally smoke-stained walls. The atmosphere is perfect for reading and deep (and long) conversation. They usually stay open to the wee hours.

café/kroeg   ka·*fey*/krookh
not a café, but a pub – an establishment mainly serving beer and other types of alcohol. Coffee and soft drinks are available as a sideline. Many also serve snacks or simple meals. The 'local' around the corner is known as *stamkroeg* stam·khrookh, *stamcafé* stam·ka·fey or *buurtcafé* bewrt·ka·fey.

de muur   duh mewr
'the wall' – in the Netherlands, wall-mounted rows of small coin-operated windows with warm, deep-fried snacks. They're popular as a late-night (or early-morning) snack when everything else is closed.

eetcafé   eyt·ka·fey
café where people go not only to drink, but to have a good meal without having to fork out restaurant prices. The aim is to have a good conversation over a meal and a few drinks. The menu is often extensive and the food yummy. Local specialities and daily specials might be available.

grand café   gra·ka·fey
more spacious *café* with comfortable seating and classy furnishings – they serve alcohol as well as nonalcoholic drinks and meals. The perfect place for a stylish and relaxed lunch or brunch.

haringstand   haa·ring·stant
'herring stand' – sells the best and freshest herring

koffiehuisje n   ko·fee·höy·shuh
'coffee house' – espresso bar or café specialising in coffee and other hot drinks (alcohol is the sideline here). They serve cakes and pastries to go with the coffee, as well as light meals. Not unlike a *theehuisje* tey·höy·shuh (tea room); sometimes more like an espresso bar or *broodjeszaak* broh·chus·zaak (sandwich shop).

koffieshop
ko·fee·shop

coffee shop – café authorised to sell soft drugs such as the ubiquitous home-grown *nederwiet* *ney·duhr·weet* (meaning 'pot from the Netherlands'). They also serve coffee and cake – but inquire about the ingredients first or you'll be putting your teeth into a space cake before you know it!

pannenkoekenhuisje n ®
pa·nuh·koo·kuh·höys·shuh

pancake parlour – a Dutch institution

patatkraam/frietkot ®/®
pa·tat·kraam/freet·kot

chips shop – place specialising in Flemish-style fries. It can be a simple shack or van, or a small shop (often called *frituur* *free·tewr*) dealing in take-away fries and deep-fried snacks .

praatcafé n ®
praat·ka·fey

pub set up and laid out specifically to promote conversation over a drink or two (of the alcoholic variety or not) – it's all about meeting up with friends and conversation here. Snacks or light meals are often available.

proeflokaal
proof·loh·kaal

tasting house that used to be attached to distilleries – type of café or pub offering a large variety of gins and liqueurs (or beers) and where people go specifically to taste and appreciate what's on offer. Staff can help you choose and are generally subject matter experts. In the Netherlands, they usually specialise in *jenever* *yuh·ney·vuhr/zhuh·ney·vuhr* ®/® (gin). In Belgium, it's often about *bier* *beer* (beer), although they also have their *druppelkot* n *dru·puhl·kot* or *jeneverkot* n *zhuh·ney·vuhr·koht* (gin shack) – sometimes a shack but often a pub with a bewildering *jenever* list.

terras
tuh·ras

outdoor terrace – a fixture in many *cafés* and a great place to relax, watch passers-by, read the paper or catch up with friends. At the first sign of spring, people flock here to soak up the sun. Many are now covered and heated in winter.

theatercafé
tey·yaa·tuhr·ka·fey

café in or near a theatre district where people tend to go before and after performances. They usually attract a mix of bohemian and chic clientele; struggling artists, would-be models, treehuggers, baby-boomers, yups and business people all rub shoulder here with each other.

finding a place to eat

Can you recommend a bar/restaurant?
Kunt u een bar/restaurant   kunt ew uhn bar/res·toh·*rant*
aanbevelen? pol   *aan*·buh·vey·luhn

Where would you go for ...?	*Waar zou u heen gaan voor ...?* pol	waar zaw ew heyn khaan vohr ...
a celebration	*een feestelijke maaltijd*	uhn *feys*·tuh·luh·kuh *maal*·teyt
a cheap meal	*een goedkope maaltijd*	uhn khoot·*koh*·puh *maal*·teyt
local specialities	*plaatselijke specialiteiten*	*plaat*·suh·luh·kuh spey·sya·lee·*tey*·tuhn

Where would you go to taste ...?	*Waar zou u heen gaan om ... te proeven?* pol	waar zaw ew heyn khaan om ... tuh *proo*·vuhn
good Indonesian food	*goed Indonesisch eten*	khoot in·doh·*ney*·sis *ey*·tuhn
the local beer	*met bier*	met beer
cuisine	*bereide gerechten*	buh·*rey*·duh khuh·*rekh*·tuhn

I'd like to reserve a table for ...	*Ik wil graag een tafel voor ... reserveren.*	ik wil khraakh uhn *taa*·fuhl vohr ... rey·ser·*vey*·ruhn
(two) people	*(twee) personen*	(twey) puhr·*soh*·nuhn
(eight) o'clock	*(acht) uur*	(akht) ewr

listen for ...

We zijn gesloten.	wuh zeyn khuh·*sloh*·tuhn	**We're closed.**
We zitten vol.	wuh *zi*·tuhn vol	**We're full.**
Een momentje.	uhn moh·*men*·chuh	**One moment.**

Are you still serving food?
Is de keuken nog open?   is duh *keu*·kuhn nokh *oh*·puhn

How long is the wait?
Hoelang moeten we wachten?   hoo·*lang* moo·tuhn wuh *wakh*·tuhn

at the restaurant

What would you recommend?
Wat kan u aanbevelen? pol   wat kan ew *aan*·buh·vey·luhn

What are they having?
Wat hebben zij?   wat *he*·buhn zey

What's in that dish?
Wat zit er in dat gerecht?   wat zit uhr in dat khuh·*rekht*

What's it/that called?
Hoe heet het/dat?   hoo heyt huht/dat

I'll have that.
Ik neem dat.   ik neym dat

Does it take long to prepare?
Duurt het lang om het te bereiden?   dewrt huht lang om huht tuh buh·*rey*·duhn

Is it self-serve?
Is het zelfbediening?   is huht *zelf*·buh·dee·ning

Is service included in the bill?
Is bediening inbegrepen?   is buh·*dee*·ning in·buh·grey·puhn

Are these complimentary?
Zijn deze gratis?   zeyn *dey*·zuh *khraa*·tis

Could I please see the wine list?
Mag ik de wijnkaart?   makh ik duh *weyn*·kaart

Which beers do you serve?
Welke bieren heeft u? pol   *wel*·kuh *bee*·ruhn heyft ew

I'm ready to order.
Ik wil graag bestellen.   ik wil khraakh be·*ste*·luhn

To call the waiter or waitress over, address them as *Meneer* muh·*neyr* (Sir) or *Mevrouw* muh·*vraw* (Miss), or *Juffrouw* yu·fraw (Miss, for a teenage girl only – see also page 109).

Don't ask for a doggie bag – it's just not done in the Low Countries. When paying, never ask 'to go Dutch' in a Dutch restaurant – if you're that way inclined, ask to split the bill by saying:

Kunnen we apart betalen alstublieft? pol
  ku·nuhn wuh a·*part*   **Could we pay separately,**
  buh·*taa*·luhn al·stew·*bleeft* **please?**

Tips aren't compulsory or expected – but they will be appreciated, of course.

I'd like (a/the) …, please.	*Ik wil graag …*	ik wil khraakh …
children's menu	*de kindermenu*	duh *kin*·duhr·muh·new
child seat	*een kinderstoel*	uhn *kin*·duhr·stool
drink list	*de drankkaart*	duh *drang*·kaart
half portion	*een halve portie*	uhn *hal*·vuh *por*·see
local speciality	*een plaatselijke specialiteit*	uhn *plaat*·suh·luh·kuh spey·sya·lee·*teyt*
menu (in English)	*een menu (in het Engels)*	uhn me·*new* (in huht *eng*·uhls)
nonsmoking	*niet-roken*	*neet*·roh·kuhn
smoking	*roken*	*roh*·kuhn
table for (five)	*een tafel voor (vijf)*	uhn *taa*·fuhl vohr (veyf)
that dish	*dat gerecht*	dat khuh·*rekht*

I'd like it with/	Ik wil het graag	ik wil huht khraakh
without …	met/zonder …	met/zon·duhr …
cheese	kaas	kaas
chilli (sauce)	chili(saus)	chee·lee(·saws)
cream	room	rohm
garlic	knoflook	knof·lohk
(curried) ketchup	(curry)ketchup	(ku·ree·)ke·chup
(tomato)	(tomaten)	(toh·maa·tuhn·)
ketchup	ketchup	ke·chup
lemon	citroen	see·troon
mayonnaise	mayonaise	ma·yoh·ney·zuh
mustard	mosterd	mos·tuhrt
nuts	noten	noh·tuhn
oil	olie	oh·lee
pepper	peper	pey·puhr
salt	zout	zawt
sugar	suiker	söy·kuhr
tartare sauce	tartaarsaus	tar·taar·saws
tomato sauce	tomatensaus	toh·maa·tuhn·saws
vinegar	azijn	a·zeyn

For other specific meal requests, see **vegetarian & special meals**, page 181.

---

listen for …

Waar wilt u zitten? **pol**
  waar wilt ew *zi*·tuhn — **Where would you like to sit?**

Wilt u al bestellen? **pol**
  wilt ew al buh·*ste*·luhn — **Are you ready to order?**

Wat mag het zijn?
  wat makh huht zeyn — **What can I get for you?**

Houdt u van …? **pol**
  hawt ew van … — **Do you like …?**

Ik kan … aanbevelen.
  ik kan …
  aan·buh·*vey*·luhn — **I suggest the …**

Alstublieft. **pol**
  al·stew·*bleeft* — **Here you go!**

Eet smakelijk.
  eyt *smaa*·kuh·luhk — **Enjoy your meal.**

Hors D'oeuvre/	hor·döy·vruh/	Appetisers
Hapjes	hap·yuhs	
Soep	soop	Soups
Voorgerechten	vohr·khuh·rekh·tuhn	Entrées
Salades	sa·laa·duhs	Salads
Hoofdgerechten	hohft·khuh·rekh·tuhn	Main Courses
Tussengerechten	tu·suhn·khuh·rekh·tuhn	Entremets
Bijgerechten/	bey·khuh·rekh·tuhn/	Side Dishes
Tussengerechten	tu·suhn·khuh·rekh·tuhn	
Desserts/	dey·sers/	Desserts
Nagerechten	naa·khuh·rekh·tuhn	
Aperitieven	a·pey·ree·tee·vuhn	Aperitifs
Dranken	drang·kuhn	Drinks
Frisdranken	fris·drang·kuhn	Soft Drinks
Sterke Dranken	ster·kuh drang·kuhn	Spirits
Bier	beer	Beers
Mousserende	moo·sey·ruhn·duh	Sparkling Wines
Wijn ®	weyn	
Schuimwijn ®	skhöym·weyn	Sparkling Wines
Witte Wijn	wi·tuh weyn	White Wines
Rode Wijn	roh·duh weyn	Red Wines
Dessertwijn	dey·sert·weyn	Dessert Wines
Likeuren	lee·keu·ruhn	Digestifs/
		Liqueurs

at the table

aan tafel

Please bring a/the ...	*Mag ik ... alstublieft?* pol	makh ik ... al·stew·bleeft
bill	*de rekening*	duh rey·kuh·ning
cutlery	*bestek*	buh·stek
(wine)glass	*een (wijn)glas*	uhn (weyn·)khlas
serviette	*een servet*	uhn ser·vet
tablecloth	*een*	uhn
	tafellaken	taa·fuhl·laa·kuhn

I didn't order this.
 Ik heb dit niet besteld.   ik hep dit neet be·*stelt*

There's a mistake in the bill/check.
 Er zit een fout in de   uhr zit uhn fawt in duh
 rekening.   *rey*·kuh·ning

talking food

I love this dish.
 Dit gerecht is erg lekker.   dit khuh·*rekht* is erkh *le*·kuhr

I love the local cuisine.
 Ik vind de plaatselijke   ik vint duh *plaat*·suh·luh·kuh
 keuken erg lekker.   *keu*·kuhn erkh *le*·kuhr

Delicious!
 Heerlijk/Lekker!   *heyr*·luhk/*le*·kuhr

To lick thumbs and fingers!
 Om de vingers bij   om duh *ving*·uhrs bey
 af te likken!   af tuh *li*·kuhn

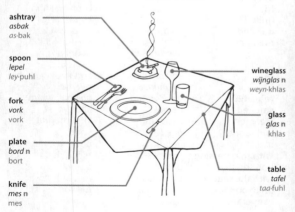

ashtray
asbak
as·bak

spoon
lepel
ley·puhl

fork
vork
vork

plate
bord n
bort

knife
mes n
mes

wineglass
wijnglas n
weyn·khlas

glass
glas n
khlas

table
tafel
taa·fuhl

My compliments to the chef.
Mijn complimenten   meyn kom·plee·*men*·tuhn
aan de chef.   aan duh shef

I'm full.
Ik heb genoeg gegeten.   ik hep khuh·*nookh* khuh·*khey*·tuhn

This is ...	Dit is ...	dit is ...
burnt	*aangebrand*	*aan*·khuh·brant
(too) cold	*(te) koud*	(tuh) kawt
off	*bedorven*	buh·*dor*·vuhn
(too) spicy	*(te) pikant*	(tuh) pee·*kant*
stale	*oudbakken*	awt·*ba*·kuhn
superb	*fantastisch*	fan·*tas*·tees

methods of preparation

bereidingswijzen

I'd like it ...	Ik wil het graag ...	ik wil huht khraakh ...
I don't want it ...	Ik wil het niet ...	ik wil huht neet ...
boiled	*gekookt*	khuh·*kohkt*
deep-fried	*gefrituurd*	khuh·free·*tewrt*
fried	*gebakken*	khuh·*ba*·kuhn
grilled	*gegrild*	khu·*khrilt*
mashed	*als puree*	als pew·*rey*
medium	*redelijk* Ⓝ	*rey*·duh·luhk
	doorbakken	dohr·*ba*·kuhn
	à point Ⓑ	a·*pwaa*
rare	*kort gebakken* Ⓝ	kort khuh·*ba*·kuhn
	saignant Ⓑ	sey·*nya*
reheated	*opgewarmd*	*op*·khuh·warmt
smoked	*gerookt*	khuh·*rohkt*
steamed	*gestoomd*	khuh·*stohmt*
well-done	*goed*	khoot
	doorbakken	dohr·*ba*·kuhn
with the dressing on the side	*met de slasaus opzij*	met duh *slaa*·saws op·*zey*
with the sauce/ mayonnaise separate	*met de saus/ mayonnaise apart*	met duh saws/ ma·yoh·*ney*·zuh a·*part*

nonalcoholic drinks

alcoholvrije dranken

flat/still mineral water	*spa blauw* Ⓝ	spa blaw
	plat water Ⓑ	plat *waa*·tuhr
mineral/bottled water	*mineraal-water*	mee·ney·*raal*·waa·tuhr
sparkling mineral water	*spa rood* Ⓝ	spa roht
	spuitwater Ⓑ	*spöyt*·waa·tuhr
buttermilk	*karnemelk* Ⓝ	*kar*·nuh·melk
	botermelk Ⓑ	*boh*·tuhr·melk
(hot) chocolate milk	*(warme) chocolade-melk*	*(war*·muh) shoh·koh·*laa*·duh·melk
(orange) juice	*(sinaasappel)sap*	(see·*naas*·a·puhl·)sap
lemonade	*limonade*	lee·moh·*naa*·duh
soft drink	*frisdrank*	*fris*·drangk
(hot) water	*(warm) water*	(warm) *waa*·tuhr
(cup of)	*(een kopje)*	(uhn *kop*·yuh)
tea/coffee	*thee/koffie*	tey/*ko*·fee
with/without …	*met/zonder …*	met/*zon*·duhr …
coffee milk	*koffiemelk*	*ko*·fee·melk
lemon	*citroen*	see·*troon*
milk	*melk*	melk
sugar	*suiker*	*söy*·kuhr
whipped cream	*slagroom*	*slakh*·rohm

coffee time

black	*zwart*	zwart
decaffeinated	*decaf*	*dey*·kaf
iced	*met ijs*	met eys
strong	*sterk*	sterk
weak	*flauw*	flaw
white	*met melk*	met melk

alcoholic drinks

Vodka, whisky, rum, tequila, gin and tonic, Campari and popular cocktails such as Bloody Mary are all known by their English names, so you shouldn't have any trouble getting your order. However, you might want to delve into the local beer and gin terminology for the huge number of local varieties on offer (for beers and gin, see the **culinary reader**, page 183).

advocaat	*advocaat*	at·voh·*kaat*
beer	*bier*	beer
brandy	*brandewijn* Ⓝ	*bran*·duh·weyn
	cognac Ⓑ	koh·*nyak*
champagne	*champagne*	sham·*pa*·nyuh
cocktail	*cocktail*	*kok*·teyl
gin	*jenever*	yuh·*ney*·vuhr Ⓝ
		zhuh·*ney*·vuhr Ⓑ
herb-based schnapps	*Beerenburg*	*bey*·ruhn·burkh
a shot of (whisky)	*een glas (whisky)*	uhn khlas (*wis*·kee)
strong alcoholic drink	*borrel*	*bo*·ruhl
a bottle/glass of … wine	*een fles/glas …*	uhn fles/khlas …
dessert	*dessertwijn*	dey·*sert*·weyn
red	*rode wijn*	*roh*·duh weyn
rosé	*rosé*	roh·*zey*
sparkling	*mousserende wijn* Ⓝ	moo·*sey*·ruhn·duh weyn
	schuimwijn Ⓑ	*skhöym*·weyn
white	*witte wijn*	*wi*·tuh weyn
a … of beer	*een … bier*	uhn … beer
glass	*glas*	khlas
jug	*karaf*	ka·*raf*
large bottle	*fles*	fles
small bottle	*flesje*	*fle*·shuh

Additional items are in the **culinary reader**, page 183, and the **dictionary**.

in the bar

Excuse me!
Excuseer mij!   ek·skew·*zeyr* mey

I'm next.
Het is mijn beurt.   huht is meyn beurt

I'll have (a lemon-flavoured gin).
Voor mij (een   vohr mey (uhn
citroenjenever).   see·*troon*·yuh·*ney*·vuhr/
    see·*troon*·zhuh·*ney*·vuhr) Ⓝ/Ⓔ

Same again, please.
Hetzelfde alstublieft. pol   huht·*zelf*·duh al·stew·*bleeft*

No ice, thanks.
Zonder ijs asltublieft. pol   *zon*·duhr eys al·stew·*bleeft*

How much alcohol does this contain?
Hoeveel alcohol zit hierin?   hoo·*veyl* al·koh·*hol* zit heer·*in*

I'll buy you a drink.
Ik trakteer je op een   ik trak·*teyr* yuh op uhn
drankje.   *drangk*·yuh

What would you like?
Wat wil je drinken?   wat wil yuh *dring*·kuhn

I don't drink alcohol.
Ik drink geen alcohol.   ik dringk kheyn al·koh·*hol*

It's my round.
Mijn rondje.   meyn *ron*·chuh

Do you serve meals here?
Serveert u hier   ser·*veyrt* ew heer
maaltijden? pol   *maal*·tey·duhn

not just a beer

een biertje	uhn *beer*·chuh	**normal glass of lager**
een fluitje	uhn *flöy*·chuh	**tall narrow glass of lager**
een kleintje pils Ⓝ	uhn *kleyn*·chuh pils	**small glass of lager**
een pilsje	uhn *pil*·shuh	**normal glass of lager**
een pintje Ⓔ	uhn *pin*·chuh	**normal glass of lager**

eating out

175

Wat zal het zijn?
   wat zal huht zeyn   **What are you having?**

Ik denk dat je genoeg op hebt.
   ik dengk dat yuh   **I think you've had enough.**
   khuh·*nookh* op hept

drinking up

stevig drinken

Cheers!
   Proost!   prohst

This is hitting the spot.
   Dat ging recht naar   dat khing rekht naar
   m'n hoofd.   muhn hohft
   (lit: that went straight to my head)

I feel fantastic!
   Ik voel me heerlijk!   ik vool muh *heyr*·luhk

I think I've had one too many.
   Ik denk dat ik er   ik dengk dat ik uhr
   eentje teveel op heb.   *eyn*·chuh tuh·*veyl* op hep

I'm feeling drunk.
   Ik voel me dronken.   ik vool muh *drong*·kuhn

I feel ill.
   Ik voel me ziek.   ik vool muh zeek

Where's the toilet?
   Waar is het toilet?   waar is huht twa·*let*

I'm tired, I'd better go home.
   Ik ben moe.   ik ben moo
   Ik ga best naar huis.   ik khaa best naar höys

Can you call a taxi for me?
   Kunt u een taxi   kunt ew uhn *tak*·see
   voor me bellen? **pol**   vohr muh *be*·luhn

I don't think you should drive.
   Je zou niet mogen   yuh zaw neet *mo*·khuhn
   rijden.   *rey*·duhn

buying food

eten inkopen

What's the local speciality?
Wat is het streekgerecht?   wat is huht *streyk*·khuh·rekht

What's the special regional beer here?
Wat is het streekbier?   wat is huht *streyk*·beer

What's that?
Wat is dat?   wat is dat

Can I taste it?
Kan ik het eens proeven?   kan ik huht eyns *proo*·vuhn

Can I have a bag, please?
Mag ik een draagtasje   makh ik uhn *draakh*·ta·shuh
alstublieft? pol   al·stew·*bleeft*

I don't need a bag, thanks.
Ik heb geen draagtasje   ik hep kheyn *draakh*·ta·shuh
nodig, dank u. pol   *noh*·dikh dangk ew

How much is (a kilo of cheese)?
Hoeveel kost   hoo·*veyl* kost
(een kilo kaas)?   (uhn *kee*·lo kaas)

food stuff

cooked (boiled)	*gekookt*	khuh·*kohkt*
cooked (prepared)	*bereid*	buh·*reyt*
cured (pickled)	*gepekeld*	khuh·*pey*·kuhlt
cured (preserved)	*ingemaakt*	*in*·khuh·maakt
dried	*gedroogd*	kuh·*drohkht*
fresh	*vers*	vers
frozen	*ingevroren*	*in*·khuh·vroh·ruhn
raw	*rauw*	raw
smoked	*gerookt*	khuh·*rohkt*

I'd like ...	Ik wil graag ...	ik wil khraakh ...
(one) of each	(één) van elk	(eyn) van elk
(two) of those	(twee) van die soort	(twey) van dee sohrt
them mixed/ assorted	een mengeling	uhn *meng*·uh·ling
your selection	uw selectie pol	ew sey·*lek*·see

I'd like ...	Ik wil graag ...	ik wil khraakh ...
(200) grams	(tweehonderd) gram	(twey·*hon*·duhrt) khram
half a dozen	een half dozijn	uhn half doh·*zeyn*
a dozen	een dozijn	uhn doh·*zeyn*
a quarter kilo	een half pond	uhn half pont
half a kilo	een halve kilo/ een pond	uhn *hal*·vuh *kee*·loh/ uhn pont
a kilo	een kilo	uhn *kee*·loh
(two) kilos	(twee) kilo	(twey) *kee*·loh
a bottle	een fles	uhn fles
a jar	een pot ⓝ	uhn pot
	een bokaal ⓑ	uhn boh·*kaal*
a packet	een pak	uhn pak
a piece	een stuk	uhn stuk
(three) pieces	(drie) stuks	(dree) stuks
a slice	een plak ⓝ	uhn plak
	een snee ⓑ	uhn sney
(six) slices	(zes) plakken ⓝ	(zes) *pla*·kuhn
	(zes) sneetjes ⓑ	(zes) *sney*·chus
a tin	een blik	uhn blik
(just) a little	een (klein) beetje	uhn (kleyn) *bey*·chuh
more	meer	meyr
some	enkele	*eng*·kuh·luh
that one	die	dee
this one	deze	*dey*·zuh

Less.	Minder.	*min*·duhr
A bit more.	Een beetje meer.	uhn *bey*·chuh meyr
Enough.	Dat is genoeg.	dat is khuh·*nookh*

For food items, see the **culinary reader**, page 183, and the **dictionary**.

Do you have …?	*Heeft u …?* pol	heyft ew …
anything	*iets*	eets
cheaper	*goedkopers*	khoot·*koh*·puhrs
other kinds	*nog andere*	nokh *an*·duh·ruh
Where can I find the … section?	*Waar vind ik …?*	waar vint ik …
dairy	*de zuivel-produkten*	duh *zöy*·vuhl·proh·duk·tuhn
fish	*de visafdeling*	duh *vis*·af·dey·ling
frozen goods	*de diepvries-produkten*	duh *deep*·vrees·proh·duk·tuhn
fruit and vegetable	*de groente-en fruitafdeling*	duh *khroon*·tuh·en·*fröyt*·af·dey·ling
meat	*het vlees*	huht vleys
poultry	*het gevogelte*	huht khuh·*voh*·khul·tuh

food finds

bakery	*bakker* Ⓝ	*ba*·kuhr
	bakkerij Ⓑ	ba·kuh·*rey*
bottle shop/ liquor store	*slijterij* Ⓝ	*sley*·tuh·rey
	drankenhandel Ⓑ	*drang*·kuhn·han·duhl
butcher's shop	*slagerij*	*slaa*·khuh·rey
cake shop	*banketbakker* Ⓝ	bang·*ket*·ba·kuhr
	patisserie Ⓑ	pa·ti·suh·*ree*
chocolate shop	*chocolatier*	shoh·koh·la·*tye*
fishmonger	*vishandel*	*vis*·han·duhl
greengrocer	*groenteboer*	*khroon*·tuh·boor
grocery store	*kruidenier*	kröy·duh·*neer*
health-food store	*reformwinkel*	rey·*form*·wing·kuhl
market	*markt*	markt
night shop	*nachtwinkel*	*nakht*·wing·kuhl
supermarket	*supermarkt*	*sew*·puhr·markt

cooking utensils

Could I please borrow a ...?	*Kan ik alstublieft een ... lenen?* pol	kan ik al·stew·*bleeft* uhn ... *ley*·nuhn
I need a ...	*Ik heb een ... nodig.*	ik hep uhn ... *noh*·dikh
chopping board	*snijplank*	*sney*·plangk
frying pan	*koekenpan* ⓝ	*koo*·kuh·pan
	pan ⓑ	pan
knife	*mes*	mes
saucepan	*pan* ⓝ	pan
	kookpot ⓑ	*kohk*·pot

For more cooking implements, see the **dictionary**.

---

holland vs netherlands: what's the score?

You've often heard and probably even used the term 'Holland' when talking about the Netherlands. Maybe you also wondered which of the two terms is correct – a country has to have one official name, after all, even one as tolerant as the land of the Dutch obviously is, right? Rest assured – the Dutch are no more confused about their own country than, say, the British, if you take the linguistic (and political) issue of 'Great Britain' vs 'England' as a comparison.

The official name of the country is indeed *Nederland* *ney*·duhr·lant, whereas the term *Holland* ho·lant, strictly speaking, refers to the combined provinces of *Noord* nohrt (North) and *Zuid* zöyt (South) *Holland*. However, it's now a colloquial name for the whole country, since Holland (which used to be independent) united with the rest of what's now the Netherlands back in the 16th century. Likewise, both *Nederlander* *ney*·duhr·lan·duhr and *Hollander* ho·lan·duhr are words used to refer to a Dutch person, and the adjectives *Nederlands* *ney*·duhr·lants and *Hollands* ho·lants can both be used to mean 'Dutch'. On the other hand, the Dutch language is known only as *Nederlands* *ney*·duhr·lants, just like the language all this is written in is only called 'English'!

vegetarian & special meals
vegetarische & speciale maaltijden

ordering food

Is there a …	Is er hier een …	is uhr heer uhn …
restaurant	restaurant	res·toh·rant
near here?	in de buurt?	in duh bewrt
halal	halal	ha·lal
kosher	kosher	koh·shuhr
vegetarian	vegetarisch	vey·khey·taa·ris

Do you have (vegetarian) food?
Heeft u (vegetarische) heyft ew (vey·khey·taa·ri·suh)
maaltijden? pol *maal·tey·duhn*

I don't eat …
Ik eet geen … ik eyt kheyn …

Is it cooked in/with …?
Is het bereid in/met …? is huht buh·reyt in/met …

Are these free-range eggs?
Zijn dit scharreleieren? zeyn dit skha·ruhl·ey·yuh·ruhn

Could you	Zou u een	zaw ew uhn
prepare a meal	maaltijd zonder	maal·teyt zon·duhr
without …?	… kunnen	… ku·nuhn
	klaarmaken? pol	klaar·maa·kuhn
butter	boter	boh·tuhr
eggs	eieren	ey·yuh·ruhn
fish	vis	vis
fish stock	visbouillon	vis·boo·yon
meat stock	vleesbouillon	vleys·boo·yon
oil	olie	oh·lee
pork	varkensvlees	var·kuhns·vleys
poultry	gevogelte	khuh·voh·khul·tuh
red meat	rood vlees	roht vleys

Is this ...?	Is het ...?	is huht ...
decaffeinated	cafeïnevrij/ decaf	ka·fey·ee·nuh·vrey/ dey·kaf
free of animal produce	zonder dierlijke producten	zon·duhr deer·luh·kuh proh·duk·tuhn
genetically modified	genetisch ge- modificeerd	khey·ney·tis khuh· ·moh·dee·fee·seyrt
gluten-free	glutenvrij	khlew·tuhn·vrey
low-fat	vetarm	vet·arm
low in sugar	suikerarm	söy·kuhr·arm
organic	organisch	or·khaa·nis
salt-free	zoutloos	zawt·lohs
sugar-free	suikervrij	söy·kuhr·vrey

special diets & allergies

speciale diëten & allergieën

I'm on a special diet.
Ik volg een speciaal dieet. ik volkh uhn spey·syaal dee·yeyt

I'm (a) vegan/vegetarian.
Ik ben veganist/ vegetariër. ik ben vey·kha·nist/ vey·khey·taa·ree·yuhr

I'm allergic to ... *Ik ben allergisch voor ...* ik ben a·ler·khees vohr ...

chocolate	chocolade	shoh·koh·laa·duh
dairy produce	zuivel- producten	zöy·vuhl· proh·duk·tuhn
eggs	eieren	ey·yuh·ruhn
gelatine	gelatine	zhuh·la·tee·nuh
gluten	gluten	khlew·tuhn
honey	honing	hoh·ning
MSG	MSG/ vetsin	em·es·khey/ vet·seen
nuts	noten	noh·tuhn
seafood	vis, schaal- en schelpdieren	vis skhaal en skhelp·dee·ruhn
shellfish	schaal- en schelpdieren	skhaal en skhelp·dee·ruhn

This culinary reader covers the most common ingredients and dishes in both the Netherlands and Belgium, as well as some specialities. Dishes that are known under different names have been cross-referenced. Indonesian dishes which have become commonplace in the Netherlands are indicated with Ind. We've used the symbols Ⓝ/Ⓑ for words which are different in the Netherlands and Belgium respectively. Note that we've only indicated the Dutch nouns that have neuter gender with Ⓝ after the translation – the nouns which have common gender are left unmarked (for more on gender in Dutch, see the **phrasebuilder**). If it's a plural noun, you'll also see pl.

A

aardappels *aart·a·puhls potatoes*
— **op z'n Vlaams** *op zuhn vlaams
potatoes Flemish-style – baked in
onions, bay leaf & beef broth (Flanders)*
aardbeien *aart·bey·yuhn strawberries*
aardnoot *aart·noht groundnut/peanut*
abdijbier *ap·dey·beer abbey-style beer –
produced at non-Trappist abbeys or in
other breweries, some of which are asso-
ciated (sometimes only in name) with
abbeys; examples are Affligem, Corsen-
donck, Grimbergen, Leffe & Tongerlo*
abrikoos *a·bree·kohs apricot*
advocaat *at·voh·kaat
a type of egg liqueur similar to eggnog*
afgeroomde melk
af·khuh·rohm·duh melk skim milk
ajuin *a·yöyn onion (see also ui)*
alcoholarm beer *al·koh·hol·arm beer
beer low in alcohol*
alcoholvrij beer *al·koh·hol·vrey beer
nonalcoholic beer*
amandel *a·man·duhl almond*
amandelbroodje Ⓝ
*a·man·duhl·broh·chuh
sweet roll with almond filling*
ananas *a·na·nas pineapple*
andalouse *an·da·loo·zuh Andalusian
sauce – tangy sauce of mayonnaise, peppers, onion, tomato sauce & lemon juice*
andijvie *an·dey·vee endive*
anijs *a·neys aniseed*

ansjovis *an·sho·vis anchovies*
apennoot *aa·puh·noht
groundnut/peanut*
à point *a·pwaa medium (Belgium)*
appel *a·puhl apple*
appelbol *a·puhl·bol
warm, round, sweet pastry with apple*
appelflap *a·puhl·flap apple turnover*
appelgebak Ⓝ *a·puhl·khuh·bak apple pie*
appeljenever *a·puhl·yuh·ney·vuhr/
a·puhl·zhuh·ney·vuhr Ⓝ/Ⓑ
apple-flavoured gin*
appelmoes *a·puhl·moos apple sauce*
appelpannenkoek *a·puhl·pa·nuh·kook
apple pancake with lemon juice &
caramelised sugar*
appelsien *a·puhl·seen orange (Belgium)*
appeltaart *a·puhl·taart apple pie*
arachideolie *a·ra·khee·duh·oh·lee
groundnut oil*
artisjok *ar·tee·shok artichoke*
asperge *a·sper·zhuh asparagus*
asperges op Vlaamse wijze
*a·sper·zhus op vlaam·suh wey·zuh
asparagus Flemish-style – white asparagus with a sauce of melted butter & egg*
aubergine *oh·ber·zhee·ruh eggplant*
augurk *aw·khurk gherkin*
avocado *a·voh·kaa·doh avocado*
azijn *a·zeyn vinegar*

B

baars *baars bream*
babbelut *ba·buh·lut butterscotch*

balletjes ⓝ pl *ba·luh·chus*
  small meatballs (often in soup)
bami Ind *baa·mee* noodles
  — goreng Ind *khoh·reng* fried noodles
  with veggies, pork & shrimp; often served
  with a fried egg or shredded omelette
  — hap hap rectangular croquette filled
  with noodles
  — rames Ind *raa·mes*
  noodles covered in various condiments
banaan ba·*naan* banana
banketletter bang·*ket·le·tuhr*
  almond pastry
Barbar bar·*ber*
  white beer with honey (Belgium)
basilicum ba·*zee·lee·kum* basil
bataat ba·*taat* sweet potato
beenham *beyn·ham* country ham
beignet bey·*nye* fritter
belegd broodje ⓝ buh·*lekht broh·chuh*
  filled sandwich (usually a half baguette)
belegen kaas buh·*ley·khun kaas*
  cheese ripened for 16 weeks
beschuit buh·*shöyt* typical Dutch light
  crisp bread (often round)
beslag ⓝ buh·*slakh* batter
bessen be·*suhn* berries
bessenjenever be·suhn·yuh·*ney·vuhr*/
  be·suhn·zhuh·*ney·vuhr* ⓝ/Ⓑ
  berry-flavoured gin
beuling *beu·ling* see **bloedworst**
biefstuk *beef·stuk* steak
  — tartaar tar·*taar*
  raw minced beef with eggs & spices
bier ⓝ beer beer
bière brut byer brewt
  champagne-like sparkling beer like Brut
  des Flandres from the Deus brewery
  (Belgium)
bier op fles beer op fles bottled beer
bier van 't vat beer vant vat beer on tap
bieslook *bees·lohk* chives
biet beet beet
(rode) bietjes ⓝ pl (*roh·duh*) *bee·chus*
  beetroot
bitterballen *bi·tuhr·ba·luhn* savoury
  crumbed & deep-fried meatballs
blad ⓝ blat leaf
bladerdeeg ⓝ *blaa·duhr·deykh* puff pastry
bladgroenten *blat·khroon·tuhn*
  leafy vegetables

blanche blansh alternative (originally
  French) term for **witbier** (Belgium)
bleekselderij bleyk·sel·duh·*rey* see **selderij**
blikgroenten *blik·khroon·tuhn*
  canned vegetables
blinde vink *blin·duh vingk* meat roll of
  veal or beef wrapped in bacon
bloedworst *bloot·worst* black pudding ·
  blood sausage – also called **beuling** or
  pens in Belgium
bloem bloom flour · flower
bloemkool *bloom·kohl* cauliflower
Blond blont term used to refer to the
  amber-coloured version of beers that
  come both as **Blond** (blonde) & **Donker**
  (dark) varieties, such as some of the
  Trappist beers (Belgium); sometimes also
  used to indicate any beer of the light-
  coloured variety, such as **witbier**
boeren- *boo·ruhn·*
  farmer-style · from the farm
boerenjongens *boo·ruhn·yong·uhns*
  brandy with spices & raisins
boerenkool *boo·ruhn·kohl* kale
boerenmeisjes *boo·ruhn·mey·shus*
  brandy with spices & apricots
boerenomelet *boo·ruhn·oh·muh·let*
  omelette with vegetables & bacon
bokbier *bok·beer* Dutch seasonal beer –
  Grolsch does Lentebok (Spring Bock) &
  Herfstbok (Autumn Bock)
bolleke *bo·luh·kuh* 'little ball' – Antwerp
  locals order their De Koninck Ale referring to the shape of the glass it comes in
bolus *boh·lus* type of (Dutch) pastry
bonbons *bon·bons* chocolates (Holland)
bonen *boh·nuhn* beans
borrel bo·*ruhl* alcoholic drink · aperitif
borrelhapjes ⓝ pl bo·*ruhl·hap·yuhs*
  titbits to go with alcoholic drinks
borst borst breast (meat)
bosbessen *bos·be·suhn* blueberries
bosuitjes ⓝ pl bos·*öy·chus*
  spring onions (also called **lente-uitjes**)
boter *boh·tuhr* butter
boterbabbelaar *boh·tuhr·ba·buh·laar*
  sweet containing butterscotch
boterham *boh·tuhr·ham*
  sandwich (of sliced bread)
boterletter *boh·tuhr·le·tuhr* pastry

botermelk *boh-tuhr-melk*
  buttermilk (Belgium)
bouillon *boo-yon consommé stock*
bouletten *boo-le-tuhn*
  big meatballs (Flanders)
bout *bawt leg (meat)*
braambessen *braam-be-suhn raspberries*
Brabantse koffietafel *braa-bant-suh
  ko-fee-taa-fuhl buffet-style meal consist-
  ing of various breads, cheeses, cold meats,
  savoury & sweet spreads, pies & cakes*
brandewijn *bran-duh-weyn brandy*
brood ⓝ *broth bread*
broodje ⓝ *broh-chuh bread roll*
bruidstaart *bröyts-taart wedding cake*
bruin bier *bröyn beer brown beer – also
  known as oud bruin (lit: old brown)*
Brusselse wafel *bru-suhl-suh waa-fuhl
  big, light & crispy rectangular waffle
  served on a plate with icing sugar,
  whipped cream and/or fruit*
Brussels lof ⓝ *bru-suhls lof see witlof*
Bush *boosh the strongest beer at 12%
  alcohol (not to be confused with the
  American lager Busch) – also comes as a
  Christmas beer, Bush de Noël (Belgium)*

C

cacao *ka-kaw/ka-ka-oh* ⓝ/ⓑ *cocoa*
cake *keyk cake*
caramelpudding *ka-ra-me-pu-ding
  crème caramel*
cashewnoot *ka-shoo-noht cashew*
champignons *sham-pee-nyons
  button mushrooms*
charcuterie *shar-kut-ree
  prepared/cooked/cured meats*
chili *chee-lee chilli*
chilisaus *chee-lee-saws chilli sauce*
chipolataworst *shee-poh-laa-ta-worst
  long thin sausage, rolled up*
chips *ships crisps*
chocolade *sho-koh-laa-duh chocolate*
chocoladejenever
  *shoh-koh-laa-duh-yuh-ney-vuhr/
  shoh-koh-laa-duh-zhuh-ney-vuhr* ⓝ/ⓑ
  chocolate-flavoured gin
chocoladereep *sho-koh-laa-duh-reyp
  chocolate bar*
chocomel *sho-koh-mel
  bottled chocolate drink – ask for it
  warme (warm) or koude (cold)*
citroen *see-troon lemon*

citroenjenever *see-troon-yuh-ney-vuhr/
  see-troon-zhuh-ney-vuhr* ⓝ/ⓑ
  lemon-flavoured gin
cocktailsaus *kok-teyl-saws
  sauce of mayonnaise, ketchup, whiskey,
  pepper & cream*
commiesiekaas *koh-mee-see-kaas
  Dutch Mimolette – a cow's milk cheese
  with orange skin*
confituur *kon-fee-tewr
  jam • marmalade (Flanders)*
courgette *koor-zhet zucchini*
crème fraîche *kreym fresh fresh whipped
  cream (Belgium) – more like sour cream
  in the Netherlands*
croque monsieur *krok muh-sye toasted
  sandwich with cheese & ham – croque
  madame krok ma-dam has an egg
  added, while croque Hawaii krok
  ha-way comes with a slice of pineapple*
curryworst *ku-ree-worst long, skinless,
  deep-fried mincemeat sausage
  (Flanders) – in Holland called frikandel*

D

dadel *daa-duhl date (fruit)*
daging Ind *da-khing beef*
dagschotel *dakh-skhoh-tuhl
  dish of the day (also called plat du jour)*
deeg ⓝ *deykh dough*
Delirium Tremens
  *dey-lee-ree-yuhm trey-mens
  bright blonde beer of 9% alcohol –
  comes in a distinctive ceramic-looking
  bottle with pink elephants (Belgium)*
dessert ⓝ *de-sert
  dessert – also called nagerecht*
doner kebab *deu-nuhr kuh-bap
  see shoarma*
dooier *doh-yuhr egg yolk*
doorbakken *dohr-ba-kuhn well-done*
doperwten *dop-erw-tuhn garden peas*
droog *drokh dry*
drop *drop sweet or salty liquorice*
druiven *dröy-vuhn grapes – blauwe
  druiven blaw-wuh dröy-vuhn (black
  grapes) or witte druiven wi-tuh
  dröy-vuhn (white grapes)*
Dubbel *du-buhl 'double' – Trappist or
  abbey-style beer higher in alcohol content
  than the Single but lower than the Tripel*
duif *döyf pigeon*

Duvel *dew·vuhl*
'devil' – a unique strong golden ale of 8.5% alcohol with a clean, firm body & fresh & fruity hop aromas (Belgium)

E

Edammerkaas *ey·da·muhr·kaas a small round cheese from Edam with red or orange skin – traditionally weighs 1.7 kg*
eend *eynt duck*
ei/eieren Ⓑ/Ⓝ *pl ey/ey·yuh·ruhn egg/eggs*
eierdooier *ey·yuhr·doh·yuhr egg yolk*
eierplant *ey·yuhr·plant eggplant (see also* **aubergine**)
eiwit Ⓝ *ey·wit egg white*
erwtensoep *erw·tuhn·soop thick pea soup with smoked sausage & bacon (also called* **snert**)
erwtjes *erw·chus peas*
escargots *es·kar·khohs snails (Belgium)*
everzwijn Ⓝ *ey·vuhr·zweyn boar*
extra belegen kaas *ek·stra buh·ley·khuhn kaas cheese ripened for seven months*

F

fazant *fa·zant pheasant*
filet *fee·ley fillet*
flan *fla flan*
flensje Ⓝ *flen·shuh thin pancake*
flessebier Ⓝ *fle·suh·beer bottled beer*
forel *fo·rel trout*
frambozen *fram·boh·zuhn raspberries*
frambozenbier Ⓝ *fram·boh·zuhn·beer raspberry beer – the traditional ones are based on* **Lambic** *(Belgium)*
Friese kaas *free·suh kaas a hard cheese flavoured with a combination of cumin & cloves*
Friese nagelkaas *free·suh naa·khul·kaas 'Frisian clove cheese' – a spiced cheese with a firm texture*
friet/frieten/frit/frites *freet/free·tuhn/frit/freet chips – also called* **patat** *in Holland*
frikandel *free·kan·del long, skinless, deep-fried mincemeat sausage (Holland) – in Flanders called* **curryworst** • *spicy meatball or meat patty (Belgium)*

frisdrank *fris·drangk soft drink*
fruit Ⓝ *fröyt fruit*
fruitbier *fröyt·beer fruit beer*

G

gado-gado *Ind ga·doh·ga·doh steamed vegetables & a hard-boiled egg served with peanut sauce & rice*
ganache *ga·nash a blend of chocolate, fresh cream & cocoa butter flavoured with coffee, cinnamon or liqueurs*
gans *khans goose*
garnalen *khar·naa·luhn shrimps*
garnalenkroket *khar·naa·luhn·kroh·ket deep-fried croquette filled with (grey) shrimps*
garnering *khar·ney·ring garnish*
gazeus *kha·zeus carbonated*
gebak Ⓝ *khuh·bak cakes & pastries*
gebakken *khuh·ba·kuhn baked • fried*
gebarbecued *khuh·bar·buh·kewt barbecued*
gebraad Ⓝ *khuh·braat roast*
gebraden *khu·braa·duhn roasted*
— aan 't spit *aant·spit spit-roasted*
gedroogd *khuh·drohkht dried*
geflambeerd *khuh·flam·beyrt flambéed*
gefrituurd *khuh·free·tewrt deep-fried*
gegratineerd *khuh·khra·te·neyrt browned on top with cheese (au gratin)*
gegrild *khuh·khrilt grilled*
gehakt Ⓝ *khuh·hakt mincemeat*
gehaktballetjes Ⓝ *pl khuh·hakt·ba·luh·chuhs small meatballs*
geit *kheyt goat*
geitenkaas *khey·tuh·kaas goat's cheese*
gekoeld *khuh·koolt chilled*
gekonfijt fruit Ⓝ *khu·kon·feyt fröyt candied fruit*
gekookt *khuh·kohkt boiled*
gekruid (met ...) *khuh·kröyt (met ...) seasoned (with ...)*
gemarineerd *khuh·ma·ree·neyrt marinated*
gember *khem·buhr ginger*
gemberpannenkoek *khem·buhr·pa·nuh·kook pancake laced with small chunks of ginger & ginger syrup*
gemengd *khuh·mengt assorted • mixed*

gemengde salade
khuh·*meng*·duh sa·*laa*·duh *mixed salad*

gepaneerd khuh·pa·*neyrt*
coated in breadcrumbs

gepocheerd khuh·po·*sheyrt poached*

geraspt khuh·*raspt grated*

gerookt khuh·*rohkt smoked*

gerookte Goudse kaas khuh·*rohk*·tuh *khawt*·suh kaas *'smoked Gouda cheese' –*
a sausage-shaped hard cheese that's
smoked slowly in brick ovens

geroosterd khuh·*roh*·stuhrt *roasted*
— brood ⓝ broht
toast (of bread slices)

gesauteerd khuh·soh·*teyrt sautéed*

gesmolten khuh·*smol*·tuhn *melted*

gesmoord khuh·*smohrt braised*

gesneden khuh·*sney*·duhn *cut · sliced*

gestoofd khuh·*stohft stewed*

gestoomd khu·*stohmt stecmed*

getapt beer khuh·*tapt* beer *beer on tap*

gevogelte ⓝ khuh·*voh*·khuhl·tuh
fowl · poultry

gevuld khuh·*vult stuffed*

gezouten khuh·*zaw*·tuhn *salted*

gianduja zhan·*doo*·cha
a blend of chocolate & hazelnut paste

glazuur ⓝ khla·*zewr icing*

goed doorbakken khoot dohr·*ba*·kuhn
well-done

Goudse kaas *khawt*·suh kaas
'Gouda cheese' – a popular Dutch cheese

graanjenever *khraan*·yuh·ney·vuhr/
khraan·zhuh·ney·vuhr ⓝ/ⓑ
see **jenever**

granaatappel khra·*naat*·a·puhl
pomegranate

griesmeelpudding *khrees*·meyl·pu·ding
semolina pudding often served with a
berry sauce

groene paprika *khroo*·nuh pa·*pree*·ka
green capsicum

groentebouillon *khroon*·tuh·boo·yon
vegetable broth · vegetable stock

groenten *khroon*·tuhn *vegetables*

groentenkrans *khroon*·tuh·krans
assortment of warm vegetables served
with a meal

Gueuze *kheu*·zuh *a blend of two or more*
Lambic *beers, resulting in a more*
sparkling variety (Belgium)

gyros *khee*·ros *see* **shoarma**

Haagse bluf *haakh*·suh bluf
egg whites beaten stiff & served with red
currant or berry juice

haan haan *cock*

haas haas *hare*

hagelslag *haa*·khuhl·slakh
chocolate sprinkles

half doorbakken half dohr·*ba*·kuhn
medium – in Belgium à point

ham ham *ham*

hammetje ⓝ *ha*·muh·chuh
whole ham on the bone

hapjes ⓝ pl *hap*·yuhs
appetisers · snacks · titbits

harde kaas *har*·duh kaas *hard cheese*

hardgekookt ei ⓝ *hart*·khuh·kohkt ey
hard-boiled egg

haring *haa*·ring *herring*
— met groene bonen
met *khroo*·r·uh boh·nuhn *herring with*
green beans, bacon & potatoes

haringsla *haa*·ring·slaa *cold salad of*
chopped herring with boiled potatoes,
other cooked vegetables & mayonnaise –
often served on a bread roll

hartig/hartelijk
har·tikh/*har*·tuh·luhk ⓝ/ⓑ *savoury*

havermout *haa*·vuhr·mawt *oats*

havermoutpap *haa*·vuhr·mawt·pap
milk-based oatmeal porridge

hazelnoot *haa*·zuhl·noht *hazelnut*

heet heyt *hot (temperature) · spicy*

helder *hel*·duhr *clear (eg soup)*

hersenen/hersentjes
her·suh·nuhn/*her*·suhn·chus *brains*

hert ⓝ hert *venison*

hesp hesp *ham (Belgium)*

hete bliksem *hey*·tuh *blik*·suhm
'hot lightning' – Dutch stew of potatoes,
apples, onions & bacon

Hollandse nieuwe ho·lant·suh *nee*·wuh
filleted herring – the first catch of the
season (from late May)

honing *hoh*·ning *honey*

hoofdgerecht ⑩ hohft·khuh·rekht
main course

hoorntje ⑩ hohrn·chuh custard-filled,
horn-shaped pastry · ice-cream cone

hutspot huts·pot
stew of potatoes, onions & carrots

huzarensla hew·zaa·ruhn·slaa
meat & potato salad

I

ijs ⑩ eys ice · ice cream
ingeblikt in·khuh·blikt canned
ingemaakt in·khuh·maakt preserved
— **zuur** ⑩ zewr pickles
inktvis ingkt·vis squid

J

jachtschotel yakht·skhoh·tuhl 'hunter's
stew' – oven dish with meat & potatoes

jam zhem jam

janhagel yan·haa·khul almond cookies
spiced with cinamon & allspice

jenever yuh·ney·vuhr/zhuh·ney·vuhr ⑧/⑱
gin (also called **graanjenever**) – traditionally distilled from juniper berries;
comes in a variety of strengths & tastes

jeneverbessen yuh·ney·vuhr·be·suhn/
zhuh·ney·vuhr·be·suhn ⑧/⑱
juniper berries

jong yong young
— **belegen kaas** buh·ley·khuhn kaas
cheese ripened for eight weeks

jonge jenever yong·uh yuh·ney·vuhr/
yong·uh zhuh·ney·vuhr ⑧/⑱
young jenever

jonge kaas yong·uh kaas 'young cheese' –
cheese ripened for four or five weeks

jus zhew gravy · juice (from meat)
— **d'orange** do·ransh
orange juice (Holland)

K

kaas kaas cheese

kaasaardappelen kaas·aart·a·puh·luhn
baked potatoes covered with melted
cheese

kaasblokjes ⑩ pl kaas·blok·yuhs
cheese cubes (often served with mustard
as an accompaniment to drinks)

kaaskroketten kaas·kroh·ke·tuhn
deep-fried croquettes with a cheesy/
creamy filling

kaasplank kaas·plangk cheese board
kabeljauw ka·buhl·yaw cod
kalfsoesters kalfs·oos·tuhrs veal
kalfsvlees kalfs·vleys veal
kalkoen kal·koon turkey
kammosselen ka·mo·suh·luhn scallops
kaneel ka·neyl cinnamon
kappertjes ⑩ pl ka·puhr·chus capers
karakollen ka·ra·ko·luhn snails (Belgium)
karbonade kar·boh·naa·duh
chop/cutlet – also called **kotelet**
karnemelk kar·nuh·melk buttermilk
kastanjes kas·tan·yus chestnuts
kekers key·kuhrs see **kikkererwten**
Kernhemkaas kern·nuhm·kaas a soft &
supple cheese with a mild texture
kersen ker·suhn cherries
kerstomaatjes kers·toh·maa·chus
cherry tomatoes
kervel ker·vuhl chervil
ketchap ke·tyap (Indonesian) soy sauce
kibbeling ki·buh·ling
deep-fried cod parings
kikkerbilletjes ⑩ pl ki·kuhr·bi·luh·chus
frog's legs
kikkererwten ki·kuhr·erw·tuhn chickpeas
kip kip chicken
klapstuk ⑩ klap·stuk rib of beef
knakworst knak·worst frankfurter
knoedel knoo·duhl dumpling
knoflook knof·lohk garlic – also called **look**
knolraap knol·raap swede · Swedish turnip
knolselderij knol·sel·duh·rey celeriac
koek kook biscuit · cookie
koekje ⑩ kook·yuh biscuit · cookie
koenjit Ind koon·yit ground turmeric
koffie ko·fee coffee
koffiemelk ko·fee·melk slightly sour-
tasting cream akin to condensed milk,
served separately with coffee
koffie verkeerd ko·fee vuhr·keyrt
coffee with a generous serving of milk,
similar to a caffe latte
kokosnoot koh·kos·noht coconut
komijn koh·meyn cumin
kommer kom·ko·muhr cucumber
konfituur kon·fee·tewr jam

konijn ⓝ ko-*neyn* rabbit
— **met pruimen** met *pröy*-muhn
rabbit cooked until tender in a sauce
spiked with prunes (Flanders)
koninginnehapje ⓝ
koh-ning-*khi*-nuh-hap-yuh *vol-au-vent*
(Flanders) – also see **pasteitje**
kool kohl cabbage
koolrabi kohl-*raa*-bee kohlrabi
kopstoot *kop*-stoht
'head butt' – jenever with a beer chaser
korst korst crust
korstdeeg ⓝ korst-deykh short pastry
kort gebakken kort khuh-*ba*-kuhn
rare – see also **saignant**
kotelet ko-tuh-*let* see **karbonade**
koud kawt cold
— **buffet** ⓝ bew-*fet*
buffet/smorgasbord of cold dishes
koude voorgerechten ⓟ pl *kaw*-duh
vohr-khuh-rekh-tuhn cold starters
kraanwater/kraantjeswater ⓝ Ⓝ/Ⓑ
kraan-waa-tuhr/*kraan*-chus-waa-tuhr
tap water
krab krap crab
kreeft kreyft lobster
krenten *kren*-tuhn currants
krentenbrood ⓝ *kren*-tuh-broht
bread with currants
krentewegge *kren*-tuh-we-khuh
raisin roll traditionally served with coffee
Kriek kreek cherry beer – the traditional
ones are based on **Lambic** & also known
as Oude Kriek (old Kriek) or Kriek Lambic
krieken *kree*-kuhn sour cherries
kroepoek Ind *kroo*-pook
shrimp/prawn crackers
krokant kroh-*kant* crisp
kroket kroh-*ket* croquette (often filled with
meat or cheese & eaten as a snack)
kroketjes ⓝ pl kroh-*ke*-chus
deep-fried potato croquettes
kropsla krop-slaa lettuce
kruiden *kröy*-duhn herbs & spices
kruidenkaas *kröy*-duhn-kaas
cheese with spices
kruidenpannenkoek
kröy-duhn-pa-nuh-kook
pancake with (green) herbs & spices
kruidenthee *kröy*-duh-tey herbal tea
kruidnagels *kröyt*-naa-khuls cloves

kruimeldeeg ⓝ *kröy*-muhl-deykh
shortcrust pastry
kruisbessen *kröys*-be-suhn gooseberries
krulsla krul-slaa curly-leaved lettuce
kuiken ⓝ *köy*-kuhn spring chicken
Kwak kwak amber beer of 8% alcohol with
earthy aromas, probably more famous
for its round-bottomed glass and stirrup-
like holder than for its content (Belgium)
kwark kwark quark
kwarktaart kwark-taart
cheesecake made with **kwark**
kwartel kwar-t.uhl quail
kweepeer kwey-peyr quince

L

lam ⓝ lam lamb
Lambic lam-*beek* an almost wine-like beer
from the Brussels region, brewed with wild
yeast; the Bel'e-Vue, Lindemans, Timmer-
mans & Mort Subite (lit: sudden death)
breweries are among the best-known ones
Leerdammerkaas leyr-da-muhr-kaas
a firm cheese with cherry-sized holes &
a mild, nut-like flavour (also called
Maasdammerkaas)
Leidse kaas leyt-suh kaas
'Leyden cheese' – a mild, hard cheese
spiced with cumin or caraway seeds
lekkerbekje ⓒ le-kuhr-bek-yuh
deep-fried fish fillet
lende len-duh loin
lendebiefstuk len-duh-beef-stuk
eye fillet • rump steak
lente-uitjes ⓝ *len*-tuh-öy-chus
spring onions (also called **bosuitjes**)
lever ley-vuhr liver
levertjes ⓟ pl ley-vuhr-chus
small livers (eg from chicken)
licht likht light • low-fat
— **beer** beer light beer – low-alcohol
beer (for those who are driving)
likeur lee-*keur* liqueur
limoen lee-*moon* lime
linzen lin-zuhn lentils
loempia Ind *loom*-pee-ya large spring roll
(the smaller ones are called **mini-
loempias** mee-nee-loom-pee-yas)
look lohk garlic
Luikse wafel löyk-suh waa-fuhl
heavy, sweet, sugary waffle, eaten warm

M

Maasdammerkaas *maas*·da·muhr·kaas
*a firm cheese with cherry-sized holes &
a mild, nut-like flavour (also called*
Leerdammerkaas)

maatjes ⓝ pl maa·chus
'little friends' – type of herring

magere melk *maa*·khu·ruh melk *skim milk*

makreel mak·*reyl* *mackerel*

maïs maays/ma·*yees* ⓝ/ⓑ *sweet corn*

marmelade mar·muh·*laa*·duh *marmalade*

marsepein mar·suh·*peyn* *marzipan*

mayonaise ma·yoh·*ney*·suh *mayonnaise*

Mechelse asperges me·khuhl·suh
as·*per*·khus *white asparagus –
a speciality of the Belgian town of
Mechelen*

medaillon ⓝ mey·da·*yon* *a piece of food,
usually meat, cut into a small, thin,
round or oval shape*

melk melk *milk*

meloen muh·*loon* *cantaloupe • melon*

met ... met ... *with ...*

met koolzuur/prik met *kohl*·zewr/prik
carbonated

mie Ind mee *noodles*

mierikswortel *mee*·riks·wor·tuhl
horseradish

moerbei *moor*·bey *mulberry*

moorkop *mohr*·kop *éclair (Holland)*

mosselen *mo*·suh·luhn
*mussels, usually cooked in white wine,
accompanied by chips*

mosterd *mos*·tuhrt *mustard*

(gestampte) muisjes ⓝ pl
(khuh·*stamp*·tuh) *möy*·shuhs
(ground) sugar-coated aniseed

munt munt *mint*

muntthee *munt*·tey *mint tea*

N

nagerecht ⓝ pl *naa*·khuh·rekht *dessert*

nasi Ind *na*·see *rice*
— goreng Ind *khoh*·reng
*fried rice with onions, pork, shrimp &
spices, often served with a fried egg or
shredded omelette on top*
— rames Ind *raa*·muhs
*a plate of boiled rice covered with vari-
ous vegetable & meat dishes*

niertjes ⓝ *neer*·chus *kidneys*

noedels *noo*·duhls *noodles*

noordzeegarnalen
noort·zey·khar·naa·luhn *small grey
shrimp with a distinctive taste, found
in the North Sea only – buy them fresh
from the fish market, peel them yourself
& wash them down with a glass of beer*

noot noht *nut*

nootmuskaat noht·mus·*kaat* *nutmeg*

nougatine noo·kha·*teen*
*pliable paste of sugar, syrup, crushed or
ground almonds or hazelnuts*

O

oester *oos*·tuhr *oyster*

olie *oh*·lee *oil*

oliebol *oh*·lee·bol *dough fritter*

olienoot *oh*·lee·noht *groundnut/peanut*

olijf o·*leyf* *olive*

olijfolie o·*leyf*·oh·lee *olive oil*

omelet oh·muh·*let* *omelette*

ontbijtgranen ont·*beyt*·khraa·nuhn *cereal*

ontbijtkoek ont·*beyt*·kook
gingerbread-style honey cake – called
peperkoek *in Belgium*

ossehaas *o*·suh·haas
carpaccio-style fillet of beef

ossestaart *o*·suh·staart *oxtail*

ossetong *o*·suh·tong *oxtongue*

oud awt *matured • old*

oud bruin awt bröyn *'old brown' –
brown beer (see also* **bruin beer***)*

oude jenever *aw*·duh yuh·*ney*·vuhr/
aw·duh zhuh·*ney*·vuhr ⓝ/ⓑ
old jenever

oude kaas *aw*·duh kaas
cheese ripened for at least a year

P

paard paart *horse*

paardefilet *paar*·duh·fee·ley *fillet of horse*

paddestoelen pa·duh·*stoo*·luhn
mushrooms

paling *paa*·ling *eel*
— in 't groen int khroon *'green eels' –
eel in spinach sauce (Flanders)*

Palm palm
*typical Belgian-style ale, tasty & amber
in colour – look out for the horse logo*

pannenkoek pa·nuh·kook *pancake*

(rode/groene) paprika (roh·duh/khroo·nuh) pa·pree·ka *(red/green) capsicum*

parelhoen paa·ruhl·hoon *guinea fowl*

passievrucht pa·see·vrukht *passionfruit*

pasteitje ⓝ pa·stey·chuh *vol-au-vent – in Belgium called* **koninginnehapje**

patat pa·tat *French fries (Holland)*

patrijs pa·treys *partridge*

pedis Ind puh·dees *hot (spicy)*

peer peyr *pear*

pens pens *see* **bloedworst**

peper pey·puhr *(cracked) pepper*

peperkoek pey·puhr·kook *see* **ontbijtkoek**

pepernoten pey·puhr·noh·tuhn *crunchy ginger biscuits*

perzik per·zik *peach*

peterselie pey·tuhr·sey·lee *parsley*

peultjes ⓝ pl peul·chus *sugar peas*

peulvrucht peul·vrukht *legume*

pide pee·dey *Turkish pizza*

pikant pee·kant *spicy*

pils pils *lager – the best-selling Stella Artois from Leuven is known worldwide, but other equally good pilsners include Maes, Primus & Jupiler; in Holland, there's Heineken of course, but also Amstel, Grolsch & Oranjeboom*

pinda pin·da *groundnut/peanut*

pindasaus pin·da·saws *peanut sauce*

pisang pee·sang *banana*

pistachenoot pees·tash·noht *pistachio*

pita pee·ta *stuffed pitta bread sandwiches, Middle-Eastern style*

pitabrood ⓝ pee·ta·broht *pitta bread*

plak plak *slice (Holland)*

plat du jour plat dew zhoor *French for* **dagschotel**

poffert po·fuhrt *a Dutch version of Gugelhoph – a small, round raisin cake served with coffee*

poffertjes ⓝ pl po·fuhr·chuhs *small puffed-up pancakes served with butter & icing sugar (Holland)*

pompoen pom·poon *pumpkin*

portie por·see *portion/serve*

— gemengd khuh·mengd *plate with mixed titbits, often cheese, salami, olives, etc*

pralines pra·lee·nuh *chocolates*

prei prey *leek*

prinsesseboontjes ⓝ pl prin·se·suh·boohn·chus *haricot beans*

pruimen pröy·muhn *plums • prunes*

puree pew·rey *mash*

puur pewr *pure/straight (alcohol)*

R

raap/rapen raap/raa·puhn *turnip(s)*

rabarber ra·bar·buhr *rhubarb*

radijs ra·deys *radish*

rauw raw *raw*

redelijk gebakken rey·duh·luhk khu·ba·kuhn *medium*

ree(bout) rey(·bawt) *venison*

reep (chocolade) reyp (shoh·koh·laa·duh) *(chocolate) bar*

ribstuk ⓝ rip·stuk *rib steak*

rijp reyp *ripe*

rijst reyst *rice*

rijstebrij/rijstpap Ⓝ/Ⓑ reys·tuh·brey/reyst·pap *sweet rice pudding, usually served with brown sugar*

rijsttafel reys·taa·fuhl *'rice table' – an array of savoury Indonesian dishes, like braised beef, pork satay & ribs served with white rice*

rijstvla reyst·vlaa *a tart filled with sweet, creamy rice pudding*

rivierkreeft ree·veer·kreyft *crayfish*

rode biet roh·duh beet *beetroot*

rode kool ron·duh kohl *red cabbage*

rode paprika roh·duh pa·pree·ka *red capsicum*

roerei ⓝ roo·rey *scrambled eggs*

rog rokh *ray*

roggebrood ⓝ ro·khuh·broht *pumpernickel • rye bread*

rollade ro·laa·duh *rolled slices of meat held together with string & slow-cooked in the oven*

rolmops rol·mops *rollmop*

romig roh·mikh *creamy*

rood roht *rare – in Belgium* **saignant**

roodbaars roht·baars *red mullet*

rood bier ront beer *red beer – wine-like in colour, like Rodenbach (Belgium)*

rookkaas ron·kaas *smoked cheese*

room rohm *cream*

roomijs rohm·eys *ice cream*

roomkaas *rohm*-kaas *cream cheese*
roti kip *roh*-tee kip *curried chicken served with potatoes, long beans, bean sprouts & a chickpea-flour pancake (Suriname)*
rozijnen ro-*zey*-nuhn *raisins • sultanas*
rund ⓝ runt *beef*
Russisch ei ⓝ *ru*-sis ey *sliced egg served with a vegetable mix*

S

saignant *sey*-nya
  rare – also called **kort gebakken**
salade sa-*laa*-duh *salad*
sambal Ind *sam*-bal *red chilli paste*
  — **badjak** Ind ba-*dzhak*
  dark brown, onion-based chilli paste with a mild & sweet flavour
  — **oelek** Ind *oo*-lek *hot red chilli paste*
sap ⓝ sap *juice*
sardientjes ⓝ pl sar-*deen*-chus *sardines*
saté sa-*tey* '*satay*' – *pieces of barbecued beef, chicken or pork on small skewers (sometimes covered in peanut sauce)*
saucijs saw-*seys* *sausage (Holland)*
saucijzebroodje ⓝ
  saw-*sey*-zuh-*broh*-chuh *sausage roll – in Belgium called* **worstebrood**
saus saws *sauce*
savooikool sa-*voy*-kohl *savoy cabbage*
schaal- en schelpdieren ⓝ pl skhaal en *skhelp*-dee-ruhn *crustaceans & shellfish*
schaap ⓝ skhaap *mutton • sheep*
schelvis *skhel*-vis *haddock*
schenkel *skheng*-kuhl *shank*
schimmelkaas *skhi*-muhl-kaas *blue cheese*
schol skhol *plaice*
schorsenelen skhor-suh-*ney*-luhn *black salsify*
schouderstuk ⓝ *skhaw*-duhr-stuk *shoulder (meat)*
selderij sel-duh-*rey* *celery*
shoarma shoo-*war*-ma *Lebanese & Turkish pitta bread filled with sliced lamb from a vertical spit (also known as* **gyros** *or* **doner kebab**)
sinaasappel see-*naas*-a-puhl *orange*
Single *sing*-uhl '*single*' – *Trappist or abbey-style beer most modest in alcohol*

siroop see-*rohp* *sirup*
sjalotjes ⓝ pl sha-*lo*-chus *shallots*
sla slaa *lettuce • salad*
slaatje *slaa*-chuh *salad*
slagroom *slakh*-rohm *whipped cream*
slakken *sla*-kuhn
  snails – in Belgium called **escargots**
slasaus *slaa*-saws *dressing • vinaigrette*
smeerkaas *smeyr*-kaas *spreadable cheese*
snee sney *slice*
snert snert *see* **erwtensoep**
snijbonen *sney*-boh-nuhn *haricot beans*
snoep snoop *candy • lollies • sweets*
soep soop *soup*
soesjes ⓝ pl *soo*-shuhs *profiteroles*
sojamelk *soh*-ya-melk *soy milk*
sojasaus *soh*-ya-saws
  *soy sauce – salty (***zout***) or sweet (***zoet***)*
sojascheuten *soh*-ya-*skheu*-tuhn
  see **taugé**
Spaanse pepers *spaan*-suh *pey*-puhrs
  '*Spanish peppers*' – *chillies*
spa blauw spa blaw *still mineral water*
spa rood spa roht *fizzy mineral water*
specerijen spey-suh-*rey*-yuhn *spices*
speculaas/speculoos spey-ku-*laas*/
  spey-ku-*lohs* *cinnamon-flavoured biscuit*
speenvarken ⓝ *speyn*-var-kuhn
  suckling pig
spek ⓝ spek *bacon*
spekpannenkoek *spek*-pa-nuh-kook
  crispy & aromatic bacon pancake
sperziebonen *sper*-zee-boh-nuhn
  green beans
spiegelei ⓝ *spee*-khul-ey
  fried egg, sunny side up
spinazie spee-*naa*-zee *spinach*
spruitjes ⓝ pl *sprôy*-chus *Brussels sprouts*
spuitwater ⓝ *spôyt*-waa-tuhr
  sparkling mineral water (soda water)
stamppot *stam*-pot *mashed potatoes & vegetables – in Belgium called* **stoemp**
sterk sterk *strong (of flavour)*
sterke dranken *ster*-kuh *drang*-kuhn *spirits*
steurgarnaal *steur*-khar-naal *prawn*
St Jacobsschelp sint-*yaa*-kops-skhelp
  scallop

stoemp stoomp *Flemish-style mashed potatoes, see* **stamppot**
— **met prei** met prey *creamy mashed potatoes with leeks & onion*
stokbrood ⓝ stok-broht *baguette*
stokvis stok-vis *dried cod*
stoofschotel stohf-skhoh-tuhl *casserole*
stoofvlees ⓝ stohf-vleys
*beef stew traditionally served with fries –
also called* **Vlaamse stoofkarbonade**
strandgapers strant-khaa-puhrs *clams*
strooppannenkoek strohp-pa-nuh-kook
*pancake with a light-brown syrup
derived from the sugar beet*
suiker söy-kuhr *sugar*

T

taart taart *pie • tart*
tahoe taa-hoo *tofu*
taptemelk tap-tuh-melk *skim milk*
tartaarsaus tar-taar-saws *tartare sauce*
taugé taw-zhey *bean sprouts – in Belgium
called* **sojascheuten**
thee tey *tea*
— **met citroen** met see-troon
tea with lemon
timbaaltje ⓝ tim-baal-chuh
*small round mould for the preparation
of puddings, puréed vegetables etc • all
dishes prepared in such a mould*
tofoe toh-foo *tofu*
tomaten toh-maa-tuhn *tomatoes*
tompoes tom-poos *custard slice with
icing*
tong tong *sole • tongue*
tonijn toh-neyn *tuna*
toost tohst *toast*
tosti tos-tee *toasted sandwich – in Belgium
called* **croque monsieur**
Trappist tra-pist *Trappist beer (Belgium has
six Trappist breweries – Achel, Chimay,
Orval, Rochefort, Westmalle & West-
vleteren; Holland has one – La Trappe)*
Tripel tri-puhl *'triple' – golden Trappist beer
or abbey-style beer with a high alcohol
content (refermented in the bottle)*
truffels tru-fuhls *truffles – subterranean
fungi that are a highly prized delicacy*
tuin- töyn- *from the garden*

tuinbonen töyn-boh-nuhn *broad beans*
tuinkers töyn-kers *cress*

U

ui/uien öy/öy-yuhn
onion/onions (also see **ajuin***)*
uitsmijter öyt-smey-tuhr
*sliced bread with cold meat covered with
fried eggs & served with a garnish*

V

van 't schap vant skhap
*'from the shelf' – the phrase to order a
beer at room temperature (Belgium)*
varkenshaasje ⓝ var-kuhns-haa-shuh
pork tenderloin
varkenspoot var-kuhns-poht *pig's trotter*
varkensvlees ⓝ var-kuhns-vleys *pork*
veenbes veyn-bes *cranberry*
venkel veng-kuhl *fennel*
venusschelpen vey-nus-skhel-puhn
clams • pipis
Verboden Vrucht vuhr-boh-duhn vrukht
*'forbidden fruit' – dark, strong beer from
the Hoegaarden family of beers (Belgium)*
verjaardagstaart vuhr-yaar-dakhs-taart
birthday cake
verloren brood ⓝ vuhr-loh-ruhn broht
'lost bread' – Flemish for **wentelteefjes**
vermicelli ver-mee-she-lee
thin noodles, often added to soup
vers vers *fresh*
vetsin vet-seen *MSG*
vijg veykh *fig*
vis vis *fish*
vla vlaa *custard*
vlaai vlaay *sweet tart/cake/pie – can contain fruit, cream, custard or chocolate*
Vlaams/Vlaamse vlaams/vlaam-suh
Flemish • Flemish-style
Vlaamse frites vlaam-suh freet
*fries/chips made from the whole potato
& smothered in mayonnaise*
Vlaamse stoofkarbonade vlaam-suh
stohf-kar-boh-naa-duh *see* **stoofvlees**
vlammetjes ⓝ pl vla-muh-chus
spicy spring rolls
vlees ⓝ vleys *meat*

vleeswaren *vleys*·waa·ruhn
cooked/prepared meats – also called
charcuterie in Belgium

vogelnestje ⓝ *voh*·khuhl·ne·shuh
'bird's nest' – meat loaf with egg inside

volkorenbrood ⓝ *vol*·koh·ruhn·broht
wholemeal bread

voorgerecht ⓝ *vohr*·khuh·rekht starter

vruchten-/fruit-… *vrukh*·tuhn·/fröyt·…
… with fruit

vruchtenvlaai *vrukh*·tuhn·vlaay
a fruit flan from the Limburg region filled
with fruits like cherries & strawberries

W

wafel *waa*·fuhl waffle

walnoten *wal*·noh·tuhn walnuts

warm warm hot (temperature)
— **buffet** ⓝ *bew*·fet
buffet/smorgasbord of hot dishes

warme chocolade *war*·muh
shoh·koh·*laa*·duh hot chocolate (drink)

warme voorgerechten ⓝ pl *war*·muh
vohr·khuh·rekh·tuhn warm starters

water ⓝ *waa*·tuhr water

waterkers *waa*·tuhr·kers watercress

watermeloen *waa*·tuhr·muh·*loon*
watermelon

waterzooi *waa*·tuhr·zoy
creamy meal soup with potatoes, vegetables & chicken or fish (Flanders)

wentelteefjes ⓝ pl *wen*·tuhl·teyf·yuhs
bread slices soaked in a mixture of milk,
egg, cinnamon & sugar & fried in an
oiled pan – also called **verloren brood**
in Flanders

wijn weyn wine

wijngaardslakken *weyn*·khaart·sla·kuhn
see **slakken**

wild ⓝ wilt game

witbier *wit*·beer
the original Belgian wheat beer – try
Hoegaarden as a refreshment

witlofsla *wit*·lof·slaa salad of raw **witloof**

witlof/witloof *wit*·lof
chicory – also called **Brussels lof**
— **met kaas en ham** met kaas en ham
witloof wrapped in ham & baked in the
oven in a creamy cheese sauce – traditionally served with mashed potatoes

witteke *wi*·tuh·kuh term used to indicate
pure **jenever** (as opposed to the ones
that have fruits added)

witte kool *wi*·tuh kohl white cabbage

worst worst sausage

worstebrood ⓝ *wor*·stuh·broht
see **saucijzebroodje**

worstjes ⓝ pl *wor*·shus small sausages

wortel *wor*·tuhl carrot

Z

zacht zakht mild • soft

zachte kaas *zakh*·tuh kaas soft cheese

zachtgekookt ei ⓝ *zakht*·khuh·koht ey
soft-boiled egg

zalm zalm salmon

zandgebak/zanddeeg ⓝ
zant·khuh·bak/*zant*·deykh shortbread

zeebaars *zey*·baars sea bass

zeebrasem *zey*·braa·suhm sea bream

zeeduivel *zey*·döy·vuhl monkfish

zeewier ⓝ *zey*·weer seaweed

zoet zoot sweet

zoetzuur zoot·*zewr* sweet & sour

zonder … *zon*·duhr … without …

zout ⓝ zawt salt

zure bom *zew*·ruh bom
big pickled gherkin

zure haring *zew*·ruh *haa*·ring
pickled herring – also see **rolmops**

zure room *zew*·ruh rohm sour cream

zuur zewr sour

zuurkool *zewr*·kohl sauerkraut

zwezeriken *zwey*·zuh·ri·kuhn
thymus (gland in chest of animals) –
usually from veal

emergencies

noodgevallen

Help!	*Help!*	help
Stop!	*Stop!*	stop
Go away! (general)	*Ga weg!*	khaa wekh
Go away! (stronger)	*Rot op!*	rot op
Thief!	*Dief!*	deef
Fire!	*Brand!*	brant
Watch out!	*Kijk uit!*	keyk öyt
Careful!	*Pas op!*	pa·*zop*
Call …!	*Bel …!*	bel …
an ambulance	*een ambulance*	uhn am·bew·*lans*
a doctor	*een dokter*	uhn *dok*·tuhr
the police	*de politie*	duh poh·*leet*·see

signs

Politiebureau	poh·*leet*·see·bew·roh	**Police Station**
Spoedafdeling	spoot·af·dey·ling	**Emergency Department**
Ziekenhuis	zee·kuhn·höys	**Hospital**

It's an emergency.
Het is een noodgeval. huht is uhn *noht*·khuh·val

There's been an accident.
Er is een ongeluk uhr is uhn *on*·khuh·luk
gebeurd. khuh·*beurt*

Could you please help?
Kunt u alstublieft kunt ew al·stew·*bleeft*
helpen? pol *hel*·puhn

Can I use your phone?
Kan ik uw telefoon kan ik ew tey·ley·*fohn*
gebruiken? pol khuh·*bröy*·kuhn

He/She is having a/an …	Hij/Zij heeft een …	hey/zey heyft uhn …
allergic reaction	*allergische reactie*	a·*ler*·khee·suh rey·*yak*·see
asthma attack	*aanval van astma*	*aan*·val van *ast*·ma
epileptic fit	*aanval van epilepsie*	*aan*·val van ey·pee·lep·*see*
heart attack	*hartaanval*	*hart*·aan·val

She's having a baby.
Zij krijgt een baby. — zey kreykht uhn *bey*·bee

I'm lost.
Ik ben verdwaald. — ik ben vuhr·*dwaalt*

Where are the toilets?
Waar zijn de toiletten? — waar zeyn duh twa·*le*·tuhn

Is it safe at night?
Is het 's nachts veilig? — is huht snakhts *vey*·likh

Is it safe on your own?
Is het veilig op je eentje? — is huht *vey*·likh op yuh *eyn*·chuh

Is it safe for …?	Is het veilig voor …?	is huht *vey*·likh vohr …
gay people	*homo- sexuelen*	hoh·moh· sek·sew·*wey*·luhn
travellers	*reizigers*	*rey*·zi·khurs
women	*vrouwen*	*vraw*·wuhn

police

Where's the police station?
Waar is het politiebureau? — waar is huht poh·*leet*·see·bew·*roh*

I want to report an offence. (minor/serious)
Ik wil aangifte doen van een overtreding/misdrijf. — ik wil *aan*·khif·tuh doon van uhn oh·vuhr·*trey*·ding/*mis*·dreyf

It was him/her.
Hij/Zij was het. — hey/zey was huht

I have insurance.
Ik heb verzekering. — ik hep vuhr·*zey*·kuh·ring

the police may say ...

U wordt beschuldigd van ... **pol**	ew wort buh·*skhul*·dikht van ...	**You're charged with ...**
aanranding	*aan*·ran·ding	**assault**
diefstal	*deef*·stal	**theft**
het bezitten van drugs	huht buh·*zi*·tuhn van drukhs	**possession of illegal substances**
openbare zedenschennis	oh·puhn·baa·ruh *zey*·duhn·skhe·nis	**indecent exposure**
verstoring van de openbare orde	vuhr·*stoh*·ring van duh oh·puhn·baa·ruh or·duh	**disturbing the peace**
winkeldiefstal	*wing*·kuhl·deef·stal	**shoplifting**
U wordt ervan beschuldigd ... **pol**	ew wort uhr·van buh·*skhul*·dikht ...	**You're charged with ...**
geen (geldig) visum te hebben	kheyn (khel·dikh) vee·zum tuh he·buhn	**not having a (valid) visa**
langer te zijn gebleven dan het visum toelaat	lang·uhr tuh zeyn khuh·*bley*·vuhn dan huht vee·zum too·laat	**overstaying a visa**
Het is een ...	huht is uhn ...	**It's a ... fine.**
boete voor een snelheids- overtreding	boo·tuh vohr uhn snel·heyts· oh·vuhr·trey·ding	**speeding**
parkeerboete	par·keyr·boo·tuh	**parking**

I've been ...	*Ik ben ...*	ik ben ...
He/She has been ...	*Hij/Zij is ...*	hey/zey is ...
assaulted	*aangevallen*	*aan*·khuh·va·luhn
raped	*verkracht*	vuhr·*krakht*
robbed	*bestolen*	buh·*stoh*·luhn
He/She tried to ... me.	*Hij/Zij probeerde me ...*	hey/zey proh·*beyr*·duh muh ...
assault	*aan te vallen*	aan tuh va·luhn
rape	*te verkrachten*	tuh vuhr·*krakh*·tuhn
rob	*te bestelen*	tuh buh·*stey*·luhn

essentials

197

My … was stolen.	Mijn … is gestolen.	meyn … is khuh·stoh·luhn
I've lost my …	Ik heb mijn … verloren.	ik hep meyn … vuhr·loh·ruhn
backpack	rugzak	rukh·zak
bag	tas	tas
credit card	kredietkaart	krey·deet·kaart
handbag	handtas	han·tas
money	geld	khelt
passport	paspoort	pas·pohrt
wallet	portemonnee	por·tuh·mo·ney

Could I please have an (English) interpreter?
Mag ik alstublieft makh ik al·stew·bleeft
een (Engelstalige) uhn (eng·uhls·taa·li·khuh)
tolk? pol tolk

What am I accused of?
Waar word ik van waar wort ik van
beschuldigd? be·skhul·dikht

I didn't realise I was doing anything wrong.
Ik was er mij niet van ik was uhr mey neet van
bewust dat ik iets buh·wust dat ik eets
verkeerd deed. ver·keyrt deyt

I didn't do it.
Ik heb het niet gedaan. ik hep huht neet khuh·daan

I want to contact my embassy/consulate.
Ik wil contact opnemen ik wil kon·takt op·ney·muhn
met mijn ambassade/ met meyn am·ba·saa·duh/
consulaat. kon·sew·laat

Can I have a lawyer (who speaks English)?
Mag ik alstublieft makh ik al·stew·bleeft
een (Engelstalige) uhn (eng·uhls·taa·li·khuh)
advocaat ? pol at·voh·kaat

This drug is for personal use.
Deze drugs zijn voor dey·zuh drukhs zeyn vohr
persoonlijk gebruik. puhr·sohn·luhk khuh·bröyk

I have a prescription for this drug.
Ik heb een recept/ ik hep uhn rey·sept/
voorschrift voor vohr·skhrift vohr
deze medicatie. Ⓝ/Ⓑ dey·zuh mey·dee·kaa·see

doctor

bij de dokter

Where's the nearest ...?	*Waar is de dichts-bijzijnde ...?*	waar is duh *dikhts*·bey·zeyn·duh ...
dentist	*tandarts*	*tan*·darts
doctor	*dokter*	*dok*·tuhr
emergency department	*spoedafdeling*	*spoot*·af·dey·ling
optometrist	*opticien*	op·tee·*sye*
(night) pharmacist	*(nacht)apotheek*	*(nakht*·)a·poh·*teyk*

Where's the nearest ...?	*Waar is het dichts-bijzijnde ...?*	waar is huht *dikhts*·bey·zeyn·duh ...
hospital	*ziekenhuis*	*zee*·kuhn·höys
medical centre	*medisch centrum*	*mey*·dis sen·trum

I need a doctor (who speaks English).
Ik heb een dokter nodig (die Engels spreekt).
ik hep uhn *dok*·tuhr *noh*·dikh (dee *eng*·uhls spreykt)

Could I see a female doctor?
Zou ik een vrouwelijke dokter kunnen zien?
zaw ik uhn *vraw*·wuh·luh·kuh *dok*·tuhr *ku*·nuhn zeen

Could the doctor come here?
Kan de dokter naar hier komen?
kan duh *dok*·tuhr naar heer *koh*·muhn

Is there an after-hours emergency number?
Is er een noodnummer voor buiten de normale uren?
is uhr uhn *noht*·nu·muhr vohr *böy*·tuhn duh nor·*maa*·luh *ew*·ruhn

I've run out of my medication.
Mijn medicijnen zijn op.
meyn mey·dee·*sey*·nuhn zeyn op

This is my usual medicine.
Dit zijn mijn normale   dit zeyn meyn nor·*maa*·luh
medicijnen.   mey·dee·*sey*·nuhn

My child weighs (20 kilos).
Mijn kind weegt (twintig)   meyn kint weykht (*twin*·tikh)
kilo.   *kee*·loh

What's the correct dosage?
Wat is de juiste   wat is duh *yöy*·stuh
dosering?   doh·*zey*·ring

I don't want a blood transfusion.
Ik wil geen bloedtransfusie.   ik wil kheyn *bloot*·trans·few·zee

Please use a new syringe.
Gebruik alstublieft een   khuh·*bröyk* al·stew·*bleeft* uhn
nieuwe injectiespuit. **pol**   *nee*·wuh in·*yek*·see·spöyt

I have my own syringe.
Ik heb mijn eigen   ik hep meyn *ey*·khuhn
injectiespuit.   in·*yek*·see·spöyt

I've been vaccinated against …	*Ik ben ingeënt tegen …*	ik ben *in*·khuh·ent tey·khuhn …
He/She has been vaccinated against …	*Hij/Zij is ingeënt tegen …*	hey/zey is *in*·khuh·ent tey·khun …
hepatitis A/B/C	*hepatitis A/B/C*	hey·paa·*tee*·tees aa/bey/sey
tetanus	*tetanus*	*tey*·ta·nus
typhoid	*typhus*	*tee*·fus

I need new …	*Ik heb … nodig.*	ik hep … *noh*·dikh
contact lenses	*nieuwe contactlenzen*	*nee*·wuh kon·*takt*·len·zuhn
glasses	*een nieuwe bril*	uhn *nee*·wuh bril

My prescription is …
Mijn recept/voorschrift   meyn rey·*sept*/*vohr*·skhrift
is … ⑧/⑧   is …

How much will it cost?
Hoeveel kost het?   hoo·*veyl* kost huht

Can I have a receipt for my insurance?

Kan ik een kwitantie   kan ik uhn kwee·*tan*·see
hebben voor mijn   he·buhn vohr meyn
verzekering?   vuhr·*zey*·kuh·ring

---

the doctor may say ...

Wat is het probleem?
  wat is huht pro·*bleym*   **What's the problem?**

Waar doet het pijn?
  waar doot huht peyn   **Where does it hurt?**

Heeft u koorts? **pol**
  heyft ew kohrts   **Do you have a temperature?**

Hoe lang heeft u dit al? **pol**
  hoo lang heyft ew   **How long have you been**
  dit al   **like this?**

Heeft u dat nog ooit gehad? **pol**
  heyft ew dat nokh   **Have you had this before?**
  oyt khuh·*hat*

Drinkt u? **pol**   dringkt ew   **Do you drink?**
Gebruikt u   khuh·*bröykt* ew   **Do you take**
  drugs? **pol**   drukhs   **drugs?**
Rookt u? **pol**   rohkt ew   **Do you smoke?**

Bent u ergens allergisch voor? **pol**
  bent ew *er*·khuhns   **Are you allergic**
  a·*ler*·khees vohr   **to anything?**

Neemt u medicijnen? **pol**
  neymt ew   **Are you on**
  mey·dee·*sey*·nuhn   **medication?**

Bent u seksueel actief? **pol**
  bent ew sek·sew·*weyl*   **Are you sexually active?**
  ak·*teef*

Heeft u onbeschermde seks gehad? **pol**
  heyf ew   **Have you had**
  on·buh·*skherm*·duh   **unprotected sex?**
  seks khuh·*hat*

Voor hoelang bent u op reis? **pol**
  vohr hoo·*lang* bent   **How long are you**
  ew op reys   **travelling for?**

the doctor may say ...

Ik verwijs u door naar een specialist. **pol**
ik vuhr·*weys* ew dohr naar
uhn spey·sya·*list*
**I'm referring you to
a specialist.**

U moet in het ziekenhuis opgenomen worden. **pol**
ew moot in huht
zee·kuhn·höys
op·khuh·noh·muhn *wor*·duhn
**You need to be admitted
to hospital.**

U moet het laten onderzoeken wanneer u weer thuis bent. **pol**
ew moot huht *laa*·tuhn
on·duhr·*zoo*·kuhn wa·*neyr*
ew weyr töys bent
**You should have it
checked when you
go home.**

U moet naar huis gaan voor de behandeling. **pol**
ew moot naar höys khaan
vohr duh be·*han*·duh·ling
**You should return home
for treatment.**

U bent een hypochonder! **pol**
ew bent uhn
hee·poh·*khon*·duhr
You're a hypochondriac!

symptoms & conditions

symptomen & aandoeningen

I'm sick.
Ik ben ziek.   ik ben zeek

It hurts here.
Hier doet het pijn.   heer doot huht peyn

My child is (very) sick.
Mijn kind is (erg) ziek.   meyn kint is (erkh) zeek

I've been injured.
Ik ben gewond.   ik ben khuh·*wont*

He/She has been injured.
Hij/Zij is gewond.   hey/zey is khuh·*wont*

I've been vomiting.
Ik heb overgegeven.   ik hep oh·vuhr·khuh·*khey*·vuhn

He/She has been vomiting.
*Hij/Zij heeft
overgegeven.*   hey/zey heyft
oh·vuhr·khuh·*khey*·vuhn

I feel ...	*Ik voel me ...*	ik vool muh ...
better	*beter*	*bey*·tuhr
depressed	*gedeprimeerd*	khuh·dey·pree·*meyrt*
nauseous	*misselijk*	*mi*·suh·luhk
shivery	*rillerig*	*ri*·luh·rikh
strange	*raar*	raar
stressed	*gestresseerd*	khuh·stre·*seyrt*
weak	*zwak*	zwak
worse	*slechter*	*slekh*·tuhr

I feel anxious/dizzy.
Ik ben angstig/duizelig.   ik ben *ang*·stikh/*döy*·zuh·likh

I feel hot and cold.
Ik heb het koud en warm.   ik hep huht kawt en warm

I'm dehydrated.
Ik ben gedehydrateerd.   ik ben khuh·dey·hee·dra·*teyrt*

I can't sleep.
Ik kan niet slapen.   ik kan neet *slaa*·puhn

I fainted.
Ik ben flauw gevallen.   ik ben flaw khuh·*va*·luhn

I think it's the medication I'm on.
Ik denk dat het aan mijn   ik denk dat huht aan meyn
medicijnen ligt.   mey·dee·*sey*·nuhn likht

I'm on medication for ...
Ik neem medicijnen   ik neym mey·dee·*sey*·nuhn
voor ...   vohr ...

He/She is on medication for ...
Hij/Zij neemt   hey/zey neymt
medicijnen voor ...   mey·dee·*sey*·nuhn vohr ...

I have (a/an) ...
Ik heb (een) ...   ik hep (uhn) ...

He/She has (a/an) ...
Hij/Zij heeft (een) ...   hey/zey heyft (uhn) ...

I've recently had (a/an) …
Ik heb onlangs (een)   ik hep on·*langs* (uhn)
… gehad.   … khuh·hat

He/She has recently had (a/an) …
Hij/Zij heeft onlangs   hey/zey heyft on·*langs*
(een) … gehad.   (uhn) … khuh·hat

asthma	*astma*	*ast*·ma
backache	*rugpijn*	*rukh*·peyn
bronchitis	*bronchitis*	bron·*khee*·tis
cold n	*kou*	kaw
constipation	*constipatie*	kon·stee·*paa*·see
cough n	*hoest*	hoost
diabetes	*diabetes/*	dee·ya·*bey*·tes/
	suikerziekte	*söy*·kuhr·zeek·tuh
diarrhoea	*diarree*	dee·ya·*rey*
eczema	*eczema*	ek·*zey*·ma
epilepsy	*epilepsie*	ey·pee·lep·*see*
fever	*koorts*	kohrts
flu	*griep*	khreep
food	*voedsel-*	*voot*·suhl·
poisoning	*vergiftiging*	vuhr·*khif*·ti·khing
fracture	*breuk*	breuk
gastritis	*maagontsteking*	*maakh*·ont·stey·king
headache	*hoofdpijn*	*hohft*·peyn
heart attack	*hartaanval*	*hart*·aan·val
heart condition	*hartkwaal*	*hart*·kwaal
high/low blood	*hoge/lage*	hoh·khuh/*laa*·khuh
pressure	*bloeddruk*	*bloo*·druk
infection	*ontsteking*	ont·*stey*·king
nausea	*misselijkheid*	*mi*·suh·luhk·heyt
pain n	*pijn*	peyn
pneumonia	*longontsteking*	*long*·ont·stey·king
rash	*huiduitslag*	*höyt*·öyt·slakh
sore throat	*keelpijn*	*keyl*·peyn
sprain	*verstuiking*	vuhr·*stöy*·king
stomachache	*maagpijn*	*maakh*·peyn
toothache	*kiespijn* ⓝ	*kees*·peyn
	tandpijn ⓑ	*tant*·peyn

Gebruikt u een anticonceptiemiddel? pol	
khu·*bröykt* ew uhn	**Are you using**
an·tee·kon·*sep*·see·mi·duhl	**contraception?**
Bent u ongesteld? pol	
bent ew on·khuh·*stelt*	**Are you menstruating?**
Bent u zwanger? pol	
bent ew *zwang*·uhr	**Are you pregnant?**
Wanneer was u laatst ongesteld? pol	
wa·*neyr* was ew laatst	**When did you last have**
on·khuh·*stelt*	**your period?**
U bent zwanger. pol	
ew bent *zwang*·uhr	**You're pregnant.**

women's health

gynaecologie

I'm pregnant.	*Ik ben zwanger.*	ik ben *zwang*·uhr
I'm on the pill.	*Ik neem de pil.*	ik neym duh pil

I think I'm pregnant.
Ik denk dat ik zwanger ben.   ik dengk dat ik *zwang*·uhr ben

I haven't had my period for (six) weeks.
Ik ben al (zes) weken   ik ben al (zes) *wey*·kuhn
niet ongesteld geweest.   neet on·khuh·*stelt* khuh·*weyst*

I've noticed a lump here.
Ik heb hier een   ik hep heer uhn
gezwel gevoeld.   khu·*zwel* khuh·*voolt*

Do you have something for (period pain)?
Heeft u iets tegen   heyft ew eets *tey*·khuhn
(menstruatiepijn)? pol   (men·strew·*waa*·see·peyn)

I have (a) ...	*Ik heb een ...*	ik hep uhn ...
cystitis	*blaasontsteking*	*blaas*·ont·stey·king
urinary tract	*infectie van*	in·*fek*·see van
infection	*de urine-*	duh ew·*ree*·nuh·
	wegen	wey·khuhn
yeast infection	*schimmelinfectie*	*skhi*·muhl·in·fek·see

health

205

I need (a/the) ...	*Ik heb ... nodig.*	ik hep ... *noh*·dikh
contraception	*een anticon-*	uhn an·tee·kon·
	ceptiemiddel	*sep*·see·mi·duhl
morning-after	*de morning*	duh *mohr*·ning
pill	*after pil*	*aaf*·tuhr pil
pregnancy test	*een zwanger-*	uhn *zwang*·uhr·
	schapstest	skhaps·test

allergies

I'm allergic	*Ik ben allergisch*	ik ben a·*ler*·khees
to ...	*voor ...*	vohr ...
He/She is allergic	*Hij/Zij is allergisch*	hey/zey is a·*ler*·khees
to ...	*voor ...*	vohr ...
antibiotics	*anti-*	an·tee·
	biotica	bee·*yoh*·tee·ka
anti-	*ontstekings-*	ont·*stey*·kings·
inflammatories	*remmende*	*re*·muhn·duh
	medicijnen	mey·dee·*sey*·nuhn
aspirin	*aspirine*	as·pee·*ree*·nuh
bees	*bijen*	*bey*·yuhn
codeine	*codeine*	koh·dey·*ee*·nuh
penicillin	*penicilline*	pey·nee·see·*lee*·nuh
pollen	*pollen*	*po*·luhn
sulphur-based	*zwavel-*	*zwaa*·vuhl·
drugs	*houdende*	*haw*·duhn·duh
	medicijnen	mey·dee·*sey*·nuhn

I have a skin	*Ik heb een*	ik hep uhn
allergy.	*huidallergie.*	*höyt*·a·ler·khee
antihistamines	*anti-*	an·tee·
	histaminica	his·ta·*mee*·nee·ka
inhaler	*inhalator*	in·haa·*laa*·tor
injection	*injectie*	in·*yek*·see

For some food-related allergies, see **special diets & allergies**, page 182.

parts of the body

lichaamsdelen

My ... hurts.
Mijn ... doet pijn.   meyn ... doot peyn
I can't move my ...
Ik kan mijn ...   ik kan meyn ...
niet bewegen.   neet buh·*wey*·khuhn
I have a cramp in my ...
Ik heb kramp in mijn ...   ik hep kramp in meyn ...
My ... is swollen.
Mijn ... is gezwollen.   meyn ... is khu·*zwo*·luhn

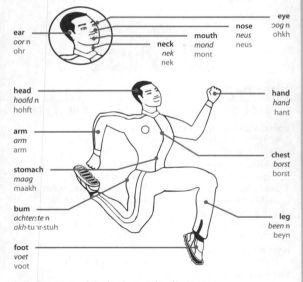

ear
oor n
ohr

nose
neus
neus

mouth
mond
mont

neck
nek
nek

eye
oog n
ohkh

head
hoofd n
hohft

hand
hand
hant

arm
arm
arm

chest
borst
borst

stomach
maag
maakh

bum
achterste n
akh·tur·stuh

leg
been n
beyn

foot
voet
voot

For other parts of the body, see the **dictionary**.

alternative treatments

I don't use (Western medicine).
Ik gebruik geen   ik khuh·*bröyk* kheyn
(Westerse geneeskunde).   (*wes*·tuhr·suh khuh·*neys*·kun·duh)

I prefer ...	*Ik verkies ...*	ik vuhr·*kees* ...
Can I see	*Kan ik iemand*	kan ik *ee*·mant
someone who	*zien die aan*	zeen dee aan
practises ...?	*... doet?*	... doot
acupuncture	*acupunctuur*	a·kew·punk·*tewr*
naturopathy	*natuur-*	na·*tewr·*
	geneeskunde	khuh·*neys*·kun·duh
reflexology	*reflexologie*	rey·flek·soh·loh·*khee*

pharmacist

I need something for (a headache).
Ik heb iets nodig   ik hep eets *noh*·dikh
tegen (hoofdpijn).   *tey*·khuhn (*hohft*·peyn)

Do I need a prescription for (antihistamines)?
Heb ik een recept/   hep ik uhn rey·*sept*/
voorschrift nodig voor   *vohr*·skhrift *noh*·dikh vohr
(antihistaminica)? ⓝ/ⓑ   (an·tee·his·ta·*mee*·nee·ka)

I have a prescription.
Ik heb een recept/   ik hep uhn rey·*sept*/
voorschrift. ⓝ/ⓑ   *vohr*·skhrift

How many times a day?
Hoeveel keer per dag?   hoo·*veyl* keyr puhr dakh

Will it make me drowsy?
Word ik er loom van?   wort ik uhr lohm van

Twee/Drie keer per dag.
twey/dree keyr puhr dakh — **Twice/Three times a day.**

Voor/Met/Na het eten.
vohr/met/na huht ey·tuhn — **Before/With/After food.**

Heeft u dit al eerder ingenomen? pol
heyft ew dit al eyr·duhr
in·khuh·noh·muhn — **Have you taken this before?**

U moet deze medicijnen nemen tot ze op zijn. pol
ew moot dey·zuh
mey·dee·sey·nuhn
ney·muhn tot zuh op zeyn — **You must complete the course.**

antiseptic n	*ontsmettend middel* n	ont·*sme*·tuhnt *mi*·duhl
bandage	*verband* n	vuhr·*bant*
contraceptives	*anticonceptie- middelen* n pl	an·tee·kon·*sep*·see· mi·duh·luhn
diarrhoea medicine	*middel tegen diarree* n	*mi*·duhl *tey*·khuhn dee·ya·*rey*
insect repellent	*insectverdrijvend middel* n	in·sekt·vuhr·*drey*·vuhnt *mi*·duhl
laxatives	*laxeermiddelen* n pl	lak·*seyr*·mi·duh·luhn
painkillers	*pijnstillers*	*peyn*·sti·luhrs
rehydration salts	*rehydratatie- oplossing*	rey·hee·dra·*taa*·see· op·lo·sing
sleeping pills	*slaappillen*	*slaa*·pi·luhn

For more pharmaceutical items, see the **dictionary**.

dentist

bij de tandarts

I have a ...	*Ik heb ...*	ik hep ...
broken tooth	*een gebroken tand*	uhn khuh·*broh*·kuhn tant
cavity	*een gaatje*	uhn *khaa*·chuh
toothache	*kiespijn* ⓝ *tandpijn* ⓑ	*kees*·peyn *tant*·peyn

I've lost a filling.
Ik heb een vulling   ik hep uhn *vu*·ling
verloren.   vuhr·*loh*·ruhn

My dentures are broken.
Ik heb mijn kunstgebit   ik hep meyn *kunst*·khuh·bit
gebroken.   khuh·*broh*·kuhn

My gums hurt.
Mijn tandvlees doet pijn.   meyn *tant*·vleys doot peyn

I don't want it extracted!
Ik wil niet dat hij   ik wil neet dat hey
getrokken wordt!   khuh·*tro*·kuhn wort

Ouch!
Au!   aw

I need (a/an) ...   *Ik heb een ...*   ik hep uhn ...
          nodig.   *no*·dikh
    anaesthetic   *verdoving*   vuhr·*doh*·ving
    filling   *vulling*   *vu*·ling

---

the dentist may say ...

Doe je mond ver open.
    doo yuh mont ver *oh*·puhn   **Open wide.**

Dit doet helemaal geen pijn.
    dit doot hey·luh·*maal*   **This won't hurt a bit.**
    kheyn peyn

Bijt hierop.
    beyt *hee*·rop   **Bite down on this.**

Niet bewegen.
    neet buh·*wey*·khuhn   **Don't move.**

Spoelen alsjeblieft.
    spoo·luhn a·shuh·*bleeft*   **Rinse.**

Kom terug, ik ben nog niet klaar!
    kom tuh·*rukh*   **Come back,**
    ik ben nokh neet klaar   **I haven't finished!**

DICTIONARY > english–dutch

A

In this dictionary, words are marked as n (noun), a (adjective), v (verb), adv (adverb), prep (preposition), pron (pronoun), sg (singular), pl (plural), inf (informal) and pol (polite) where necessary. Note that we've only indicated Dutch nouns which have neuter gender with ⑩ after the translation – the nouns which have common gender are left unmarked. Where a word has different masculine and feminine forms, both options are given and indicated with ⑩/① (for more on gender in Dutch, see the **phrasebuilder**). If it's a plural noun, you'll also see pl. We've used the symbols ⑧/⑧ for words which are different in the Netherlands and Belgium respectively. For more food terms, see the **culinary reader**.

A

aboard *aan boord* aan bohrt
abortion *abortus* a·bor·tus
about (approximately) *ongeveer* on·khuh·veyr
about (relating to) *aangaande* aan·khaan·duh
above *boven* boh·vuhn
abroad *in het buitenland* in huht böy·tuhn·lant
accident *ongeval* ⑩ on·khuh·val
accommodation *accommodatie* a·koh·moh·daa·see
account (bill) n *rekening* rey·kuh·ning
across *tegenover* tey·khuhn·oh·vuhr
actor *acteur/actrice* ⑩/① ak·teur/ak·tree·suh
acupuncture *acupunctuur* a·kew·punk·tewr
adaptor *adapter* a·dap·tuhr
addiction *verslaving* vuhr·slaa·ving
address n *adres* ⑩ a·dres
administration *administratie* at·mee·nee·straa·see
administrator *bestuurder* buh·stewr·duhr
admission (price) *toegangsprijs* too·khangs·preys
admit (let in) v *toelaten* too·laa·tuhn
adult n *volwassene* vol·wa·suh·nuh
advertisement *advertentie* at·vuhr·ten·see
advice *advise* ⑩ at·vees
aeroplane *vliegtuig* ⑩ vleekh·töykh

after *na* naa
afternoon *middag/namiddag* ⑧/⑧ mi·dakh/naa·mi·dakh
again *opnieuw* op·neew
age n *leeftijd* leyf·teyt
(three days) ago *(drie dagen) geleden* (dree daa·khun) khuh·ley·duhn
agree *overeenkomen* oh·vuhr·eyn·koh·muhn
agriculture *landbouw* lant·baw
ahead (clock/distance) *voorop* vohr·op
ahead (in the future) *in de toekomst* in duh too·komst
air n *lucht* lukht
air-conditioned *met airconditioning* met eyr·kon·di·shuh·ning
airline *luchtvaartmaatschappij* lukht·vaart·maat·skha·pey
airmail *luchtpost* lukht·post
airplane *vliegtuig* ⑩ vleekh·töykh
airport *luchthaven* lukht·haa·vuhn
airport tax *luchthavenbelasting* lukht·haa·vuhn·buh·las·ting
aisle (on plane) *gangpad* ⑩ khang·pat
alarm clock *wekker* we·kuhr
all *alle* a·luh
allergy *allergie* a·ler·khee
almond *amandel* a·man·duhl
almost *bijna* bey·naa
alone *alleen* a·leyn
already *al* al
also *ook* ohk
altar *altaar* ⑩ al·taar
altitude *hoogte* hohkh·tuh
always *altijd* al·teyt

english–dutch

211

ambassador *ambassadeur/ambassadrice* ⓜ/ⓕ am·ba·sa·*deur*/am·ba·sa·*dree*·suh
ambulance *ambulance* am·bew·*lans*
anaemia *bloedarmoede bloot*·ar·moo·duh
ancient *oud* awt
adventure *avontuur* ⓝ a·von·*tewr*
and *en* en
angry *boos* bohs
animal *dier* ⓝ deer
ankle *enkel* eng·kuhl
another *een andere* uhn *an*·duh·ruh
answer n *antwoord* ⓝ *ant*·wohrt
answer v *antwoorden* ant·wohr·duhn
ant *mier* meer
antibiotics *antibiotica* ⓝ pl an·tee·bee·yo·tee·ka
antinuclear *antinucleair* an·tee·nu·kley·yer
antique n *antiek* an·*teek*
antiseptic a *ontsmettend* ont·*sme*·tuhnt
any *enige* ey·ni·khuh
apartment *flat/appartement* ⓝ ⓝ/ⓑ flet/a·par·tuh·*ment*
apple *appel* a·puhl
appointment *afspraak af*·spraak
apricot *abrikoos* a·bree·*kohs*
archaeological *archeologisch* ar·khey·oh·*loh*·khis
architecture *architectuur* ar·khee·tek·*tewr*
argue (a point) *argumenteren* ar·khew·men·*tey*·ruhn
argue (with someone) *ruzie maken* rew·zee *maa*·kuhn
arm (body) *arm* arm
arrest v *arresteren* a·res·*tey*·ruhn
arrivals *aankomst aan*·komst
arrive *aankomen aan*·koh·muhn
art *kunst* kunst
art gallery *kunstgalerie* kunst·kha·luh·*ree*
artist *artiest* ar·*teest*
ashtray *asbak as*·bak
Asia *Azië aa*·zee·yuh
ask v *vragen vraa*·khun
asparagus *asperge* a·*sper*·khuh
aspirin *aspirine* as·pee·*ree*·nuh
asthma *astma ast*·ma
at *bij* bey
athletics *atletiek* at·*ley*·teek
atmosphere *atmosfeer* at·mos·*feyr*
attractive *aantrekkelijk* aan·*tre*·kuh·luhk
aunt *tante tan*·tuh
Australia *Australië* aw·*straa*·lee·yuh
ATM *pin-automaat/geldautomaat* ⓝ/ⓑ *pin*·aw·toh·maat/*khelt*·aw·toh·maat

autumn *herfst* herfst
avenue *laan* laan
awful *verschrikkelijk* vuhr·*skhri*·kuh·luhk

B

B&W (film) *zwart-wit (film)* zwart·*wit* (film)
baby food *babyvoeding bey*·bee·voo·ding
baby powder *talkpoeder* ⓝ *talk*·poo·duhr
back (body) *rug* rukh
back (position) *achterkant akh*·tuhr·kant
backpack *rugzak rukh*·zak
bacon *spek* ⓝ spek
bad *slecht* slekht
bag *tas* tas
baggage *bagage* ba·*khaa*·zhuh
baggage allowance *toegestane hoeveelheid bagage* too·khuh·*staa*·nuh hoo·*veyl*·heyt ba·*khaa*·zhuh
baggage claim *bagage-inleverpunt* ⓝ/ *bagage band* ba·*khaa*·zhuh·*in*·ley·vuhr·punt/ba·*khaa*·zhuh bant
bakery *bakker/bakkerij* ⓝ/ⓑ ba·kuhr/ba·kuh·*rey*
balance (account) *saldo* ⓝ *sal*·doh
balcony *balkon* ⓝ bal·*kon*
ball (sport) *bal* bal
banana *banaan* ba·*naan*
band (music) *band/groep* ⓝ/ⓑ bent/khroop
bandage *verband* ⓝ vuhr·*bant*
Band-Aid *pleister pley*·stuhr
bank n *bank* bangk
bank account *bankrekening bangk*·rey·kuh·ning
banknote *bankbiljet* ⓝ *bangk*·bil·yet
baptism *doopsel* ⓝ *dohp*·suhl
bar n *bar* bar
bar of chocolate *reep chocolade* reyp shoh·koh·*laa*·duh
barber *barbier* bar·*beer*
bar work *werk als barbediende* ⓝ werk als *bar*·buh·deen·duh
basket *mand* mant
bath n *bad* ⓝ bat
bathing suit *zwempak* ⓝ *zwem*·pak
bathroom *badkamer bat*·kaa·muhr
battery (car) *accu a*·kew
battery (general) *batterij* ba·tuh·*rey*
battlefield *slagveld* ⓝ *slakh*·velt
be *zijn* zeyn
beach *strand* strant
bean *boon* bohn

bean sprouts *taugé/sojascheuten* Ⓝ/Ⓑ taw·*zhey*/*soh*·ya·skheu·tuhn
beard *baard* baart
beautician *schoonheidsspecialiste schohn*·heyt·spey·sya·*lis*·tuh
beautiful *mooi* moy
beauty salon *schoonheidssalon* skhohn·heyt·sa·*lon*
because *omdat* om·*dat*
bed *bed* Ⓝ bet
bed linen *beddegoed* Ⓝ be·duh·khoot
bedroom *slaapkamer* slaap·*kaa*·muhr
bee *bij* bey
beef *rundvlees* Ⓝ *runt*·vleys
beer *bier* Ⓝ beer
beer on tap *getapt bier* Ⓝ khuh·*tapt* beer
beetroot *rode biet* roh·duh beet
before *voor* vohr
beggar *bedelaar/bedelares* Ⓜ/Ⓕ *bey*·duh·laar/bey·cuh·*laa*·res
behind *achter* akh·tuhr
Belgian *Belgisch* bel·khis
Belgian person *Belg* belkh
Belgium *België* bel·khee·yuh
below *onder* on·duhr
berth (ship) n *hut* hut
berth (train) n *couchette* koo·*shet*
beside *naast* naast
best *beste* bes·tuh
bet n *weddenschap* we·duhn·skhap
bet v *wedden* we·duhn
better *beter* bey·tuhr
between *tussen* tu·suhn
bicycle *fiets* feets
big *groot* khroht
bigger *groter* khroh·tuhr
biggest *grootst* khrohtst
bike *fiets* feets
bike chain *fietsketting* feets·ke·ting
bike lock *fietsslot* Ⓒ feet·slot
bike path *fietspad* Ⓝ feets·pat
bike shop *fietsenwinkel* feet·suhn·wing·kuhl
bilingual *tweetalig* twey·*taa*·likh
bill (restaurant) n *rekening* rey·kuh·ning
binoculars *verrekijker* ve·ruh·key·kuhr
bird *vogel* voh·khul
birth certificate *geboorteakte* khuh·bohr·tuh·ak·tuh
birthday *verjaardag* vuhr·yaar·dakh
biscuit *koekje* Ⓝ kook·yuh
bite (dog/insect) n *beet* beyt
bitter *bitter* bi·tuhr
black *zwart* zwart

black market *zwarte markt* zwar·tuh markt
bladder *blaas* blaas
blanket *deken* dey·kuhn
blind a *blind* blint
blister n *blaar* blaar
blocked (drain) *verstopt* vuhr·stopt
blocked (access/road) *afgesloten* af·khuh·sloh·tuhn
blood *bloed* Ⓝ bloot
blood group *bloedgroep* bloot·khroop
blood pressure *bloeddruk* bloo·druk
blood test *bloedtest* bloo·test
blouse *bloes* bloos
blue *blauw* blaw
board (plane, ship) v *aan boord gaan* aan bohrt khaan
boarding house *pension* Ⓝ pen·*syon*
boarding pass *instapkaart* in·stap·kaart
boat *boot* boht
boat trip *rondvaart* ront·vaart
body *lichaam* Ⓝ li·khaam
boiled *gekookt* khuh·*kohkt*
bone *bot* Ⓝ bot
book n *boek* Ⓝ book
book (make a booking) v *reserveren* rey·ser·*vey*·ruhn
booked out *volgeboekt* vol·khuh·bockt
book shop *boekhandel* book·han·duhl
boot (footwear) *laars* laars
boots (footwear) *laarzen* pl laar·zuhn
border n *grens* khrens
bored *verveeld* vuhr·veylt
boring *saai/vervelend* Ⓝ/Ⓑ saay/vuhr·*vey*·luhnt
borrow *lenen* ley·nuhn
botanic garden *botanische tuin* boh·*taa*·ni·suh töyn
both *beide* bey·duh
bottle *fles* fles
bottle opener *flesopener* fles·oh·puh·nuhr
bottle shop *slijterij/drankenhandel* Ⓑ/Ⓑ sley·tuh·*rey*/drang·kuhn·han·duhl
bottom (body) *achterwerk* Ⓝ akh·tuhr·werk
bottom (position) *onderaan* on·duhr·*aan*
bowl (plate) n *kom* kom
box n *doos* dohs
boxing *boksen* Ⓝ bok·suhn
box of chocolates *doos bonbons/pralines* Ⓝ/Ⓑ dohs bon·bons/pra·*lee*·nuh
boy *jongen* yong·uhn
boyfriend *vriend* vreent
bra *beha* bey·haa
brakes *remmen* re·muhn

brandy *brandewijn/cognac* Ⓝ/Ⓑ
bran·duh·weyn/ko·nyak
brave *moedig* moo·dikh
bread *brood* Ⓝ broht
bread roll *broodje* Ⓝ broh·chuh
break v *breken* brey·kuhn
break down v *het begeven*
huht buh·khey·vuhn
breakfast *ontbijt* Ⓝ ont·beyt
breast (body) *borst* borst
breathe *ademen* aa·duh·muhn
bribe n *omkoperij* om·koh·puh·rey
bribe v *omkopen* om·koh·puhn
bridge (structure) n *brug* brukh
briefcase *aktetas* ak·tuh·tas
bring *brengen* breng·uhn
broken *gebroken* khuh·broh·khun
broken down *stuk* stuk
brother *broer* broor
brown *bruin* bröyn
bruise n *kneuzing* kneu·zing
brush n *borstel* bor·stuhl
bucket *emmer* e·muhr
bug n *insect* Ⓝ in·sekt
build v *bouwen* baw·uhn
builder *aannemer* aa·ney·muhr
building *gebouw* Ⓝ khuh·baw
bum bag *heuptasje* Ⓝ heup·ta·shuh
burn n *branden* bran·duhn
burnt *verbrand* vuhr·brant
bus (city) *stadsbus* stats·bus
bus (intercity) *bus* bus
business n *zaken* zaa·kuhn
businessperson *zakenman/zakenvrouw*
Ⓜ/Ⓕ *zaa·kuhn·man/zaa·kuhn·vraw*
business trip *zakenreis* zaa·kuhn·reys
busker *straatmuzikant*
straat·mew·zee·kant
bus station *busstation* Ⓝ bus·sta·syon
bus stop *bushalte* bus·hal·tuh
busy (person) *bezig* bey·zikh
busy (phone) *bezet* buh·zet
busy (place) *druk* druk
but *maar* maar
butcher *slager* slaa·khuhr
butcher's shop *slagerij* slaa·khuh·rey
butter n *boter* boh·tuhr
butterfly *vlinder* vlin·duhr
button *knoop* knohp
buy v *kopen* koh·puhn

C

cabbage *kool* kohl
cable car *cabine van een kabelbaan*
ka·bee·nuh van uhn kaa·buhl·baan
café *koffiehuisje* Ⓝ/*brasserie* Ⓝ Ⓑ
ko·fee·höy·shuh/bra·suh·ree
cake shop *banketbakker/patisserie* Ⓝ/Ⓑ
bang·ket·ba·kuhr/pa·tee·suh·ree
calculator *rekenmachine*
rey·kuhn·ma·shee·nuh
calendar *kalender* ka·len·duhr
call (phone) n *telefoongesprek* Ⓝ
tey·ley·fohn·khuh·sprek
camera (film/video) *camera* kaa·mey·ra
camera (photos) *fototoestel* Ⓝ
foh·toh·too·stel
camera shop *fotozaak* foh·toh·zaak
camp v *kamperen* kam·pey·ruhn
camping ground *camping*
kem·ping/kam·ping Ⓝ/Ⓑ
camping store *kampeerwinkel*
kam·peyr·wing·kuhl
camp site *kampeerplaats* kam·peyr·plaats
can n *blik* Ⓝ blik
can (be able) *kunnen* ku·nuhn
can (have permission) *mogen* moh·khuhn
canal (general) *kanaal* Ⓝ ka·naal
canal (in town) *gracht* khrakht
canalside house *grachtenhuis* Ⓝ
khrakh·tuhn·höys
cancel *annuleren* a·new·ley·ruhn
cancer *kanker* kang·kuhr
candle *kaars* kaars
candy *snoep* snoop
can opener *blikopener* blik·oh·puh·nuhr
cantaloupe *meloen* muh·loon
capsicum *peper* pey·puhr
captain *kapitein* ka·pee·teyn
car *wagen/auto* waa·khuhn/aw·toh
caravan *caravan* ke·ruh·ven/ka·ra·van Ⓝ/Ⓑ
carbon dioxide *koolstofdioxide*
kohl·stof·dee·yok·see·duh
carbon dioxide emissions
koolstofdioxide-emissie
kohl·stof·dee·yok·see·duh·ey·mee·see
cardiac arrest *hartstilstand* hart·stil·stant
cards (playing) *speelkaarten*
speyl·kaar·tuhn
care (for a sick person) v *(iemand)
verzorgen* (ee·mant) vuhr·zor·khuhn
care (have feelings for) v *(om iemand)
geven* (om ee·mant) khey·vuhn

car hire *autoverhuur* aw·toh·vuhr·hewr
car park *parking* par·king
carpenter *timmerman* ti·muhr·man
carpet *kleed* ⓝ/*tapijt* ⓝ ⓝ/ⓑ kleyt/ta·peyt
car registration *inschrijvingsbewijs* ⓝ
    in·skhrey·vings·buh·weys
carrot *wortel* wor·tuhl
carry *dragen* draa·khuhn
cash n *baar geld* ⓝ baar khelt
cash (a cheque) v *(een cheque) innen*
    (uhn shek) i·nuhn
cashew *cashewnoot* ka·shoo·noht
cashier *kassier/kassierster* ⓜ/ⓕ
    ka·seer/ka·seer·stuhr
cash register *kassa* ka·sa
castle *kasteel* ⓝ kas·teyl
casual work
    tijdelijke baan ⓝ/*interimwerk* ⓝ ⓑ
    tey·duh·luh·kuh baan/in·tuh·rim·werk
cat *kat* kat
cathedral *katedraal* ka·tey·draal
cauliflower *bloemkool* bloom·kohl
cave n *grot* khrot
CD *cd* sey·dey
celebration *viering* vee·ring
cell phone *mobiele telefoon* ⓝ/*gsm* ⓑ
    moh·bee·luh tey·ley·fohn/khey·es·em
cemetery *kerkhof* ⓝ kerk·hof
centre n *centrum* ⓝ sen·trum
ceramics *keramiek* key·ra·meek
cereal (breakfast) *ontbijtgranen* ⓝ pl
    ont·beyt·khraa·nuhn
certificate *certificaat* ⓝ ser·tee·fee·kaat
chain n *ketting* ke·ting
chair n *stoel* stool
chairperson *voorzitter* vohr·zi·tuhr
chairlift (skiing) *stoeltjeslift* stool·chuhs·lift
championships *kampioenschap* ⓝ
    kam·pee·yoon·skhap
chance n *kans* kans
change (general) n *verandering*
    vuhr·an·duh·ring
change (loose coins) n *kleingeld* ⓝ
    kleyn·khelt
change (money given back) n
    wisselgeld ⓝ wi·suhl·khelt
change (money) v *(geld) wisselen*
    (khelt) wi·suh·luhn
changing room (shop) *paskamer*
    pas·kaa·muhr
changing room (sport, individual)
    kleedhokje ⓝ kleyt·hok·yuh

changing room (sport, communal)
    kleedkamer kleyt·kaa·muhr
charming *charmant* shar·mant
chat up v *opvrijen* op·vrey·yuhn
cheap *goedkoop* khoot·kohp
cheat (at games) n *valsspeler* val·spey·luhr
cheat (in business) n *oplichter* op·likh·tuhr
check (banking) n *cheque* shek
check (bill) n *rekening* rey·kuh·ning
check v *controleren* kon·troh·ley·ruhr
check-in (desk) *incheckbalie* in·shek·ba·lee
checkpoint *controlepost* kon·troh·luh·post
cheese *kaas* kaas
cheese shop *kaaswinkel* kaas·wing·kuhl
chef *chef-kok* shef·kok
chemist (pharmacist)
    apotheker/apothekeres ⓜ/ⓕ
    a·poh·tey·kuhr/a·poh·tey·kuh·res
chemist (pharmacy) *apotheek* a·pch·teyk
cheque (banking) *cheque* shek
cherry *kers* kers
chess *schaakspel* ⓝ skhaak·spel
chessboard *schaakbord* ⓝ skhaak·bort
chest (body) *borst* borst
chestnut *hazelnoot* haa·zuhl·noht
chewing gum *kauwgom* kaw·khom
chicken *kip* kip
chicken pox *windpokken* wint·po·kuhn
chickpeas *kekers/kikkererwten* ⓝ/ⓑ
    key·kuhrs/ki·kuhr·erw·tuhn
child *kind* ⓝ kint
child-minding service *kinderoppasdienst*
    kin·duhr·o·pas·deenst
children *kinderen* ⓝ pl kin·duh·ruhn
child seat *kinderzitje* ⓝ kin·duhr·zi·chuh
chilli sauce *chilisaus* chee·lee·saws
chiropractor *chiropractor* chee·roh·prak·tor
chocolate *chocolade* shoh·koh·laa·duh
chocolate bar *chocoladereep*
    shoh·koh·laa·duh·reyp
choose *kiezen* kee·zuhn
chopping board *snijplank* sney·plangk
chopsticks *eetstokjes* ⓝ pl eyt·stok·yuhs
Christmas *Kerstmis* kerst·mis
Christmas Day *kerstdag* kerst·dakh
Christmas Eve *kerstavond* kerst·aa·vont
church *kerk* kerk
cigar *sigaar* see·khaar
cigarette *sigaret* see·kha·ret
cigarette lighter *aansteker* aan·stey·kuhr
cinema *bioscoop* bee·yos·kohp
citizenship *staatsburgerschap* ⓝ
    staats·bur·khuhr·skhap

city *stad* stat
city centre *stadscentrum* ⑥ *stat*·sen·trum
civil rights *burgerrechten*
  bur·khuh·rekh·tuhn
class (category) n *klas/klasse* klas/*kla*·suh
classical *klassiek* kla·*seek*
class system *klassesysteem* ⑥
  kla·suh·sees·*teym*
clean a *schoon/proper* ⑧/⑧
  skhohn/*proh*·puhr
clean v *schoonmaken* skhohn·*maa*·kuhn
cleaning *schoonmaak* skhohn·maak
client *klant* klant
cliff *rotswand* rots·want
climate change *klimaatverandering*
  klee·*maat*·vuhr·an·duh·ring
climb v *klimmen* kli·muhn
cloakroom *garderobe/vestiaire*
  khar·duh·roh·buh/ves·*tyer*
clock n *klok* klok
clogs *klompen* klom·puhn
close a *dichtbij* dikht·*bey*
close v *sluiten* slöy·tuhn
closed *gesloten* khuh·*sloh*·tuhn
clothesline *waslijn* was·leyn
clothing *kleding* kley·ding
clothing store *kledingzaak* kley·ding·zaak
cloud n *wolk* wolk
cloudy *bewolkt* buh·*wolkt*
clutch (car) *koppeling* ko·puh·ling
coach (bus) n *touringcar* too·ring·kar
coach v *coachen* koh·chuhn
coast n *kust* kust
coat n *jas/mantel* yas/*man*·tuhl
coat hanger *kleerhanger* kleyr·hang·uhr
cobblestones *kasseien* ka·*sey*·yuhn
cockroach *kakkerlak* ka·kuhr·lak
coconut *kokosnoot* koh·kos·noht
coffee *koffie* ko·fee
coins *muntstukken* munt·stu·kuhn
cold (illness) n *kou* kaw
cold (weather) n *kou/koude* kaw/*kaw*·duh
cold a *koud* kawt
colleague *collega* ko·*ley*·kha
collect call *gesprek voor rekening
  van de ontvanger* khuh·*sprek* vohr
  rey·kuh·ning van duh ont·*vang*·uhr
college *college* ⑥ ko·*ley*·zhuh
colour n *kleur* kleur
comb n *kam* kam
come *komen* koh·muhn
comedy *komedie* ko·*mey*·dee
comfortable *comfortabel* kom·for·*taa*·buhl

commission *commissie* ko·*mee*·see
communications (profession)
  communicatie ko·mew·nee·*kaa*·see
communion (religious) *communie*
  ko·*mew*·nee
companion *metgezel* met·khuh·zel
company (firm) *zaak* zaak
compass *kompas* ⑥ kom·*pas*
complain *klagen* klaa·khuhn
complaint *klacht* klakht
complimentary (free) *gratis* khraa·tis
computer game *computerspel* ⑥
  kom·*pyoo*·tuhr·spel
concussion *hersenschudding*
  her·suhn·skhu·ding
condom *condoom* ⑥ kon·*dohm*
conference (big) *conferentie*
  kon·fey·*ren*·see
conference (small) *bespreking*
  buh·*sprey*·king
confession (religious) *biecht* beekht
confirm (a booking) *bevestigen*
  be·*ves*·ti·khuhn
congratulations *gelukwensen*
  khuh·*luk*·wen·suhn
conjunctivitis *bindvliesontsteking*
  bint·vlees·ont·stey·king
connection (concepts) *verband* ⑥
  vurh·*bant*
connection (objects/transport)
  verbinding vuhr·*bin*·ding
conservative *conservatief* kon·ser·va·*teef*
constipation *constipatie* kon·stee·*paa*·see
consulate *consulaat* ⑥ kon·su·*laat*
contact lenses *contactlenzen*
  kon·*takt*·len·zuhn
contact lens solution
  oplossing voor contactlenzen
  op·*lo*·sing vohr kon·*takt*·len·zuhn
contagious *besmettelijk* buh·*sme*·tuh·luhk
contraceptives *anticonceptiemiddelen*
  an·tee·kon·sep·see·mi·duh·luhn
convenience store *avondwinkel*
  aa·vont·wing·kuhl
convent *klooster* ⑥ *kloh*·stuhr
cook n *kok* kok
cook v *koken* koh·kuhn
cookie *koekje* ⑥ *kook*·yuh
cooking *koken* koh·kuhn
cool (groovy) *leuk* leuk
cool (temperature) *koel* kool
corkscrew *kurkentrekker* kur·kuh·tre·kuhr
corn *maïs* maays/ma·*yees* ⑧/⑧

corner n *hoek* hook
corrupt a *corrupt* ko·rupt
corruption *corruptie* ko·rup·see
cost n *kost* kost
cost v *kosten* kos·tuhn
cotton n *katoen* ⓝ ka·toon
cotton balls *wattenproppen*
    wa·tuh·pro·puhn
cotton buds *wattenstaafjes*
    wa·tuh·staaf·yuhs
cough n *hoest* hoost
cough v *hoesten* hoos·tuhn
cough medicine *hoestmiddel* ⓝ
    hoost·mi·duhl
count v *tellen* te·luhn
counter (at bar) *toog* tohk
country *land* ⓝ lant
countryside *platteland* ⓝ pla·tuh·lant
court (legal) *gerecht* ⓝ khuh·rekht
court (tennis) *plein* ⓝ pleyn
cover charge *bedieningsgeld* ⓝ
    buh·dee·nings·khelt
cow *koe* koo
cracker *beschuit* be·skhöyt
crafts *handwerk* ⓝ hant·werk
crash (car) n *aanrijding* aan·rey·ding
crash (plane) n *vliegtuigongeluk* ⓝ
    vleekh·töykh·on·khuh·luk
crazy *gek* khek
cream (food) *room* rohm
cream (lotion) *crème* kreym
credit n *krediet* ⓝ krey·deet
credit card *kredietkaart* krey·deet·kaart
cross (religious) n *kruis* ⓝ kröys
crowded *stampvol* stamp·vol
cucumber *komkommer* kom·ko·muhr
cup *kop* kop
cupboard *kast* kast
currency exchange *wisselkantoor* ⓝ
    wi·suhl·kan·tohr
current (electricity) *stroom* strohm
current affairs *actualiteiten*
    ak·tew·wa·lee·tey·tuhn
custom *gewoonte* khuh·wohn·tuh
customs *douane* doo·waa·nuh
cut n *snede* sney·duh
cut v *snijden* sney·duhn
cutlery *bestek* ⓝ buh·stek
CV *cv* ⓝ sey·vey
cycle (ride) v *fietsen* feet·suhn
cycling (casual) *fietsen* feet·suhn
cycling (competitive) *wielersport*
    wee·luhr·sport

cyclist (casual) *fietser* feet·suhr
cyclist (competitive) *wielrenner*
    weel·re·nuhr
cystitis *blaasontsteking* blaas·ont·stey·king

D

dad *pa* paa
daily a&adv *dagelijks* daa·khuh·luhks
dam *dam* dam
damage *schade* skhaa·duh
damage from water *waterschade*
    waa·tuhr·skhaa·duh
dance n *dans* dans
dance v *dansen* dan·suhn
dancing *dansen* dan·suhn
dangerous *gevaarlijk* khuh·vaar·luhk
dark (colour/night) *donker* dong·kuhr
date (appointment) n *afspraak* af·spraak
date (day) *dag* dakh
date (fruit) *dadel* daa·duhl
date (go out with) v *uitgaan met*
    öyt·khaan met
date of birth *geboortedatum*
    khuh·bohr·tuh·daa·tum
daughter *dochter* dokh·tuhr
dawn *dageraad* daa·khuh·raat
day *dag* dakh
day after tomorrow *overmorgen*
    oh·vuhr·mor·khun
day before yesterday *eergisterer*
    eyr·khis·tuh·ruhn
dead *dood* doht
deaf *doof* dohf
deal (cards) v *delen* dey·leyn
decide *beslissen* buh·sli·suhn
deep (water) *diep* deep
deforestation *ontbossing* ont·bo·sing
degrees (temperature) *graden* kraa·duhn
delay n *vertraging* vuhr·traa·khing
delicious *lekker* le·kuhr
deliver *bezorgen* be·zor·khuhn
democracy *democratie* dey·moh·kra·see
demonstration (display) *demonstratie*
    dey·mon·straa·see
demonstration (rally) *betoging*
    buh·toh·khing
Denmark *Denemarken* dey·nun·mar·kuhn
dental floss *tandzijde* tant·zey·duh
dentist *tandarts* tan·darts
deodorant *deodorant* dey·yoh·doh·rant
depart *vertrekken* vuhr·tre·kuhn

department store
  warenhuis ⓝ/*grootwarenhuis* ⓝ/ⓑ
  waa·ruhn·höys/khroht·waa·ruhn·höys
departure *vertrek* ⓝ *vuhr·trek*
departure gate *vertrekhal* vuhr·trek·hal
deposit (money) n *storting* stor·ting
descendant *afstammeling* af·sta·muh·ling
desert n *woestijn* woos·teyn
design n *ontwerp* ⓝ ont·werp
dessert *dessert* ⓝ de·seyr
destination *bestemming* buh·ste·ming
details *details* ⓝ pl dey·tays
diabetes *suikerziekte/diabetes*
  söy·kuhr·zeek·tuh/dee·ya·bey·tis
dial tone *kiestoon* kees·tohn
diamond *diamant* dee·ya·mant
diaper *luier* löy·yuhr
diaphragm (contraceptive) *pessarium* ⓝ
  pe·saa·ree·yuhm
diarrhoea *diarree* dee·ya·rey
diary (agenda) *agenda* a·khen·da
diary (personal notes) *dagboek* ⓝ
  dakh·book
dice n *dobbelstenen* do·buhl·stey·nuhn
dictionary *woordenboek* ⓝ
  wohr·duhn·book
die v *sterven* ster·vuhn
diet n *dieet* ⓝ dee·yeyt
different *verschillend* vuhr·skhi·luhnt
difficult *moeilijk* mooy·luhk
digital a *digitaal* dee·khee·taal
dining car *restauratiewagen*
  res·toh·raa·see·waa·khuhn
dinner *diner* ⓝ/*avondmaal* ⓝ
  dee·ney/aa·vont·maal
direct a *rechtstreeks* rekh·streyks
direct-dial *rechtstreekse lijn*
  rekh·streyk·suh leyn
direction *richting* rikh·ting
director *directeur/directrice* ⓜ/ⓕ
  dee·rek·teur/dee·rek·tree·suh
dirty *vuil* vöyl
disabled *gehandicapt* khuh·hen·dee·kept/
  khuh·han·dee·kapt ⓝ/ⓑ
discount n *korting* kor·ting
discrimination *discriminatie*
  dis·kree·mee·naa·see
disease *ziekte* zeek·tuh
dish n *schotel* skhoh·tuhl
disk (CD-ROM) *schijf* skheyf
diving *duiken* döy·kuhn
diving equipment *duikuitrusting*
  döyk·öyt·rus·ting

divorced *gescheiden* khuh·skhey·duhn
dizzy *duizelig* döy·zuh·likh
do *doen* doon
doctor *dokter* dok·tuhr
dog *hond* hont
dole *werkloosheidsuitkering*
  werk·lohs·heyts·öyt·key·ring
doll *pop* pop
door *deur* deur
double a *dubbel* du·buhl
double bed *tweepersoonsbed* ⓝ
  twey·puhr·sohns·bet
double room *tweepersoonskamer*
  twey·puhr·sohns·kaa·muhr
down *naar beneden* naar buh·ney·duhn
downhill *bergaf* berkh·af
downtown *stadscentrum* ⓝ stat·sen·trum
dozen *dozijn* ⓝ do·zeyn
draught beer *getapt bier* ⓝ khuh·tapt beer
dream n *droom* drohm
dress n *jurk/kleed* ⓝ yurk/kleyt
dried *gedroogd* khuh·drohkht
dried fruit *gedroogd fruit* ⓝ
  khuh·drohkht fröyt
drink (alcoholic) n *drank/drankje* ⓝ
  drangk/drang·kyuh
drink (general) n *drank* drangk
drink v *drinken* dring·kuhn
drive v *rit* rit
drivers licence *rijbewijs* ⓝ rey·buh·weys
drug n *drugs* drukhs
drug addiction *drugsverslaving*
  drukhs·vuhr·slaa·ving
drug dealer *drugdealer* drukh·dee·luhr
drugs (illicit) *drugs* drukhs
drugstore *drogisterij* droh·khis·tuh·rey
drug trafficking *drugshandel*
  drukhs·han·duhl
drug user *(drugs)gebruiker*
  (drukhs·)khuh·bröy·kuhr
drum n *trommel* tro·muhl
drums (kit) *drumstel* ⓝ drum·stel
drunk a *dronken* drong·kuhn
dry a *droog* drohkh
dry (clothes) v *drogen* droh·khuhn
dry (oneself) v *afdrogen* af·droh·khuhn
duck n *eend* eynt
dummy (pacifier) *fopspeen* fop·speyn
Dutch *Nederlands/Hollands*
  ney·duhr·lants/ho·lants
Dutch (language) *Nederlands* ⓝ
  ney·duhr·lants
Dutch gable *klokgevel* klok·khey·vuhl

Dutch person *Nederlander/Hollander*
ney-duhr-lan-duhr/ho-lan-duhr
Dutch-speaking *Nederlandstalig* ney-duhr-lants-*taa*-lihk
duty-free shop *taksvrije winkel*
taks-vrey-yuh wing-kuhl
DVD *dvd* dey-vey-*dey*
dyke *dijk* deyk

E

each *elke* elk-kuh
ear *oor* ⑩ ohr
early adv *vroeg* vrookh
earn *verdienen* vuhr-*dee*-nuhn
earplugs *oorstopper* ohr-sto-puhn
earrings *oorringen* oh-ring-uhn
Earth *aarde* ɑar-duh
earthquake *aardbeving* aart-bey-ving
east n *oosten* ⑩ oh-stuhn
Easter *Pasen* paa-suhn
easy *gemakkelijk* khuh-*ma*-kuh-luhk
eat v *eten* ey-tuhn
education (at home) *opvoeding*
op-voo-ding
education (at school) *onderwijs* ⑩
on-duhr-weys
egg *ei* ⑩ ey
eggplant *aubergine* oh-ber-khee-nuh
election *verkiezing* vuhr-*kee*-zing
electrical store
handel in elektrische apparaten
han-duhl in ey-*lek*-tri-suh a-pa-*raa*-tuhn
electrician *electricien* ey-lek-tree-*sye*
electricity *elektriciteit* ey-lek-tree-see-*teyt*
elevator *lift* lift
embarrassed *gegeneerd* khuh-zhuh-*neyrt*
embassy *ambassade* am-ba-*saa*-duh
emergency *noodgeval* ⑩ noot-khuh-val
emotional *emotioneel* ey-moh-syoh-*neyl*
employee *werknemer* werk-*ney*-muhr
employer *werkgever* werk-*khey*-vuhr
empty a *leeg* leykh
end n *einde* ⑩ eyn-duh
endangered species *bedreigde soort*
buh-*dreykh*-duh sohrt
engaged (phone) *bezet* buh-*zet*
engaged (to be married)
verloofd vuhr-*lohft*
engagement (to marry)
verloving vuhr-*loh*-ving
engine *motor* mʳ oh-tor
engineer n *ingenieur* in-zhey-*nyeur*

engineering (civil) *burgerlijke bouwkunde*
bur-khur-luh-kuh baw-kun-duh
engineering (mechanical) *machine-bouwkunde* ma-*shee*-nuh-baw-kun-duh
England *Engeland* eng-uh-lant
English *Engels* eng-uhls
English (language) *Engels* ⑩ eng-uhls
English-speaking
Engelstalig eng-uhls-*taa*-lihk
enjoy (oneself) *(zich) amuseren*
(zikh) a-mew-sey-ruhn
enough *genoeg* khuh-*nookh*
enter *binnengaan* bi-nuhn-khaan
entertainment guide *uitgaansgids*
öyt-khaans-khits
entry n *ingɑng* in-khang
environment *milieu* ⑩ mil-*yeu*
equality *gelijkheid* khuh-*leyk*-heyt
equal opportunity *gelijke kansen* pl
khuh-*ley*-kuh kan-suhn
equipment *uitrusting* öyt-rus-ting
escalator *roltrap* rol-trap
estate agency *makelaarskantoor* ⑩
maa-kuh-laars-kan-tohr
euro *euro/euro's* sg/pl eu-roh/eu-rohs
Europe *Europa* eu-roh-pa
European Union *Europese Unie*
eu-roh-pey-suh ew-nee
euthanasia *euthanasie* eu-ta-na-*zee*
evening *avond* aa-vont
every a *elke* el-kuh
everyone *iedereen* ee-duh-*reyn*
everything *alles* ɑ-luhs
exactly *juist* yöyst
example *voorbeeld* ⑩ vohr-beylt
excellent *uitmuntend* öyt-*mun*-tuhnt
excess baggage *overvracht* oh-vuhr-vrakht
exchange (general) v *ruilen* röy-luhn
exchange (money) v *wisselen* wi-suh-luhn
exchange rate *wisselkoers* wi-suhl-koors
excluded *niet inbegrepen*
neet in-buh-khrey-puhn
exhaust (car) *uitlaat* öyt-laat
exhibition *tentoonstelling*
tuhn-*tohn*-ste-ling
exit n *uitgang* öyt-khang
expensive *duur* dewr
experience n *ervaring* er-*vaa*-ring
exploitation *uitbuiting* öyt-böy-ting
express mail *exprespost* eks-pres-post
extension (visa) *verlenging* vuhr-*leng*-ing
eye *oog* ⑩ ohkh
eye drops *oogdruppels* ohkh-dru-puhls

F

fabric *stof* (n) stof
façade *gevel* khey-vuhl
face n *gezicht* (n) khuh-zikht
face cloth *washandje* (n) was-han-chuh
factory *fabriek* fa-breek
factory worker
  fabrieksarbeider/fabrieksarbeidster
  (m)/(f) fa-breeks-ar-bey-duhr/
  fa-breeks-ar-beyt-stuhr
fairground *kermis* ker-mis
fall (autumn) *herfst* herfst
fall (down) v *val* val
family *familie* fa-mee-lee
family name *familienaam* fa-mee-lee-naam
famous *bekend* buh-kent
fan (machine) *ventilator* ven-tee-laa-tor
fan belt *ventilatorriem* ven-tee-laa-to-reem
far *ver* ver
fare n *tarief* (n) ta-reef
farm n *boerderij* boor-duh-rey
farmer *boer/boerin* (m)/(f) boor/boo-rin
fashion n *mode* moh-duh
fast a *snel* snel
fat (food) a *vet* vet
fat (objects/people) a *dik* dik
father *vader* vaa-duhr
father-in-law *schoonvader* skhohn-vaa-duhr
faucet *kraantje* (n) kraan-chuh
fault (someone's) n *fout* fawt
faulty *stuk* stuk
feed *voeden* voo-duhn
feel (emotions/touch) v *voelen* voo-luhn
feeling (physical) *gevoel* (n) khuh-vool
feelings *gevoelens* (n) pl khuh-voo-luhns
female a *vrouwelijk* vraw-wuh-luhk
fence n *omheining* om-hey-ning
fencing (sport) *schermen* skher-muhn
ferry n *veerboot/ferry* (n)/(e)
  veyr-boht/fe-ree
fever *koorts* kohrts
few *enkele* eng-kuh-luh
fiancé/fiancée *verloofde* vuhr-lohf-duh
fiction *fictie* fik-see
field *veld* (n) velt
field hospital *veldhospitaal* (n)
  velt-hos-pee-taal
fig *vijg* veykh
fight (argument) n *ruzie* rew-zee
fight (physical) n *gevecht* (n) khuh-vekht
fill v *vullen* vu-luhn

film speed *filmgevoeligheid*
  film-khuh-voo-likh-heyt
filtered *gefilterd* khuh-fil-tert
find v *vinden* vin-duhn
fine n *boete* boo-tuh
fine a *fijn* feyn
finger *vinger* ving-uhr
finish n *einde* (n) eyn-duh
finish v *eindigen* eyn-di-khuhn
fire (general) n *vuur* (n) vewr
fire (out of control) n *brand* brant
fire brigade *brandweer* brant-weyr
firewood *brandhout* (n) brant-hawt
first a *eerste* eyrs-tuh
first aid *eerste hulp* eyrs-tuh hulp
first-aid kit *EHBO-kist* ey-haa-bey-yoh-kist
first class *eerste klas* eyrs-tuh klas
first name *voornaam* vohr-naam
fish n *vis* vis
fishing *vissen* vi-suhn
fishmonger *vishandelaar* vis-han-duh-laar
fish shop *vishandel* vis-han-duhl
flag n *vlag* vlakh
Flanders *Vlaanderen* vlaan-duh-ruhn
flannel (face cloth) *washandje* (n)
  was-han-chuh
flash (camera) *flits* flits
flashlight (torch) *zaklantaarn* zak-lan-taarn
flat (apartment) n *flat/appartement* (n)
  (n)/(e) flet/a-par-tuh-ment
flat a *vlak* vlak
flea *vlo* vloh
flea market *vlooienmarkt* vloh-yuhn-markt
Flemish *Vlaams* vlaams
Flemish (language) *Vlaams* (n) vlaams
Flemish Community
  Vlaamse Gemeenschap
  vlaam-suh khuh-meyn-skhap
Flemish person *Vlaming* vlaa-ming
Flemish-speaking
  Vlaamstalig vlaams-taa-likh
flight *vlucht* vlukht
flood n *overstroming* oh-vuhr-stroh-ming
floor n *vloer* vloor
floor (storey) *verdieping* vuhr-dee-ping
florist *bloemist* bloo-mist
flour *bloem* bloom
flower n *bloem* bloom
flu *griep* khreep
fly n *vlieg* vleekh
fly v *vliegen* vlee-khuhn
foggy *mistig* mis-tikh
follow *volgen* vol-khuhn

food *voedsel* voot·suhl
food supplies *voedselvoorraad* sg
　voot·suhl·voh·raat
foot (body) *voet* voot
football (soccer) *voetbal* ⑩ voot·bal
footpath *voetpad* ⑩ voot·pat
foreign *buitenlands* böy·tuhn·lants
forest *woud* ⑩ wawt
forever *voor altijd* vohr al·teyt
forget *vergeten* vuhr·khey·tuhn
forgive *vergeven* vuhr·khey·vuhn
fork *vork* vork
fortnight *veertien dagen*
　veyr·teen daa·khuhn
fortune teller *waarzegger/waarzegster*
　⑩/① waar·ze·khuhr/waar·zekh·stuhr
foul (soccer) n *overtreding*
　oh·vuhr·trey·ding
fragile *breekbaar* breyk·baar
France *Frankrijk* frank·reyk
free (available/not bound) a *vrij* vrey
free (gratis) a *gratis* khraa·tis
freeze v *vriezen* vree·zuhn
French *Frans* frans
French (language) *Frans* ⑩ frans
French-speaking *Franstalig* frans·taa·likh
fresh *vers* vers
fridge *ijskast* eys·kast
fried *gebakken* khuh·ba·kuhn
friend *vriend/vriendin* ⑩/①
　vreent/vreen·din
Frisian (language) *Fries* ⑩ frees
from *van* van
frost *vorst* vorst
frozen *bevroren* buh·vroh·ruhn
fruit *fruit* ⑩ fröyt
fruit-picking *fruitoogst* fröyt·ohkhst
fry v *bakken* ba·kuhn
frying pan *koekenpan/pan* ⑩/⑧
　koo·kuh·pan/pan
full *vol* vol
full-time *voltijds* vol·teyts
fun a *leuk* leuk
funeral *begrafenis* buh·graa·fuh·nis
funny *grappig* khra·pikh
furniture *meubilair* ⑩ meu·bee·*leyr*
future n *toekomst* too·komst

G

game (sport) *spel* ⑩ spel
garage *garage* kha·raa·zhuh
garbage *vuilnis* ⑩ vöyl·nis
garbage can *vuilbak* vöyl·bak

garden n *tuin* töyn
gardener *tuinier* töy·*neer*
gardening *tuinieren* töy·*nee*·ruhn
garlic *knoflook* knof·lohk
gas (for cooking) *gas* ⑩ khas
gas (petrol) *benzine* ben·*zee*·nuh
gas cartridge *gasvulling* khas·vu·ling
gauze *gaas* ⑩ khaas
gay (homosexual) *homo* hoh·moh
gears (car, bicycle) *versnellingen* pl
　vuhr·*sne*·ing·uhn
Germany *Duitsland* döyts·lant
get *bekomen* buh·koh·muhn
get off (bus, train) *uitstappen* öyt·sta·puhn
gift *geschenk* ⑩ khuh·*skhengk*
gig *optreden* op·trey·duhn
gin *jenever* yuh·*ney*·vuhr/
　zhuh·*ney*·vuhr ⑩/⑧
girl *meisje* ⑩ mey·shuh
girlfriend *vriendin* vreen·din
give *geven* khey·vuhn
given name *voornaam* vohr·naam
glandular fever *klierkoorts* kleer·kohrts
glass (drinking) *glas* ⑩ khlas
glasses (spectacles) *bril* sg bril
gloves (clothing/latex) *handschoenen* pl
　hant·skhoo·nuhn
glue n *lijm* leym
go *gaan* khaan
goalkeeper *doelverdediger/keeper*
　dool·vuhr·dey·di·khuhr/*kee*·puhr
goat *geit* kheyt
god *god* ⑩ khot
goggles (skiing) *skibril* skee·bril
goggles (swimming) *zwembril* zwem·bril
gold n *goud* ⑩ khawt
golf course *golfterrein* ⑩ kholf·tuh·reyn
good *goed* khoot
goodbye *afscheid* ⑩ af·skheyt
go out *uitgaan* öyt·khaan
go out with (date) *uitgaan met*
　öyt·khaan met
go shopping *gaan winkelen*
　khaan *wing*·kuh·luhn
government *overheid* oh·vuhr·heyt
grandchild *kleinkind* ⑩ kleyn·kint
grandfather *grootvader*
　khroht·vaa·duhr
grandmother *grootmoeder*
　khroht·moo·duhr
grapes *druiven* dröy·vuhn
grateful *dankbaar* dangk·baar
grave n *graf* ⑩ khraf
great (fantastic) *fantastisch* fan·*tas*·tis

green *groen* khroon
greengrocer *groenteboer* khroon·tuh·boor
grey *grijs* khreys
grocery shop *kruidenierszaak* krôy·duh·neers·zaak
groceries *boodschappen* boht·skha·puhn
group *groep* khroop
grow *groeien* khroo·yuhn
guarantee n *garantie* kha·ran·see
guess v *raden* raa·duhn
guesthouse *pension* ⓝ pen·syon
guide (audio/person) *gids* khits
guidebook *gids* khits
guide dog *geleidehond* khuh·ley·duh·hont
guided tour *rondleiding* ront·ley·ding
guilty *schuldig* skhul·dikh
gum *kauwgom* kaw·khom
gun *geweer* ⓝ khuh·weyr
gym (place) *fitnesscentrum* ⓝ fit·nuhs·sen·trum
gymnastics *gymnastiek* kheem·nas·teek
gynaecologist *gynaecoloog* khee·ney·koh·lohkh

H

hair *haar* ⓝ haar
hairbrush *haarborstel* haar·bor·stuhl
haircut *kapsel* ⓝ kap·suhl
hairdresser *kapper* ka·puhr
half n *helft* helft
hallucination *hallucinatie* ha·lew·see·naa·see
hammer n *hamer* haa·muhr
hammock *hangmat* hang·mat
hand *hand* hant
handbag *handtas* han·tas
handicraft *handwerk* ⓝ hant·werk
handkerchief *zakdoek* zak·dook
handlebars *stuur* ⓝ sg stewr
handmade *handgemaakt* hant·khuh·maakt
handsome *knap* knap
hangover *kater* kaa·tuhr
happy *gelukkig* khuh·lu·kikh
harassment (sexual) *ongewenste intimiteiten* on·khuh·wens·tuh in·tee·mee·tey·tuhn
harbour n *haven* haa·vuhn
hard (not soft) *hard* hart
hardware store *doe-het-zelfzaak* doo·huht·zelf·zaak
hat *hoed* hoot
have *hebben* he·buhn

have a cold *verkouden zijn* vuhr·kaw·duhn zeyn
have fun *plezier hebben* pley·zeer he·buhn
hay fever *hooikoorts* hoy·kohrts
hazelnut *hazelnoot* haa·zuhl·noht
he *hij* hey
head (body) *hoofd* ⓝ hohft
head on beer *schuimkraag* skhöym·khraakh
headache *hoofdpijn* hohft·peyn
headlights *koplampen* kop·lam·puhn
health *gezondheid* khuh·zont·heyt
health-food store *reformwinkel* rey·form·wing·kuhl
hear *horen* hoh·ruhn
hearing aid *hoorapparaat* ⓝ hohr·a·pa·raat
heart *hart* ⓝ hart
heart attack *hartaanval* hart·aan·val
heart condition *hartkwaal* hart·kwaal
heat n *hitte* hi·tuh
heated (food) *opgewarmd* op·khuh·warmt
heated (place) *verwarmd* vuhr·warmt
heater *verwarmingstoestel* ⓝ vuhr·war·mings·too·stel
heating *verwarming* vuhr·war·ming
heavy (weight) *zwaar* zwaar
height *hoogte* hohkh·tuh
height of water *waterstand* waa·tuhr·stant
helmet *helm* helm
help n *hulp* hulp
help v *helpen* hel·puhn
hemp *hennep* he·nuhp
her (possessive) *haar* haar
herb *kruid* ⓝ kröyt
herbalist *kruidkundige* kröyt·kun·di·khuh
here *hier* heer
herring *haring* haa·ring
high (height) *hoog* hohkh
highchair *kinderstoel* kin·duhr·stool
high school *middelbare school* mi·duhl·baa·ruh skhohl
highway *snelweg* snel·wekh
hike v *trekken* tre·kuhn
hiking *trekken* tre·kuhn
hiking boots *wandellaarzen* wan·duhl·laar·zuhn
hiking route *wandelroute* wan·duhl·roo·tuh
hill *heuvel* heu·vuhl
hire v *huren* hew·ruhn
his *zijn* zeyn
historical *historisch* his·toh·ris
history *geschiedenis* khuh·skhee·duh·nis
hitchhike *liften* lif·tuhn

HIV-positive *seropositief*
sey·roh·poh·see·*teef*

holiday (day off) n *feestdag* feys·dakh

holiday (vacation) *vakantie* va·*kan*·see

holiday resort *vakantieoord* ⓝ
va·*kan*·see·ohrt

holidays *vakantie* va·*kan*·see

Holland *Holland* ho·lant

home *thuis* töys

homeless *dakloos* dak·lohs

homemaker *huisman/huisvrouw* ⓜ/ⓕ
höys·man/höys·vraw

homesickness *heimwee* heym·wey

homosexual n *homoseksueel*
hoh·moh·sek·sew·*weyl*

honey *honing* hoh·ning

honeymoon (period) *wittebroodsweken*
wi·tuh·brohts·wey·kuhn

honeymoon (trip) *huwelijksreis*
hew·wuh·luhks·reys

horse *paard* ⓝ paart

horse racing *paardenwedrennen*
paar·duhn·wet·re·nuhn

horse riding *paardrijden* ⓝ paart·rey·duhn

hospital *ziekenhuis* ⓝ zee·kuhn·höys

hospitality *gastvrijheid* khast·vrey·heyt

hot *warm* warm

(very) hot *heet* heyt

hotel *hotel* ⓝ hoh·*tel*

hot water *warm water* ⓝ warm *waa*·tuhr

hot water bottle *warmwaterfles*
warm·*waa*·tuhr·fles

hour *uur* ⓝ ewr

house n *huis* ⓝ höys

housework *huishoudelijk werk* ⓝ
höys·haw·duh·luhk werk

how *hoe* hoo

how much/many *hoeveel* hoo·*veyl*

hug v *omhelzen* om·*hel*·zuhn

huge *zeer groot* zeyr khroht

humanities *humaniora* hew·man·*yoh*·ra

human resources *personeelszaken*
per·soh·*neyls*·zaa·kuhn

human rights *mensenrechten* ⓝ pl
men·suhn·rekh·tuhn

hundred *honderd* hon·duhrt

hungry *hongerig* hong·uh·rikh

hunting *jacht* yakht

hurt v *pijn doen* peyn doon

husband *echtgenoot* ekht·khuh·noht

hydroponics *watercultuur*
waa·tuhr·kul·tewr

I *ik* ik

ice *ijs* ⓝ eys

ice axe *ijshouweel* ⓝ eys·haw·weyl

ice cream *(room)ijs* ⓝ (rohm·)eys

ice-cream parlour *ijssalon* ⓝ ey·sa·lcn

ice hockey *ijshockey* ⓝ eys·ho·kee

icy (road) *glad* khlat

identification *identificatie*
ee·den·tee·fee·kaa·see

identification card (ID) *identiteitsbewijs* ⓝ
ee·den·tee·*teyts*·buh·weys

idiot n *idioot* ee·dee·*yoht*

if *als* als

ill *ziek* zeek

immigration *immigratie* ee·mee·*graa*·see

important *belangrijk* buh·*lang*·ruhk

impossible *onmogelijk* on·*moh*·khul·luhk

in *in* in

in a hurry *gehaast* khuh·haast

included *inbegrepen* in·buh·*khrey*·puhn

income tax *inkomstenbelasting*
in·kom·stuhn·buh·las·ting

indicator *richtingsaanwijzer*
rikh·tings·aan·wey·zuhr

indigestion *indigestie* in·dee·*khes*·tee

indoor a *binnen-* bi·nuhn·

indoors adv *binnenshuis* bi·nuhns·höys

(brief) industrial action *prikactie* prik·ak·see

industry *industrie* in·dus·*tree*

infection *infectie* in·*fek*·see

inflammation *ontsteking* ont·*stey*·king

influenza *griep* khreep

information *informatie* in·for·*maa*·see

in front of *tegenover* tey·khuhn·*oh*·vuhr

ingredient *ingrediënt* ⓝ in·khrey·*dyent*

inject *inspuiten* in·*spöy*·tuhn

injection *inspuiting* in·*spöy*·ting

injured *gekwetst* khuh·*kwetst*

injury *kwetsuur* kwet·*sewr*

inner tube *binnenband* bi·nuhn·bant

innocent *onschuldig* on·*skhul*·dikh

insect repellent *insektwerend middel*
in·sekt·wey·ruhnt mi·duhl

inside adv *binnen* bi·nuhn

instructor *instructeur* in·struk·*teur*

insurance *verzekering* vuhr·*zey*·kuh·ring

interesting *interessant* in·tey·re·*sant*

intermission *pause* paw·zuh

international *internationaal*
in·tuhr·na·syoh·*naal*

interpreter *tolk* tolk

intersection *kruispunt* ⓝ *kröys*·punt
inundation *overstroming*
⠀⠀oh·vuhr·*stroh*·ming
invite *uitnodigen* öyt·noh·di·khuhn
iron (for clothes) n *strijkijzer* ⓝ
⠀⠀*streyk*·ey·zuhr
island *eiland* ⓝ *ey*·lant
it *het* huht
IT *informatica* in·for·*maa*·tee·ka
itch n *jeuk* yeuk
itemised *gedetailleerd* khuh·dey·ta·*yeyrt*
itinerary *reisroute* reys·roo·tuh
IUD *spiraaltje* ⓝ spee·*raal*·chuh

J

jacket (casual) *jas* yas
jacket (dressy) *colbert* ⓝ/*vest* ⓝ/ⓑ
⠀⠀kol·*ber*/vest
jail n *gevangenis* khuh·*vang*·uh·nis
jam n *jam/confituur* ⓝ/ⓑ
⠀⠀zhem/kon·fee·*tewr*
jar *pot/bokaal* ⓝ/ⓑ pot/boh·*kaal*
jaw *kaak* kaak
jealous *jaloers* ya·*loors*
jeans *spijkerbroek/jeans* ⓝ/ⓑ
⠀⠀*spey*·kuhr·brook/zheens
jellyfish *kwal* kwal
jewellery *juwelen* yew·*wey*·luhn
job *baan/werk* ⓝ ⓝ/ⓑ baan/werk
jogging *joggen* ⓝ *dzho*·guhn
joke n *grap* khrap
journey n *reis* reys
judge n *rechter* rekh·tuhr
juice n *sap* ⓝ sap
jump v *sprong* sprong
jumper (sweater) *trui* tröy
jumper leads *startkabels* start·kaa·buhls

K

key (door etc) *sleutel* sleu·tuhl
keyboard *toetsenbord* ⓝ *toot*·suhn·bort
kick v *schoppen* skho·puhn
kidney *nier* neer
kill v *doden* doh·duhn
kind (nice) *aardig* aar·dikh
kindergarten *kleuterschool* kleu·tuhr·skhohl
king *koning* koh·ning
kiss n *kus* kus
kiss v *kussen* ku·suhn
kitchen *keuken* keu·kuhn
knee *knie* knee

knife n *mes* ⓝ mes
know (someone) *kennen* ke·nuhn
know (something) *weten* wey·tuhn

L

labourer *arbeider/arbeidster* ⓝ/ⓕ
⠀⠀*ar*·bey·duhr/*ar*·beyt·stuhr
lace (fabric) n *kant* kant
lake *meer* ⓝ meyr
lamb (meat) *lamsvlees* ⓝ *lams*·vleys
land n *land* ⓝ lant
landlady *huisbazin* höys·baa·zin
landlord *huisbaas* höys·baas
language *taal* taal
large *groot* khroht
last (final) *laatste* laat·stuh
last (previous) *vorige* voh·ri·khuh
late adv *laat* laat
later *later* laa·tuhr
laugh v *lachen* la·khuhn
laundrette *wasserette* wa·suh·re·tuh
laundry (clothes) *was* was
laundry (place) *wasserij* wa·suh·*rey*
laundry (room) *wasinrichting*
⠀⠀was·in·rikh·ting
law (legislation) *wet* wet
law (study/profession) *rechten* ⓝ pl
⠀⠀rekh·tuhn
lawyer *advocaat* at·voh·*kaat*
laxative *laxeermiddel* ⓝ lak·*seyr*·mi·duhl
lazy *lui* löy
leader *leider* ley·duhr
leaf n *blad* ⓝ blat
learn *leren* ley·ruhn
leather n *leder* ⓝ ley·duhr
lecturer (at university) *lector* lek·tor
lecturer (general/speaker) *spreker*
⠀⠀sprey·kuhr
ledge *richel* ri·khul
left (direction) *links* lingks
left luggage *achtergelaten bagage*
⠀⠀akh·tuhr·khuh·laa·tuhn ba·*khaa*·zhuh
left-luggage office *bagagedepot* ⓝ
⠀⠀ba·*khaa*·zhuh·dey·poh
left-wing *links* lingks
leg (body) *been* ⓝ beyn
legal *wettelijk* we·tuh·luhk
legislation *wetgeving* wet·khey·ving
legume *peulvrucht* peul·vrukht
lemon *citroen* see·*troon*
lentils *linzen* lin·zuhn
lesbian n *lesbische* les·bi·suh

less *minder* min·duhr
letter (mail) *brief* breef
lettuce *sla* slaa
liar *leugenaar* leu·khuh·naar
librarian *bibliothecaris* bi·blyoh·tey·kaa·ris
library *bibliotheek* bi·blyoh·teyk
lice *luizen* löy·zuhn
licence (general) n *vergunning*
vuhr·khu·ning
licence (driving) n *rijbewijs* ⓝ
rey·buh·weys
license plate number *kentekenplaat*
ken·tey·kuhn·plaat
licorice *drop* drop
lie (not stand) v *liggen* li·khuhn
lie (not tell the truth) v *liegen* lee·khuhn
life *leven* ley·vuhn
lifeboat *reddingsboot* re·dings·boht
life guard *redder* re·duhr
life jacket *reddingsvest* ⓝ re·dings·vest
light n *licht* ⓝ likht
light (colour/weight) a *licht* likht
light bulb *gloeilamp* khlooy·lamp
lighter (cigarette) *aansteker* aan·stey·kuhr
light meter *lichtmeter* likht·mey·tuhr
like v *houden van* haw·duhn van
lime *limoen* lee·moon
linguist *taalkundige* taal·kun·di·khuh
lip balm *lippenbalm* li·puhn·balm
lips *lippen* li·puhn
lipstick *lippenstift* li·puh·stift
liquor store *slijterij/drankenhandel* ⓝ/ⓑ
sley·tuh·rey/drang·kuhn·han·duhl
listen *luisteren* löys·tuh·ruhn
little (quantity) a *weinig* wey·nikh
little (size) a *klein* kleyn
live (life) *leven* ley·vuhn
live (somewhere) *wonen* woh·nuhn
liver *lever* ley·vuhr
lizard *hagedis* haa·khuh·dis
local a *plaatselijk* plaat·suh·luhk
lock n *slot* slot
lock v *sluiten* slöy·tuhn
locked *gesloten* khuh·sloh·tuhn
lollies *snoep* snoop
long *lang* lang
look v *kijken* key·kuhn
look after *verzorgen* vuhr·zor·khuhn
look for *zoeken* zoo·kuhn
lookout *uitkijk* öyt·keyk
loose *los* los
loose change *kleingeld* ⓝ kleyn·khelt
lose *verliezen* vuhr·lee·zuhn

lost *verloren* ver·loh·ruhn
lost-property office *gevonden voorwerpen*
ⓝ pl khuh·von·duhn vohr·wer·puhn
(a) lot *veel* veyl
loud *luid* löyt
love n *liefde* leef·duh
love v *houden van* haw·duhn van
lover *minnaar/minares* ⓜ/ⓕ
mi·naar/mi·naa·res
low *laag* laakh
lubricant *smeermiddel* ⓝ smeyr·mi·duhl
lubricant (sex) *glijmiddel* ⓝ khley·mi·duhl
luck *geluk* ⓝ khuh·luk
lucky *gelukkig* khuh·lu·kikh
(be) lucky v *boffen* bo·fuhn
luggage *bagage* ba·khaa·zhuh
luggage locker *bagagekluis*
ba·khaa·zhuh·klöys
luggage tag *bagage-etiket* ⓝ
ba·khaa·zhuh·ey·tee·ket
lump *knobbel* kno·buhl
lunch *lunch/middagmaal* ⓝ
lunsh/mi·dakh·maal
lung *long* long
Luxembourg *Luxemburg* luk·suhm·burkh
luxury *luxueus* luk·sew·weus

M

magazine *tijdschrift* ⓝ teyt·skhrift
mail (letters/postal system) n *post* post
mail v *verzenden* vuhr·zen·duhn
mailbox *brievenbus* bree·vuh·bus
main a *voornaamste/hoofd-*
vohr·naam·stuh/hohft·
main road *hoofdweg* hohft·wekh
main square *stadsplein* ⓝ stats·pleyn
mansion *herenhuis* ⓝ hey·ruhn·höys
make v *maken* maa·kuhn
man n *man* man
manual worker
handarbeider/handarbeidster ⓜ/ⓕ
hant·ar·bey·duhr/hant·ar·beyt·stuhr
many *veel* veyl
map (of building) *plattegrond*
pla·tuh·khront
map (of country/town) *kaart* kaart
marital status *wettelijke stand*
we·tuh·luh·kuh stant
market n *markt* markt
marriage *huwelijk* ⓝ hew·wuh·luhk
married *gehuwd* khuh·hewt
marry *huwen* hew·wuhn

mass (Catholic) *mis* mis
mat *mat* mat
match (sports) *wedstrijd* wet·streyt
matches (for lighting) *lucifers* lew·see·fers
mattress *matras* ma·tras
maybe *misschien* mee·skheen
mayor *burgemeester* bur·khuh·mey·stuhr
me *me* muh
meal *maaltijd* maal·teyt
measles *mazelen* maa·zuh·luhn
meat *vlees* Ⓝ vleys
mechanic *mechanicien* mey·ka·nee·sye
medicine (medication) *medicijn* Ⓝ
  mey·dee·seyn
medicine (study/profession)
  medicijnen/geneeskunde Ⓝ/Ⓑ
  mey·dee·sey·nuhn/khuh·neys·kun·duh
meditation *meditatie* mey·dee·taa·see
meet (first time) v *ontmoeten*
  ont·moo·tuhn
meet (get together) v *samenkomen*
  saa·muhn·koh·muhn
melon *meloen* muh·loon
member *lid* Ⓝ lit
memorial *gedenkteken* Ⓝ
  khuh·dengk·tey·kuhn
memory card *geheugenkaart*
  khuh·heu·khuhn·kaart
menstruation *menstruatie*
  men·strew·waa·see
menu *menu* Ⓝ muh·new
message n *bericht* Ⓝ buh·rikht
metal n *metaal* Ⓝ mey·taal
metre *meter* mey·tuhr
metro station *metrostation* Ⓝ
  mey·troh·sta·syon
microwave oven
  magnetron/microgolfoven Ⓝ/Ⓑ
  makh·ney·tron/mee·kroh·kholf·oh·vuhn
midday *middag* mi·dakh
midnight *middernacht* mi·duhr·nakht
migraine *migraine* mee·khreyn
military n *leger* Ⓝ ley·khuhr
military service *legerdienst*
  ley·khuhr·deenst
milk *melk* melk
mill *molen* moh·luhn
million *miljoen* Ⓝ mil·yoon
mince n *gehakt* Ⓝ khuh·hakt
mineral water *mineraalwater* Ⓝ
  mee·ney·raal·waa·tuhr
minute n *minuut* mee·newt
mirror n *spiegel* spee·khul

miscarriage *miskraam* mis·kraam
miss *missen* mi·suhn
mistake n *vergissing* vuhr·khi·sing
mix v *mengen* meng·uhn
mobile phone *mobiele telefoon* Ⓝ/*gsm* Ⓑ
  moh·bee·luh tey·ley·fohn/khey·es·em
moisturiser (cream) *vochtinbrengende*
  crème vokht·in·breng·uhn·duh kreym
monastery *klooster* Ⓝ kloh·stuhr
money *geld* Ⓝ khelt
monk *kloosterling* kloh·stuhr·ling
month *maand* maant
monument *monument* Ⓝ mo·new·ment
moon *maan* maan
more *meer* meyr
morning *ochtend/morgen* Ⓝ/Ⓑ
  okh·tuhnt/mor·khuhn
morning sickness
  zwangerschapsmisselijkheid
  zwang·uhr·skhaps·mi·suh·luhk·heyt
mosque *moskee* mos·key
mosquito *mug* mukh
mosquito net *muskietennet* Ⓝ
  mus·kee·tuhn·net
mother *moeder* moo·duhr
mother-in-law *schoonmoeder*
  skhohn·moo·duhr
motorbike *motorfiets* moh·tor·feets
motorboat *motorboot* moh·tor·boht
motorway *autoweg* aw·toh·wekh
mountain *berg* berkh
mountaineering *bergsport* berkh·sport
mountain path *bergpad* Ⓝ berkh·pat
mountain range *bergketen* berkh·key·tuhn
mouse *muis* möys
moustache *snor* snor
mouth *mond* mont
movie *film* film
mud *modder* mo·duhr
mum *mam* mam
mumps *bof* bof
murder n *moord* mohrt
murder v *vermoorden* vuhr·mohr·duhn
muscle *spier* speer
museum *museum* Ⓝ mew·zey·yuhm
mushroom *paddenstoel* pa·duh·stool
music *muziek* mew·zeek
musician *muzikant* mew·zee·kant
music shop *muziekwinkel*
  mew·zeek·wing·kuhl
mussel *mossel* mo·suhl
mute *doofstom* dohf·stom
my *mijn* meyn

N

nail clippers *nagelknipper* sg
naa·khuhl·kni·puhr
name n *naam* naam
napkin *servet* ser·vet
nappy *luier* lõy·yuhr
nappy rash *uieruitslag* lõy·yuhr·õyt·slakh
narrow *smal* smal
nationality *nationaliteit* na·syoh·na·lee·teyt
national park *national park*
na·syoh·naal park
nature *natuur* na·tewr
naturopathy *natuurgeneeskunde*
na·tewr·khuh·neys·kun·duh
nausea *misselijkheid* mi·suh·luhk·heyt
near prep *bij* bey
nearby *dichtbij* dikht·bey
nearest *dichtstbijzijnde* dikhts·bey·zeyn·duh
necessary *noodzakelijk* noht·zaa·kuh·luhk
neck *nek* nek
necklace *halsketting* hals·ke·ting
need v *nodig hebben* noh·dikh he·buhn
needle (sewing/syringe) *naald* naalt
negative a *negatief* ney·kha·teef
negatives (photos) *negatieven*
ney·kha·tee·vuhn
neither adv *evenmin* ey·vuh·min
nephew *neef* neyf
(The) Netherlands *Nederland* ney·duhr·lant
network (phone) *netwerk* net·werk
never *nooit* noyt
new *nieuw* neew
news *nieuws* neews
newsagency (selling newspapers)
krantenzaak kran·tuh·zaak
newspaper *krant* krant
newsstand *krantenkiosk* kran·tuh·kee·yosk
New Year's Day *nieuwjaarsdag*
neew·yaars·dakh
New Year's Eve *oudejaarsavond*
aw·duh·yaars·aa·vont
New Zealand *Nieuw-Zeeland* neew·zey·lant
next (following) *volgend* vol·khuhnt
next to *naast* naast
nice *leuk/fijn* leuk/feyn
nickname *bijnaam* bey·naam
niece *nicht* nikht
night *nacht* nakht
nightclub *nachtclub* nakht·klup
night out *avondje-uit* aa·vont·chuh·õyt
no *nee* ney
noisy *lawaaierig* la·waa·yuh·rikh

none *geen* kheyn
nonsmoking *niet-roken* neet·roh·kuhn
noodles *noedels* noo·duhls
noon *middag* mi·dakh
north n *noorden* nohr·duhn
nose *neus* neus
not *niet* neet
notebook *notitieboekje*
noh·tee·see·book·yuh
nothing *niets* neets
no vacancy *vol/volzet* vol/vol·zet /
now *nu* new
not yet *nog niet* nokh neet
nuclear energy *kernenergie*
kern·ey·ner·khee
nuclear testing *atoomtesten* pl
a·tohm·tes·tuhn
nuclear waste *atoomafval* a·tohm·af·val
number n *nummer* nu·muhr
numberplate *nummerplaat* nu·muhr·plaat
nun *non* non
nurse n *zuster* zus·tuhr
nut (food) *noot* noht

O

oats *havermout* haa·vuhr·mawt
ocean *oceaan* oh·sey·yaan
occupied *bezet* buh·zet
off (power) *uit* õyt
off (spoilt) *bedorven* buh·dor·vuhn
office *kantoor* kan·tohr
office worker *kantoorwerker*
kan·tohr·wer·kuhr
often *vaak* vaak
oil (cooking) *olie* oh·lee
oil (petrol) *benzine* ben·zee·nuh
old *oud* awt
old city *oude stad* aw·duh stat
olive *olijf* oh·leyf
olive oil *olijfolie* oh·leyf·oh·lee
on *op* op
on (power) *aan* aan
once *één keer* eyn keyr
one *één* eyn
one-way ticket *enkele reis* eng·kuh·luh reys
onion *ui* õy
only adv *alleen* a·leyn
on time *op tijd* op teyt
open v *openen* oh·puh·nuhn
opening hours *openingsuren* pl
oh·puh·nings·ew·ruhn

opera house *operagebouw* ⓝ
oh·pey·ra·khuh·*baw*
operation (medical) *operatie*
oh·pey·*raa*·see
operator (telephone) *telefonist*
tey·ley·foh·*nist*
opinion *opinie* o·*pee*·nee
opposite prep *tegenover*
tey·khuhn·*oh*·vuhr
optometrist *opticien* op·tee·*sye*
or *of* of
orange (colour) *oranje* oh·*ran*·yuh
orange (fruit) *sinaasappel/appelsien*
ⓝ/ⓑ see·*naas*·a·puhl/a·puhl·*seen*
orchestra *orkest* ⓝ or·*kest*
order n *bestelling* buh·*ste*·ling
order v *bestellen* be·*ste*·luhn
ordinary *gewoon* khuh·*wohn*
orgasm *orgasme* ⓝ or·*khas*·muh
original a *origineel* o·ree·zhee·*neyl*
other *andere* an·duh·ruh
our *onze* on·zuh
out of order *stuk* stuk
outside adv *buiten* böy·tuhn
ovarian cyst *gezwel op de eileiders* ⓝ
khuh·*zwel* op duh ey·ley·duhrs
ovary *eileider* ey·ley·duhr
overcoat *jas* yas
overdose n *overdosis* oh·vuhr·doh·sis
overnight (during the night) adv
gedurende de nacht
khuh·*dew*·ruhn·duh duh nakht
overnight (lasting one night) adv
één nacht durend eyn nakht *dew*·ruhnt
overseas *overzees* oh·vuhr·zeys
overseas (abroad) adv *in het buitenland*
in huht *böy*·tuhn·lant
owe *schuldig zijn* skhul·dikh zeyn
owner *eigenaar/eigenares* ⓜ/ⓕ
ey·khuh·naar/ey·khuh·naa·res
oxygen *zuurstof* zewr·stof
oyster *oester* oos·tuhr
ozone layer *ozonlaag* oh·zon·laakh

P

pacifier (dummy) *fopspeen* fop·speyn
package n *pak* ⓝ/*pakket* ⓝ pak/pa·*ket*
packet (general) *pak* ⓝ/*pakket* ⓝ
pak/pa·*ket*
padlock *hangslot* ⓝ *hang*·slot
page n *pagina* paa·khee·na
pain n *pijn* peyn

painful *pijnlijk* peyn·luhk
painkiller *pijnstiller* peyn·sti·luhr
painter (artist/tradesperson) *schilder*
skhil·duhr
painting (the art) *schilderkunst*
skhil·duhr·kunst
painting (a work) *schilderij* ⓝ skhil·duh·rey
pair (couple) n *paar* ⓝ paar
palace *paleis* ⓝ pa·leys
pan *pan* pan
pants (trousers) *broek* brook
pantyhose *panty* pen·tee/*pan*·tee ⓝ/ⓑ
panty liners *inlegkruisjes* ⓝ pl
in·lekh·kröy·shuhs
paper n *papier* ⓝ pa·peer
paperwork *papieren* ⓝ pl pa·*pee*·ruhn
pap smear *uitstrijkje* ⓝ öyt·streyk·yuh
paraplegic n *aan beide benen verlamd*
aan bey·duh bey·nuhn vuhr·*lamt*
parcel n *pak* ⓝ/*pakket* ⓝ pak/pa·*ket*
parents *ouders* aw·duhrs
park (a car) v *parkeren* par·key·ruhn
parliament *parlement* ⓝ par·luh·*ment*
part (component) n *onderdeel* ⓝ
on·duhr·deyl
part-time *deeltijds* deyl·teyts
party (entertainment) *feestje* ⓝ/*fuif* ⓝ/ⓑ
fey·shuh/föyf
party (politics) *partij* par·tey
pass (go by) v *voorbijgaan* vohr·*bey*·khaan
pass (kick/throw) v *passen* pa·suhn
passenger *passagier* pa·sa·*kheer*
passionfruit *passievrucht* pa·see·vrukht
passport *paspoort* ⓝ *pas*·pohrt
passport number *paspoortnummer* ⓝ
pas·pohrt·nu·muhr
past n *verleden* ⓝ vuhr·*ley*·duhn
pastry *gebak* ⓝ khuh·*bak*
path *pad* ⓝ pat
pavement *voetpad* ⓝ *voot*·pat
pay v *betalen* buh·*taa*·luhn
payment *betaling* buh·*taa*·ling
pea *erwt* erwt
peace *vrede* vrey·duh
peach *perzik* per·zik
peak (mountain) *piek* peek
peak hour *piekuur* ⓝ *peek*·ewr
peanut *pinda* pin·da
pear *peer* peyr
pedal n *pedaal* ⓝ pey·*daal*
pedal boat *waterfiets* waa·tuhr·feets
pedestrian n *voetganger* voot·gang·uhr
pencil *potlood* ⓝ pot·loht

penknife *zakmes* ⓝ *zak·mes*
pensioner *gepensioneerde*
khuh·pen·syoh·*neyr*·duh
people *mensen* *men*·suhn
pepper (bell) *paprika* pa·*pree*·ka
per (day) *per (dag)* puhr (dakh)
per cent *procent* proh·*sent*
performance *voorstelling* *vohr*·ste·ling
perfume n *parfum* ⓝ par·*föy*
period pain *menstruatiepijn*
men·strew·*waa*·see·peyn
permission *toestemming* *too*·ste·ming
permit n *toestemmen* *too*·ste·muhn
person *persoon* puhr·*sohn*
petition n *petitie* pey·*tee*·see
petrol *benzine* ben·*zee*·nuh
petrol station *benzinestation* ⓝ
ben·*zee*·nuh·sta·syon
pharmacist *apotheker/apothekeres* ⓜ/ⓕ
a·poh·*tey*·kuhr/a·poh·tey·kuh·*res*
pharmacy *apotheek* a·poh·*teyk*
phone book *telefoonboek* ⓝ
tey·ley·*fohn*·book
phone box *telefooncel* tey·ley·*fohn*·sel
phonecard *telefoonkaart* tey·ley·*fohn*·kaart
photograph v *fotograferen*
foh·toh·khra·*fey*·ruhn
photographer *fotograaf* foh·toh·*khraaf*
photography *fotografie* foh·toh·khraa·*fee*
phrasebook *taalgids* *taal*·khits
pickaxe *houweel* ⓝ *haw*·weyl
pickles *inmaakt zuur* ⓝ
in·khuh·maakt zewr
pie (big) *taart* taart
pie (small) *pastei* pas·*tey*
piece n *stuk* stuk
pig *varken* ⓝ *var*·kuhn
(the) pill *de pil* duh pil
pillow *kussen* ⓝ *ku*·suhn
pillowcase *kussensloop* ku·suhn·slohp
pineapple *ananas* a·na·nas
pink *roze* *roh*·zuh
pistachio *pistachenoot* pees·*ta*·shuh·noht
place n *plaats* plaats
place of birth *geboorteplaats*
khuh·*bohr*·tuh·plaats
plane *vliegtuig* ⓝ *vleekh*·töykh
plastic a *plastic/plastieken*
ples·tik/plas·*tee*·kuhn
plate *bord* ⓝ bort
platform (train station) *perron* ⓝ pe·*ron*
play (cards) v *kaartspelen* *kaart*·spey·luhr
play (instrument) v *spelen* *spey*·luhn

play (theatre) n *toneelstuk* ⓝ toh·*neyl*·stuk
pleasant *prettig* *pre*·tikh
plug (bath) n *stop* stop
plug (electricity) n *stekker* *ste*·kuhr
plum *pruim* pröym
plumber *loodgieter* loht·*khee*·tuhr
poached *gepocheerd* khuh·po·*sheyrt*
pocket n *zak* zak
pocketknife *zakmes* ⓝ *zak*·mes
poetry *dichtkunst* *dikht*·kunst
point v *wijzen* *wey*·zuhn
poisonous *giftig* *khif*·tikh
police *politie* poh·*leet*·see
police officer *politieagent*
poh·*leet*·see·a·khent
police station *politiebureau* ⓝ
poh·*leet*·see·bew·roh
policy (code of conduct) *gedragslijn*
khuh·*drakhs*·leyn
policy (insurance) *polis* *pon*·lis
politician *politicus* poh·*lee*·tee·kus
politics *politiek* poh·*lee*·teek
pollution *vervuiling* vuhr·*vöy*·ling
pond *vijver* *vey*·vuhr
pool (game) *biljart* ⓝ *bil*·yart
pool (swimming) *zwembad* ⓝ *zwem*·bat
poor (wealth) *arm* arm
popular *populair* poh·pew·*leyr*
pork *varkensvlees* ⓝ *var*·kuhns·vleys
port (river/sea) *haven* *haa*·vuhn
positive a *positief* poh·zee·*teef*
possible *mogelijk* *moh*·khuh·luhk
post (mail) n *post* post
post v *op de post doen* op *duh* post doon
postage *portkosten* *port*·kos·tuhn
postcard *ansichtkaart/postkaart* ⓝ/ⓑ
an·zikht·kaart/*post*·kaart
poster *poster/affiche* ⓝ *pos*·tuhr/a·*fee*·shuh
post office *postkantoor* ⓝ *post*·kan·tohr
pot (cooking) *kookpot* *kohk*·pot
potato *aardappel* *aart*·a·puhl
pottery *aardewerk* ⓝ/*keramiek*
aar·duh·werk/*key*·ra·meek
pound (money) *pond* ⓝ pont
pound (weight) *pond* ⓝ pont
poverty *armoede* ar·*moo*·duh
powder n *poeder* ⓝ *poo*·duhr
power (electricity) n *elektriciteit*
ey·lek·tree·see·*teyt*
power (physical) n *kracht* krakht
power (politics) n *macht* makht
prawn *garnaal* *khar*·naal
prayer *gebed* ⓝ khuh·*bet*

prayer book *gebedenboek* ⓝ
khuh·*bey*·duhn·book
prefer *verkiezen* vuhr·*kee*·zuhn
pregnancy test kit *zwangerschapstest*
zwang·uhr·skhaps·test
pregnant *zwanger* zwang·uhr
premenstrual tension *pms*
(premenstrueel syndroom) pey·em·es
(prey·men·strew·*weyl* seen·drohm)
prepare (for something) *voorbereiden*
vohr·buh·rey·duhn
prepare (food) *klaarmaken* klaar·maa·kuhn
prescription *recept* ⓝ/*voorschrift* ⓝ/ⓑ
rey·sept/vohr·skhrift
present (gift) n *geschenk* ⓝ khuh·*skhengk*
present (time) n *heden* ⓝ *hey*·duhn
president *president* prey·zee·*dent*
pressure (tyre) n *druk* druk
pretty *mooi* moy
price n *prijs* preys
priest *priester* prees·tuhr
prime minister *minister-president* ⓝ/*eerste
minister* ⓑ *mee*·nis·tuhr·prey·zee·*dent*/
eyr·stuh mee·*nis*·tuhr
prince *prins* prins
prince consort *prins-gemaal*
prins·khuh·*maal*
prince regent *prins-regent* prins·rey·*khent*
princess *prinses* prin·*ses*
prison *gevangenis* khuh·*vang*·uh·nis
prisoner *gevangene* khuh·*vang*·uh·nuh
private *privé* pree·*vey*
produce v *produceren* proh·dew·*sey*·ruhn
profit n *winst* winst
program n *programma* ⓝ proh·*khra*·ma
projector *projector* proh·*yek*·tor
promise v *beloven* buh·*loh*·vuhn
prostitute n *prostituée* pros·tee·tew·*wey*
prostitution *prostitutie* pros·tee·*tew*·see
protect v *beschermen* buh·*skher*·muhn
protected *beschermd* buh·*skhermt*
protest v *protesteren* proh·tes·*tey*·ruhn
provisions (food) *proviand* proh·*vyant*
pub (bar) *café* ⓝ/*kroeg* ka·*fey*/krookh
public gardens *openbaar park* ⓝ
oh·puhn·baar park
public phone *openbare telefoon*
oh·puhn·bah·ruh tey·ley·*fohn*
public relations *pr* pey·*eyr*
public toilet *openbaar toilet* ⓝ
oh·puhn·baar twa·*let*
pull v *trekken* tre·kuhn

pump n *pomp* pomp
pumpkin *pompoen* pom·*poon*
puncture n *lek* ⓝ lek
puppet theatre *marionettentheater* ⓝ
mar·yoh·ne·tuhn·tee·*yaa*·tuhr
pure *puur* pewr
purple *purper* pur·puhr
purse *portemonnee* por·tuh·moh·*ney*
push v *duwen* dew·wuhn
put *zetten* ze·tuhn

Q

quadriplegic n *volledig verlamd*
vo·ley·dikh vuhr·*lamt*
qualifications *kwalificaties*
kwa·lee·fee·*kaa*·sees
quality n *kwaliteit* kwa·lee·*teyt*
quarantine *quarantaine* ka·ran·*tey*·nuh
quarter (15 minutes) n *kwartier* ⓝ
kwar·*teer*
quarter (a fourth) n *kwart* ⓝ kwart
quay *kaai/kade* kaay/*kaa*·duh
queen *koningin* koh·ning·*khin*
Queen Mother *koningin-moeder*
koh·ning·*khin*·moo·duhr
question n *vraag* vraakh
queue n *rij* rey
quick *snel* snel
quiet *stil* stil
quit (job) *ontslag nemen*
ont·*slakh* ney·muhn
quit (something) *ophouden met*
op·how·duhn met

R

rabbit *konijn* ⓝ koh·*neyn*
race (sport) n *wedstrijd* wet·streyt
racetrack *renbaan* ren·baan
racing bike *racefiets* reys·feets
racism *racisme* ⓝ ra·*sis*·muh
radiator *radiator* ra·dee·*yaa*·tor
radio n *radio* raa·dee·yoh
radish *radijs* ra·*deys*
railway *spoorweg* spohr·wekh
railway station *(trein)station* ⓝ
(treyn)·sta·*syon*
rain n *regen* rey·khuhn
raincoat *regenjas* rey·khuhn·yas
raisin *rozijn* roh·*zeyn*
rally (protest) n *betoging* buh·*toh*·khing

rape n *verkrachting* vuhr·*krakh*·ting
rape v *verkrachten* vuhr·*krakh*·tuhn
rare (steak) *kort gebakken* Ⓝ/*saignant* Ⓑ
kort khuh·*ba*·kuhn/sey·*nya*
rare (uncommon) *zeldzaam* zelt·zaam
rash *uitslag* öyt·slakh
raspberry *framboos* fram·*bohs*
rat *rat* rat
raw *rauw* raw
razor (electric) *scheerapparaat* Ⓝ
skheyr·a·pa·raat
razor (manual) *scheermes* Ⓝ skheyr·mes
razor blade *scheermesje* Ⓝ skheyr·me·shuh
read v *lezen* ley·zuhn
reading *lectuur* lek·*tewr*
ready a *klaar* klaar
real estate agent *makelaar* maa·kuh·laar
realistic *realistisch* rey·ya·*lis*·tis
rear (location) a *aan de achterkant*
aan duh akh·tuhr·kant
reason n *reden* rey·duhn
receipt n *kwitantie* kwee·*tan*·see
recently *onlangs* on·*langs*
recommend *aanbevelen* aan·buh·vey·luhn
record (in writing) v *optekenen*
op·*tey*·kuh·nuhn
record (music) v *opnemen* op·ney·muhn
recording *opname* op·naa·muh
recyclable *recyclebaar/herbruikbaar*
ree·*say*·kuhl·baar/her·*bröyk*·baar
recycle *recyclen/herbruiken*
ree·*say*·kluhn/her·*bröy*·kuhn
red *rood* roht
red wine *rode wijn* roh·duh weyn
referee n *scheidsrechter* skheyts·rekh·tuhr
reference *referentie* rey·fey·*ren*·see
refrigerator *koelkast* kool·kast
refugee *vluchteling* vlukh·tuh·ling
refund n *terugbetaling*
tuh·*rukh*·buh·taa·ling
refuse v *weigeren* wey·khuh·ruhn
regional *regionaal* rey·khyoh·*naal*
registered mail *aangetekende post*
aan·khuh·tey·kuhn·duh post
rehydration salts *rehydratie-oplossing*
rey·hee·*dra*·see·op·lo·sing
relationship *relatie* ruh·*laa*·see
relax *ontspannen* ont·*spa*·nuhn
religion *godsdienst* khots·deenst
religious *godsdienstig* khots·*deens*·tikh
remote a *afgelegen* af·khuh·ley·khuhn
remote control *afstandsbediening*
af·stants·buh·dee·ning

rent n *huur* hewr
rent v *huren* hew·ruhn
repair v *herstellen* her·ste·luhn
republic *republiek* rey·pew·*bleek*
reservation (booking) *reservatie*
rey·ser·*vaa*·see
rest v *rusten* rus·tuhn
restaurant *restaurant* Ⓝ res·toh·*ra*nt
retired *gepensioneerd* khuh·pen·syo·*neyrt*
return v *terugkomen* tuh·*rukh*·koh·muhn
return ticket
retourtje Ⓝ/*heen- en terug·reis* Ⓝ/Ⓑ
ruh·*toor*·chuh/heyn·en·tuh·*rukh*·reys
review n *recensie* rey·sen·see
rice *rijst* reyst
rich (wealthy) *rijk* reyk
ride n *rijden* rey·duhn
ride (bike, horse) v *rijden* rey·duhn
ridiculous *belachelijk* buh·*lakh*·khuh·luhk
right (correct) *juist* yöyst
right (direction) *rechts* rekhs
right-wing *rechts* rekhs
ring (phone) v *rinkelen* ring·kun·luhn
rip-off n *bedrog* Ⓝ be·*drokh*
risk n *risico* Ⓝ ree·zee·koh
river *rivier* ree·veer
road *weg* wekh
road map *wegenkaart* wey·khuhn·kaart
rob *overvallen* oh·vuhr·*va*·luhn
rock n *rots* rots
rock (music) *rockmuziek* rok·*mew*·zeek
rock climbing *rotsklimmen* Ⓝ rots·kli·muhn
rock group *band/groep* Ⓝ/Ⓑ bent/khroop
roll (bread) *broodje* Ⓝ *broh*·chuh
rollerblading *inlineskaten* Ⓝ
in·layn·*skey*·tuhn
rollerskating *rolschaatsen* Ⓝ
rol·*skhaat*·suhn
romantic a *romantisch* roh·*man*·tees
room n *kamer* kaa·muhr
room number *kamernummer* Ⓝ
kaa·muhr·nu·muh
rope n *touw* Ⓝ taw
round (drinks) n *rondje* Ⓝ ron·chuh
round a *rond* ront
roundabout *rotonde* roh·*ton*·duh
route n *route* roo·tuh
rowing *roeien* Ⓝ roo·yuhn
rubbish *afval* Ⓝ *af*·val
rubella *rodehond* roh·duh·hont
rug *kleed* Ⓝ/*mat* Ⓑ/Ⓝ kleyt/mat
ruins *ruïnes* rew·wee·nuhs
rule (historic) n *heerschappij* heyr·skha·pey

R

english–dutch

231

rule (law) n *regel* rey·khuhl
rum *rum* rum
run v *rennen/lopen* ⑧/⑧
  re·nuhn/*loh*·puhn
runny nose *loopneus* lohp·neus
rush hour *spitsuur/piekuur* ⑧
  spits·ewr/*peek*·ewr

S

sad *droevig* droo·vikh
saddle *zadel* ⑩ *zaa*·duhl
safe n *kluis* klöys
safe a *veilig* vey·likh
safe sex *veilig vrijen* ⑩ *vey*·likh *vrey*·yuhn
sailboarding *plankzeilen* ⑧/*windsurfen* ⑧
  plank·zey·luhn/*wint*·sur·fuhn
saint *heilige* hey·li·khuh
salary *loon* ⑩ lohn
sale n *verkoop* vuhr·kohp
sale (specials) *koopjes* ⑩ pl *kohp*·yuhs
sales assistant *verkoper/verkoopster* ⑩/①
  vuhr·*koh*·puhr/vur·*kohp*·stuhr
sales tax *verkoopbelasting*
  vuhr·*kohp*·buh·las·ting
salmon *zalm* zalm
salt *zout* ⑩ zawt
same *dezelfde* ⑩&①/*hetzelfde* ⑩
  duh·*zelf*·duh/huht·*zelf*·duh
sand *zand* ⑩ zant
sandals *sandalen* san·*daa*·luhn
sanitary napkin *maandverband* ⑩
  maant·vuhr·bant
sardine *sardientje* ⑩ sar·*deen*·chuh
saucepan *pan/kookpot* ⑧/⑧ pan/*kohk*·pot
sausage *saucijs/worst* ⑧/⑧ saw·*seys*/worst
say *zeggen* ze·khuhn
scalp *hoofdhuid* hohft·höyt
scarf *sjaal* shaal
school *school* skhohl
science *wetenschap* wey·tuhn·skhap
scientist *wetenschapper*
  wey·tuhn·skha·puhr
scissors *schaar* sg skhaar
score v *scoren* skoh·ruhn
sculpture *beeldhouwwerk* ⑩
  beylt·haw·werk
sea *zee* zey
seal (animal) n *zeehond* zey·hont
seasick *zeeziek* zey·zeek
seaside n *kust* kust
season *seizoen* ⑩ sey·zoon
seat (place) *zitje* ⑩ *zi*·chuh

seatbelt *veiligheidsriem* vey·likh·heyts·reem
second n *seconde* suh·kon·duh
second a *tweede* twey·duh
second class n *tweede klas* twey·duh klas
secondhand *tweedehands* twey·duh·*hants*
secondhand shop *tweedehandswinkel*
  twey·duh·*hants*·wing·kuhl
secretary *secretaris/secretaresse* ⑩/①
  sey·krey·*taa*·ris/sey·krey·taa·*re*·suh
see *zien* zeen
self-employed *zelfstandig* zelf·*stan*·dikh
selfish *egoïstisch* ey·khoh·*wis*·tis
self-service a *zelfbediening*
  zelf·buh·dee·ning
sell *verkopen* vuhr·*koh*·puhn
send *sturen* stew·ruhn
sensible *verstandig* vuhr·*stan*·dikh
sensitive *gevoelig* khuh·*voo*·likh
sensual *sensueel* sen·sew·*weyl*
separate a *afzonderlijk* af·zon·duhr·luhk
serious *ernstig* ern·stikh
service n *dienst* deenst
service charge *bedieningstoeslag*
  buh·*dee*·nings·too·slakh
service station *benzinestation* ⑩
  ben·zee·nuh·sta·syon
serviette *servet* ⑩ ser·*vet*
several *verscheidene* vuhr·*skhey*·duh·nuh
sew *naaien* naa·yuhn
sex education *seksuele voorlichting*
  sek·sew·*wey*·luh vohr·likh·ting
sexism *seksisme* ⑩ sek·*sis*·muh
shade *schaduw* skhaa·dew
shadow *schaduw* skhaa·dew
shallow *ondiep* on·deep
shape n *vorm* vorm
share (with) v *delen* dey·luhn
shave v *scheren* skhey·ruhn
shaving cream *scheerschuim* ⑩
  skheyr·skhöym
she *zij* zey
sheep *schaap* ⑩ skhaap
sheet (bed) *laken* ⑩ *laa*·kuhn
shelf *plank* plangk
shingles (illness) *gordelroos* khor·duhl·rohs
ship n *schip* ⑩ skhip
shirt *hemd* ⑩ hemt
shoes *schoenen* skhoo·nuhn
shoelace *schoenveters* skhoon·*vey*·tuhrs
shoe shop *schoenenzaak* skhoo·nuhn·zaak
shoot v *schieten* skhee·tuhn
shop n *winkel* wing·kuhl
shop v *winkelen* wing·kuh·luhn

shopping *winkelen* ⓝ wing·kuh·luhn
shopping centre *winkelcentrum* ⓝ wing·kuh·sen·trum
short (height) *klein* kleyn
short (length) *kort* kort
shortage *tekort* ⓝ tuh·kort
shorts *short* sg short
shoulder *schouder* skhaw·duhr
shout v *roepen* roo·puhn
show v *tonen* toh·nuhn
shower n *douche* doo·shuh
shrine *schrijn* ⓝ skhreyn
shut a *gesloten* khuh·sloh·tuhn
shy *verlegen* vuhr·ley·khuhn
sick *ziek* zeek
sick bag *papieren zak* pa·pee·ruhn zak
side *kant* kant
sidewalk *voetpad* ⓝ voot·pat
sign (general) n *teken* ⓝ tey·kuhn
sign (traffic) n *bord* ⓝ bort
sign v *tekenen* tey·kuh·nuhn
signature *handtekening* hant·tey·kuh·ning
silk n *zijde* zey·duh
silver n *zilver* ⓝ zil·vuhr
similar *gelijkaardig* khuh·leyk·aar·dikh
simple *eenvoudig* eyn·vaw·dikh
since (time) *sinds* sins
sing v *zingen* zing·uhn
singer *zanger/zangeres* ⓜ/ⓕ zang·uhr/zang·uh·res
single (person) *vrijgezel* vrey·khuh·zel
single room *éénpersoonskamer* eyn·puhr·sohns·kaa·muhr
singlet *hemdje* ⓝ hem·chuh
sister *zus* zus
sit v *zitten* zi·tuhn
size (general) *maat* maat
skate v *schaatsen* skhaat·suhn
ski v *skiën* skee·yuhn
skiing *skisport* skee·sport
skim milk *taptemelk* ⓝ/*afgeroomde melk* ⓑ tap·tuh·melk/af·khuh·rohm·duh melk
skin n *huid* höyt
skirt *rok* rok
skull *schedel* skhey·duhl
sky *lucht* lukht
sleep n *slaap* slaap
sleep v *slapen* slaa·puhn
sleeping bag *slaapzak* slaap·zak
sleeping berth *slaapplaats* slaap·plaats
sleeping car *slaapwagen* slaap·waa·khuhn
sleeping pills *slaappillen* slaap·pi·luhn
sleepy *slaperig* slaa·puh·rikh

slice n *plak/snee* ⓝ/ⓑ plak·sney
slide film *diafilm* dee·ya·film
slow *traag* traakh
slowly *traag* traakh
small *klein* kleyn
smaller *kleiner* kley·nuhr
smallest *kleinst* kleynst
smell n *geur* kheur
smile v *glimlachen* khlim·la·khuhn
smoke v *roken* roh·kuhn
snack n *snack* snek/snak ⓝ/ⓔ
snail *slak* slak
snake *slang* slang
snorkelling *snorkelen* ⓝ snor·kuh·luhn
snow n *sneeuw* sneyw
snow v *sneeuwen* sney·wuhr
snowball *sneeuwbal* sneyw·bal
snowboarding *snowboarden* ⓝ snohw·bor·duhn
snowman *sneeuwpop* sneyw·pop
snowscape *sneeuwlandschap* ⓕ sneyw·lant·skhap
snowy *sneeuwachtig* sneyw·akh·tikh
soap *zeep* zeyp
soccer *voetbal* ⓝ voo·bai
socialist n *socialist* son·sya·list
social welfare *sociale zekerheid* soh·syaa·luh zey·kuhr·neyt
socks *sokken* so·kuhr
soft drink *frisdrank* fris·drangk
soldier *soldaat* sol·daat
some *enkele* eng·kuh·luh
someone *iemand* ee·mant
something *iets* eets
sometimes *soms* soms
son *zoon* zohn
song *lied* ⓝ leet
soon *gauw* khaw
sore a *pijnlijk* peyn·luhk
south n *zuiden* ⓝ zöy·duhn
souvenir shop *souvenirwinkel* soo·vuh·neer·wing·kuhl
soy milk *sojamelk* soh·ya·melk
soy sauce *sojasaus* soh·ya·saws
space (room) *ruimte* röym·tuh
sparkling wine *mousserende wijn* ⓑ/*schuimwijn* ⓑ moo·sey·ruhn·duh weyn/skhöym·weyn
speak *praten* praa·tuhn
special a *pijnlijk* spey·syaal
specialist n *specialist* spey·sya·list
speed (travel) n *snelheid* snel·heyt

speed limit *maximumsnelheid*
mak·see·mum·snel·heyt
speedometer *snelheidsmeter*
snel·heyts·mey·tuhr
spider *spin* spin
spinach *spinazie* spee·*naa*·zee
spoilt (food) *bedorven* buh·*dor*·vuhn
spoke *spaak* spaak
spoon *lepel* ley·puhl
sportsperson *sportman/sportvrouw* ⓜ/ⓕ
sport·man/sport·vraw
sports store *sportwinkel* sport·wing·kuhl
sprain n *verstuiking* vuhr·stöy·king
spring (coil) *veer* veyr
spring (season) *lente* len·tuh
square (town) *plein* ⓝ pleyn
stadium *stadion* ⓝ staa·dee·yon
staff *personeel* ⓝ per·soh·neyl
stairway *trap* trap
stale *oudbakken* awt·ba·kuhn
stamp (postage) n *postzegel* post·zey·khul
star n *ster* ster
(four-)star *(vier)sterren* (veer·)ste·ruhn
start v *starten* star·tuhn
station *station* ⓝ sta·syon
stationer *kantoorboekhandel*
kan·tohr·book·han·duhl
statue *standbeeld* ⓝ stant·beylt
stay (at a hotel) v *logeren* loh·zhey·ruhn
stay (in place) v *verblijven* vuhr·bley·vuhn
STD *seksueel overdraagbare aandoening*
sek·sew·weyl oh·vuhr·draakh·baa·ruh
aan·doo·ning
steak (beef) *biefstuk* beef·stuk
steal *stelen* stey·luhn
steep *steil* steyl
step n *stap* stap
step (stair/threshold) n *trede* trey·duh
stepped gable *trapgevel* trap·khey·vuhl
still water *spa blauw* ⓝ/*plat water* ⓝ ⓑ
spa blaw/plat waa·tuhr
stock (food) *bouillon* boo·yon
stockings *kousen* kaw·suhn
stolen *gestolen* khuh·stoh·luhn
stomach *maag* maakh
stomachache *maagpijn* maakh·peyn
stone n *steen* steyn
stop (bus, tram) n *halte* hal·tuh
stop (cease) v *stoppen* sto·puhn
stop (prevent) v *tegenhouden*
tey·khuhn·haw·duhn
story *verhaal* ⓝ vuhr·haal
stove *fornuis* ⓝ for·nöys
straight *recht* rekht

strange *raar* raar
stranger n *onbekende* on·buh·ken·duh
strawberry *aardbei* aart·bey
stream n *stroom* strohm
street *straat* straat
strike n *staking* staa·king
string *touw* ⓝ taw
stroke (health) *beroerte* buh·roor·tuh
stroller *wandelwagen* wan·duhl·waa·khuhn
strong *sterk* sterk
stubborn *koppig* ko·pikh
student *student* stew·dent
stupid *dom* dom
style n *stijl* steyl
subtitles *ondertitels* on·duhr·tee·tuhls
suburb *buitenwijk* böy·tuhn·weyk
subway (train) *metro* mey·troh
sugar *suiker* söy·kuhr
suit ⓝ/*kostuum* ⓝ ⓝ/ⓑ
pak/kos·tewm
suitcase *koffer* ko·fuhr
sultana *sultanarozijn* sul·taa·na·roh·zeyn
summer *zomer* zoh·muhr
sun *zon* zon
sunburn *zonnebrand* zo·nuh·brant
sunglasses *zonnebril* sg zo·nuh·bril
sunny *zonnig* zo·nikh
sunrise *zonsopgang* zons·op·khang
sunscreen (lotion) *zonnecrème*
zo·nuh·kreym
sunset *zonsondergang* zons·on·duhr·khang
sunstroke *zonneslag* zo·nuh·slakh
superstition *bijgeloof* ⓝ bey·khuh·lohf
supporter (politics) *aanhanger*
aan·hang·uhr
surf n *branding* bran·ding
surf v *surfen* sur·fuhn
surface mail (land/sea) *gewone post*
khuh·woh·nuh post
surfboard *surfplank* surf·plangk
surfing *surfsport* surf·sport
surname *familienaam* fa·mee·lee·naam
surprise n *verrassing* vuh·ra·sing
sustainable *duurzaam* dewr·zaam
sweater *trui* tröy
sweet a *zoet* zoot
sweets sg *snoep* ⓝ snoop
swelling *gezwel* ⓝ khuh·zwel
swim v *zwemmen* zwe·muhn
swimming *zwemsport* zwem·sport
swimming pool *zwembad* ⓝ zwem·bat
swimsuit *zwempak* ⓝ zwem·pak

synagogue *synagoog* see·na·*khohkh*
synthetic *synthetisch* sin·*tey*·tis
syringe *spuit* spöyt

T

table *tafel* taa·fuhl
tablecloth *tafellaken* ⓝ taa·fuh·laa·kuhn
table tennis *tafeltennis* ⓝ taa·fuhl·te·nis
tail n *staart* staart
tailor n *kleermaker* kleyr·maa·kuhr
take v *nemen* ney·muhn
take a photo *een foto nemen*
   uhn foh·toh ney·muhn
talk v *praten* praa·tuhn
tall *groot* khroht
tampon *tampon* tam·pon
tanning lotion *zonnebrandolie*
   zo·nun·brant·oh·lee
tap n *kraantje* ⓝ kraan·chuh
tap (beer) v *(bier) tappen* (beer) ta·puhn
tapestry *tapisserie* ta·pi·suh·ree
tap water *kraantjeswater* ⓝ
   kraan·chuhs·waa·tuhr
tasty *lekker* le·kuhr
tax n *belasting* buh·las·ting
taxi stand *taxistandplaats*
   tak·see·stant·plaats
tea *thee* tey
teacher *leraar/lerares* ⓜ/ⓕ
   ley·raar/ley·raa·res
team *ploeg* plookh
teaspoon *theelepeltje* ⓝ tey·ley·puhl·chuh
technique *techniek* tekh·neek
teeth *tanden* tan·duhn
telephone n *telefoon* tey·ley·fohn
telephone v *telefoneren*
   tey·ley·foh·ney·ruhn
telephone centre *telefoonkantoor* ⓝ
   tey·ley·fohn·kan·tohr
television *televisie* tey·ley·vee·see
tell *zeggen* ze·khuhn
temperature (fever) *koorts* kohrts
temperature (weather) *temperatuur*
   tem·pey·ra·tewr
temple (body) *slaap* slaap
tennis court *tennisbaan* te·nis·baan
tent peg *(tent)haring* (tent·)haa·ring
terrible *verschrikkelijk* vuhr·skhri·kuh·luhk
terrorism *terrorisme* ⓝ te·roh·ris·muh
thank *bedanken* buh·dang·kuhn
that a *die* ⓜ&ⓕ/*dat* ⓝ dee/dat
theatre *theater* ⓝ tey·yaa·tuhr

theatre (building) *schouwburg*
   skhaw·burkh
their *hun* hun
there *daar* daar
they *zij* zey
thick *dik* dik
thief *dief* deef
thin *dun* dun
think *denken* deng·kuhn
third a *derde* der·duh
thirsty *dorstig* dors·tikh
this a *deze* ⓜ&ⓕ/*dit* ⓝ dey·zuh/dit
thread n *draad* draat
throat *keel* keyl
thrush (health) *candida* kan·dee·da
thunderstorm *onweer* on·weyr
ticket *kaartje* ⓝ/*ticket* ⓟ ⓝ/ⓑ
   kaar·chuh/ti·ket
ticket collector *kaartjesknipper*
   kaar·chus·kni·puhr
ticket machine *kaartjesautomaat*
   kaar·chus·aw·toh·maat
ticket office *loket* ⓝ loh·ket
tide *getij* ⓝ khuh·tey
tight *strak* strak
time n *tijd* teyt
time difference *tijdsverschil* ⓝ
   teyts·vuhr·skhil
timetable (general) *tijdschema* ⓝ
   teyt·skhey·ma
timetable (transport) *dienstregeling*
   deenst·rey·khuh·ling
tin (can) *blikje* ⓝ blik·yuh
tin opener *blikopener* blik·oh·puh·nuhr
tiny *miniem* mee·neem
tip (gratuity) n *fooi* foy
tire n *band* bant
tired *moe* moo
to *naar* naar
toast (food) n *geroosterd brood* ⓝ
   khuh·roh·stuhrt broht
toaster *broodrooster* broht·roh·stuhr
tobacco *tabak* ta·bak
tobacconist *sigarenhandel*
   see·khaa·ruhn·han·duhl
tobogganing *sleetje rijden* ⓝ
   sley·chuh rey·du·n
today *vandaag* van·daakh
toe *teen* teyn
tofu *tahoe/tofce* ta·hoo/to·n·foo
together *samen* saa·muhr
toilet *toilet* ⓝ twa·let
toilet paper *toiletpapier* ⓝ twa·let·pa·peer

tollway *tolweg* tol·wekh
tomato *tomaat* toh·*maat*
tomorrow *morgen* mor·khun
tonight *vanavond* van·*aa*·vont
too (also) *ook* ohk
too (much) *te* tuh
tooth *tand* tant
toothache *kiespijn/tandpijn* Ⓝ/Ⓑ
  kees·peyn/tant·peyn
toothbrush *tandenborstel*
  tan·duhn·bor·stuhl
toothpaste *tandpasta* tant·pas·ta
toothpick *tandenstoker*
  tan·duhn·stoh·kuhr
torch (flashlight) *zaklantaarn* zak·lan·taarn
touch v *aanraken* aan·raa·kuhn
tour (city/outdoors) n *tocht* tokht
tour (short, eg museum) n *rondleiding*
  ront·ley·ding
tourist *toerist* too·rist
tourist office *VVV/toerismebureau* Ⓝ
  Ⓝ/Ⓑ vey·vey·*vey*/too·ris·muh·bew·roh
towards *naar … toe* naar … too
towel *handdoek* han·dook
tower *toren* toh·ruhn
town *stad* stat
town hall *stadhuis* Ⓝ stat·*höys*
toxic waste *toxisch afval* Ⓝ tok·sis af·val
toy shop *speelgoedwinkel*
  speyl·khoot·wing·kuhl
track (path) *pad* Ⓝ pat
track (sport) *baan* baan
trade (commerce) n *handel* han·duhl
trade (profession) n *vak* Ⓝ vak
tradesperson *stielman* steel·man
traffic n *verkeer* Ⓝ vuhr·keyr
traffic jam *verkeersopstopping*
  vuhr·keyrs·op·sto·ping
traffic light *verkeerslicht* Ⓝ vuhr·keyrs·likht
trail n *pad* Ⓝ pat
train n *trein* treyn
train station *(trein)station* Ⓝ
  (treyn·)sta·*syon*
tram *tram* trem/tram Ⓝ/Ⓑ
tram stop *tramhalte* tram·hal·tuh
transit lounge *lounge voor doorgaande
  reizigers* laawnzh vohr dohr·khaan·duh
  rey·zi·khuhrs
translate *vertalen* vuhr·*taa*·luhn
translator *vertaler* vuhr·*taa*·luhr
travel v *reizen* rey·zuhn
travel agency *reisbureau* Ⓝ reys·bew·roh
travellers cheque *reischeque* reys·shek
travel sickness *reisziekte* reys·zeek·tuh

tree *boom* bohm
trenches (war) *loopgraven* lohp·khraa·vuhn
trip (journey) *reis* reys
trolley *rolwagentje* Ⓝ rol·waa·khun·chuh
trousers *pantalon* sg/*broek* sg Ⓝ/Ⓑ
  pan·ta·*lon*/brook
truck *vrachtwagen* vrakht·waa·khun
trust v *vertrouwen* vuhr·*traw*·wuhn
try (attempt) v *proberen* proh·*bey*·ruhn
tube (tyre) *binnenband* bi·nuhn·bant
tuna *tonijn* toh·neyn
tune n *deuntje* Ⓝ deun·chuh
turkey *kalkoen* kal·*koon*
turn v *draaien* draa·yuhn
turn (right/left) v *(links/rechts) afslaan*
  (lingks/rekhs) af·slaan
TV *tv* tey·vey
tweezers *pincet* Ⓝ pin·set
twice *tweemaal* twey·maal
twin beds *lits jumeaux* lee zhew·moh
twins *tweeling* twey·ling
two *twee* twey
type n *soort* sohrt
typical *typisch* tee·pis
tyre *band* bant

U

ugly *lelijk* ley·leyk
ultrasound *echografie* e·khoh·khra·*fee*
umbrella (rain) *paraplu* pa·ra·*plew*
umbrella (sun) *parasol* pa·ra·*sol*
uncle *oom* ohm
uncomfortable *ongemakkelijk*
  on·khuh·*ma*·kuh·luhk
understand *begrijpen* buh·*khrey*·puhn
underwear *ondergoed* Ⓝ on·duhr·khoot
unemployed *werkloos* werk·lohs
unfair *oneerlijk* on·eyr·leyk
universe *heelal* Ⓝ hey·*lal*
university *universiteit* ew·nee·ver·see·*teyt*
unleaded petrol *loodvrije benzine*
  loht·vrey·yuh ben·*zee*·nuh
unsafe *onveilig* on·vey·likh
until *tot* tot
unusual *ongewoon* on·khuh·*wohn*
up *omhoog* om·*hohkh*
uphill *bergop* berkh·*op*
urgent *dringend* dring·uhnt
urinary infection
  infectie van de urinewegen
  in·fek·see van duh ew·ree·nuh·wey·khun
useful *nuttig* nu·tikh

V

vacancy (accommodation) *kamer te huur*
  kaa-muhr tuh hewr
vacancy (job) *vacature* va-ka-*tew*-ruh
vacant (available) *vrij* vrey
vacant (empty) *leeg* leykh
vacation *vakantie* va-*kan*-see
vaccination *inenting* in-en-ting
vagina *vagina* vaa-*khee*-na
validate *valideren* va-lee-*dey*-ruhn
valley *vale* va-*ley*
valuable *waardevol* waar-duh-vol
value (price) n *waarde* waar-duh
van *transportwagen* trans-*port*-waa-khuhn
VAT *btw* bey-tey-wey
veal *kalfsvlees* ® kalfs-vleys
vegan n *veganist* vey-kha-*nist*
vegetable n *groente* khroon-tuh
vegetarian n *vegetariër*
  vey-khey-*taa*-ree-yuhr
vegetarian a *vegetarisch* vey-khey-*taa*-ris
vein *ader* aa-duhr
venereal disease
  seksueel overdraagbare aandoening
  sek-sew-*weel* oh-vuhr-*draakh*-baa-ruh
  aan-doo-ning
venue *plaats* plaats
very *zeer* zeyr
video tape *videofilm* vee-dey-yoo-film
view n *uitzicht* ® öyt-zikht
village *dorp* ® dorp
vine *wijnstok* weyn-stok
vinegar *azijn* a-zeyn
vineyard *wijngaard* weyn-khaart
violin *viool* vee-yohl
virgin *maagd* maakht
virus *virus* ® vee-rus
visa *visum* ® vee-zum
visit n *bezoek* ® buh-*zook*
visually impaired *visueel gehandicapt*
  vee-sew-*weel* khuh-*hen*-dee-kept/
  khuh-*han*-dee-kapt ®/®
vitamins *vitaminen* vee-ta-*mee*-nuhn
voice n *stem* stem
volunteer n *vrijwilliger* vrey-*wi*-li-khuhr
volunteer v *vrijwilligen* vrey-*wi*-li-khuhn
vote v *stemmen* ste-muhn

W

wage n *loon* ® lohn
wait v *wachten* wakh-tuhn
waiter *ober/kelner* oh-buhr/*kel*-nuhr

Waiter! *Meneer!/Mevrouw!* ®/®
  muh-*neyr*/muh-*vraw*
waitress *serveerster/dienster*
  ser-*veyr*-stuhr/*deen*-stuhr
waiting room *wachtkamer* wakht-*kaa*-muhr
wake someone up *wakker maken*
  wa-kuhr *maa*-kuhn
wake up *wakker worden* wa-kuhr *wor*-duhn
walk v *lopen/gaan* ®/® loh-puhn/khaan
walk (go for a walk) v *wandelen*
  wan-duh-luhn
wall *muur* mewr
wallet *portemonnee* por-tuh-mo-*ney*
want v *willen* wi-luhn
war n *oorlog* ohr-lokh
wardrobe *klerenkast* kley-ruhn-kast
war graves *oorlogsgraven*
  ohr-lokhs-khraa-vuhn
warm a *warm* warm
warn *waarschuwen* waar-skhew-wuhn
wash (oneself) *(zich) wassen*
  (zikh) wa-suhn
wash (something) *(iets) wassen*
  (eets) wa-suhn
wash cloth (flannel) *washandje* ®
  was-han-chuh
washing machine *wasmachine*
  was-ma-shee-nuh
wasp *wesp* wesp
watch n *horloge* ® hor-*loh*-zhuh
watch v *kijken* key-kuhn
water n *water* ® waa-tuhr
water bottle *veldfles* velt-fles
(hot) water bottle *warmwaterfles*
  warm-*waa*-tuhr-fles
water engineering *hydraulisch*
  engineering hee-draw-lis en-zhi-nee-ring
water excursion *watertocht* waa-tuhr-tokht
waterfall *waterval* waa-tuhr-val
waterfront *waterkant* waa-tuhr-kant
water gate *vloeddeur* vloot-deur
water level *waterstand* waa-tuhr-stant
waterlogged *volgelopen met water*
  vol-khuh-loh-puhn met waa-tuhr
watermelon *watermeloen*
  waa-tuhr-muh-loon
waterproof (building/structure)
  waterdicht waa-tuhr dikht
water-skiing *waterskiën* ®
  waa-tuhr-skee-yuhn
watertight *waterdicht* waa-tuhr-dikht
wave (beach) n *golf* kholf
way (method) *manier* ma-neer

way (route) *weg* wehk
we *wij* wey
weak *zwak* zwak
wealthy *rijk* reyk
wear *dragen* draa·khuhn
weather n *weer* ⓝ weyr
wedding *huwelijk* ⓝ hew·wuh·luhk
wedding cake *huwelijkstaart*
　hew·wuh·luhks·taart
wedding present *huwelijkscadeau* ⓝ
　hew·wuh·lukhs·ka·doh
week *week* weyk
weigh *wegen* wey·khuhn
weight *gewicht* ⓝ khuh·wikht
weights *gewichten* khuh·wikh·tuhn
weir *waterkering* waa·tuhr·key·ring
welcome v *verwelkomen*
　vuhr·wel·koh·muhn
welfare *welzijn* ⓝ wel·zeyn
well adv *goed* khoot
west n *westen* ⓝ wes·tuhn
wet a *nat* nat
what *wat* wat
wharf *aanlegplaats* aan·lekh·plaats
wheel *wiel* ⓝ weel
wheelchair *rolstoel* rol·stool
when *wanneer* wa·neyr
where *waar* waar
which *welke* wel·kuh
white *wit* wit
white wine *witte wijn* wi·tuh weyn
who *wie* wee
wholemeal bread *volkorenbrood* ⓝ
　vol·koh·ruhn·broht
why *waarom* waa·rom
wide *breed* breyt
wife *echtgenote* ekht·khuh·noh·tuh
win v *winnen* wi·nuhn
wind n *wind* wint
windmill *windmolen* wint·moh·luhn
window *raam* ⓝ raam
windscreen *voorruit* vohr·röyt
wine *wijn* weyn
wings *vleugels* vleu·khuls
winner *winnaar* wi·naar
winter *winter* win·tuhr
wire n *ijzerdraad* ey·zuhr·draat
wish v *wensen* wen·suhn
with *met* met
within (time) *binnen* bi·nuhn
without *zonder* zon·duhr
witness n *getuige* khuh·töy·khuh

wok *wadjan/wok* wa·dyan/wok
woman *vrouw* vraw
wonderful *prachtig* prakh·tikh
wood (forest) *bos* ⓝ bos
wood (material) *hout* ⓝ hawt
wool *wol* wol
word *woord* ⓝ wohrt
work n *baan/werk* ⓝ ⓝ/ⓑ baan/werk
work v *werken* wer·kuhn
work experience *werkervaring*
　werk·er·vaa·ring
workout n *conditietraining*
　kon·deet·see·trey·ning
work permit *werkvergunning*
　werk·vuhr·khu·ning
workshop (discussion)
　discussiebijeenkomst
　dis·kew·see·bey·eyn·komst
workshop (place) *werkplaats* werk·plaats
world *wereld* wey·ruhlt
worried *bezorgd* buh·zorkht
worse *slechter* slekh·tuhr
worship v *vereren* vuhr·ey·ruhn
wrist *pols* pols
write *schrijven* skhrey·vuhn
writer *schrijver* skhrey·vuhr
wrong *fout* fawt

Y

year *jaar* ⓝ yaar
yellow *geel* kheyl
yes *ja* yaa
yesterday *gisteren* khis·tuh·ruhn
(not) yet *al* al
you inf sg *jij/je* yey/yuh
you pol sg&pl *u* ew
you inf pl *jullie* yew·lee
young *jong* yong
your inf sg *jouw* yaw
your inf pl *jullie* yew·lee
your pol sg&pl *uw* ew
youth hostel *jeugdherberg*
　yeukht·her·berkh

Z

zebra crossing *zebrapad* ⓝ zey·bra·pat
zip/zipper *rits* rits
zodiac *dierenriem* dee·ruhn·reem
zoo *dierentuin* dee·ruhn·töyn
zucchini *courgette* koor·zhet

In this dictionary, words are marked as n (noun), a (adjective), v (verb), adv (adverb), prep (preposition), pron (pronoun), sg (singular), pl (plural), inf (informal) and pol (polite) where necessary. Note that we've only indicated Dutch nouns which have neuter gender with ⓝ after the translation – the nouns which have common gender are left unmarked. Where a word has different masculine and feminine forms, both options are given and indicated with ⓜ/ⓕ (for more on gender in Dutch, see the **phrasebuilder**). If it's a plural noun, you'll also see pl. We've used the symbols ⓝ and ⓑ for words which are different in the Netherlands and Belgium respectively. For food terms, see the **culinary reader**.

A

aanbevelen *aan*-buh-vey-luhn
 recommend
aan boord aan bohrt *aboard*
aangetekende post
 aan-khuh-tey-kuhn-duh post
 registered mail
aankomst *aan*-komst *arrival* • *arrivals*
aansteker *aan*-stey-kuhr
 cigarette lighter
aantrekkelijk aan-*tre*-kuh-luhk *attractive*
aardig *aar*-dikh *kind (nice)*
accommodatie a-koh-moh-*daa*-see
 accommodation
accu a-*kew* *battery (car)*
achter *akh*-tuhr *behind*
acteur/actrice ⓜ/ⓕ
 ak-*teur*/ak-*tree*-suh *actor*
adapter a-*dap*-tuhr *adaptor*
adres ⓝ a-*dres* *address* n
advocaat at-voh-*kaat* *lawyer*
afgesloten *af*-khuh-sloh-tuhn
 blocked (access/road)
afscheid ⓝ *af*-skheyt *goodbye*
afspraak *af*-spraak *appointment*
afstandsbediening
 af-stants-buh-dee-ning *remote control*
agenda a-*khen*-da *diary (agenda)*
aktetas *ak*-tuh-tas *briefcase*
alle *a*-luh *all*
alleen a-*leyn* *alone*
allergie a-ler-*khee* *allergy*
alles *a*-luhs *everything*
ambassade am-ba-*saa*-duh *embassy*

ambulance am-bew-*lans* *ambulance*
andere *an*-duh-ruh *other*
annuleren a-new-*ley*-ruhn *cancel*
ansichtkaart *an*-zikht-kaart *postcard*
antibiotica ⓝ pl an-tee-bee-*yo*-tee-ka
 antibiotics
antiek an-*teek* *antique* r
apotheek a-poh-*teyk* *chemist (pharmacy)*
apotheker/apothekeres ⓜ/ⓕ
 a-poh-*tey*-kuhr/a-poh-*tey*-kuh-res
 chemist (pharmacist)
architectuur ar-khee-tek-*tewr*
 architecture
arm arm *arm (body)*
artiest ar-*teest* *artist*
asbak *as*-bak *ashtray*
aspirine as-pee-*ree*-nuh *aspirin*
auto *aw*-toh *car*
autoverhuur aw-toh-vuhr-*hewr* *car hire*
autoweg *aw*-toh-wekh *motorway*
avond *aa*-vont *evening*
avondje-uit *aa*-vont-chuh-*öyt*
 night out
avondmaal ⓝ *aa*-vont-maal *dinner*
avondwinkel *aa*-vont-wing-kuhl
 convenience store

B

baan baan *job* ⓝ • *road* ⓑ
baar geld ⓝ baar khelt *cash* n
babyvoeding *bey*-bee-voo-ding
 baby food
bad ⓝ bat *bath* n
badkamer *bat*-kaa-muhr *bathroom*

bagage ba-*khaa*-zhuh luggage (baggage)
bagage band ba-*khaa*-zhuh bant
  baggage claim
bagagedepot ⓝ ba-*khaa*-zhuh-*dey*-poh
  left-luggage office
bagagekluis ba-*khaa*-zhuh-klöys
  luggage locker
bagage-inleverpunt ⓝ
  ba-*khaa*-zhuh-*in*-ley-vuhr-punt
  baggage claim
bagagekluis ba-*khaa*-zhuh-klöys
  luggage locker
bakken ba-*kuhn* bake • fry v
bakkerij ba-*kuh*-rey bakery
bakkerswinkel ⓝ
  ba-*kuhrs*-wing-kuhl bakery
band bant tire (tyre) n
band bent band (music) ⓝ
bank bangk bank n
bankbiljet ⓝ bangk-bil-yet banknote
banketbakkerij ⓝ bang-*ket*-ba-kuh-rey
  cake shop
bankrekening bangk-rey-kuh-ning
  bank account
batterij ba-tuh-*rey* battery (general)
bed ⓝ bet bed
beddegoed ⓝ be-duh-khoot bed linen
bedieningsgeld ⓝ
  buh-*dee*-nings-khelt cover charge
bedieningstoeslag
  buh-*dee*-nings-too-slakh service charge
bedlinnen ⓝ bet-li-nuhn linen (sheets)
beeldhouwwerk ⓝ
  beylt-*haw*-werk sculpture
been ⓝ beyn leg (body)
beha bey-*haa* bra
beide bey-duh both
belangrijk buh-*lang*-ruhk important
benzine ben-*zee*-nuh gas (petrol)
benzinestation ⓝ ben-*zee*-nuh-sta-syon
  petrol station (service station)
berg berkh mountain
bericht ⓝ buh-*rikht* message n
bespreking buh-*sprey*-king
  conference (small)
beste *bes*-tuh best
bestek ⓝ buh-*stek* cutlery
bestemming buh-*ste*-ming destination
betaling buh-*taa*-ling payment
beter bey-tuhr better
bevestigen be-*ves*-ti-khuhn
  confirm (a booking)
bevroren buh-*vroh*-ruhn frozen
bezig bey-zikh busy (person)

bezorgen be-*zor*-khuhn deliver
bibliotheek bi-blyoh-*teyk* library
bier ⓝ beer beer
bij bey at • near
binnengaan bi-nuhn-khaan enter
bioscoop bee-yos-*kohp* cinema
bitter bi-tuhr bitter
blaar blaar blister n
blauw blaw blue
blik ⓝ blik can (tin) n
blikopener blik-oh-puh-nuhr
  can (tin) opener
bloed ⓝ bloot blood
bloedgroep bloot-khroop blood group
bloemist bloo-*mist* florist
boek ⓝ book book n
boekhandel book-han-duhl book shop
boodschappen boht-skha-puhn groceries
boot boht boat
bord ⓝ bort plate
borst borst chest (body)
borstel bor-stuhl brush n
branden bran-duhn burn n
brandweer brant-weyr fire brigade
brasserie ⓑ bra-suh-*ree* café
breekbaar breyk-baar fragile
brief breef letter (mail)
brievenbus bree-vuh-bus mailbox
bril sg bril glasses (spectacles)
brochure broh-*shew*-ruh brochure
broek sg ⓑ brook trousers
broer broor brother
brood ⓝ broht bread
broodrooster broht-roh-stuhr toaster
brug brukh bridge (structure) n
bruin bröyn brown
budget ⓝ bu-*dzhet* budget n
buiten böy-tuhn outside adv
buitenlands böy-tuhn-lants foreign
burgerlijke bouwkunde bur-khur-luh-kuh
  baw-kun-duh civil engineering
bus bus bus
bushalte bus-hal-tuh bus stop
busstation ⓝ bus-sta-syon bus station

C

café ⓝ ka-*fey* pub (bar)
camera kaa-mey-ra camera (film/video)
centrum ⓝ sen-trum centre n
chef-kok shef-*kok* chef
cheque shek check (banking) n
chocolade shoh-koh-*laa*-duh chocolate

coachen koh-chuhn *coach* v
colbert ⓝ kol-ber *dressy jacket*
collega ko-ley-kha *colleague*
comfortabel kom-for-taa-buhl
comfortable
commissie ko-mee-see *commission*
communicatie ko-mew-nee-kaa-see
communicate • communications
condoom ⓝ kon-dohm *condom*
conferentie kon-fey-ren-see
conference (big)
constipatie kon-stee-paa-see
constipation
consulaat ⓒ kon-su-laat *consulate*
contactlenzen kon-takt-len-zuhn
contact lenses
couchette koo-shet *berth (train)* n

D

daar daar *there*
dag dakh *date • day*
dagboek ⓝ dakh-book
diary (personal notes)
dagelijks daa-khuh-luhks *daily* a&adv
dageraad daa-khuh-raat *dawn*
dankbaar dangk-baar *grateful*
dans dans *dance* n
dansen dan-suhn *dance* v • *dancing*
dat dat *that* a&pron
deken dey-kuhn *blanket*
delen dey-leyn *share (with)* v
dessert ⓝ de-seyr *dessert*
diafilm dee-ya-film *slide film*
diarree dee-ya-rey *diarrhoea*
dichtbij dikht-bey *close* a • *nearby*
dichtsbijzijnde dikhts-bey-zeyn-duh
nearest
die dee *that (one)* pron
dienst deenst *service* n
dienster deen-stuhr *waitress*
dienstregeling deenst-rey-khuh-ling
timetable (transport)
dierentuin dee-ruhn-töyn *zoo*
dik dik *fat (objects/people)* a
diner ⓝ dee-ney *dinner*
dit dit *this* a&pron
dochter dokh-tuhr *daughter*
doden doh-duhn *kill* v
dokter dok-tuhr *doctor*
donker dong-kuhr *dark*
doos dohs *box* n
dorstig dors-tikh *thirsty*

douane doo-waa-nuh *customs*
douche doo-shuh *shower* n
drank drangk *drink (general)* n
drankenhandel Ⓑ drang-kuhn-han-duhl
bottle shop (liquor store)
drankje ⓝ drang-kyuh *alcoholic drink* n
dringend dring-uhnt *urgent*
drinken dring-kuhn *drink* v
drogen droh-khuhn *dry* v
drogisterij droh-khis-tuh-rey *drugstore*
dronken drong-kuhn *drunk* a
droog drohkh *dry* a
drugs drukhs *illicit drugs*
druk druk *busy (place)*
duur dewr *expensive*

E

echtgenoot ekht-khuh-noht *husband*
echtgenote ekht-khuh-noh-tuh *wife*
één eyn *one*
een andere uhn an-duh-ruh *another*
een foto nemen
uhn foh-toh ney-muhn *take a photo*
éénpersoonskamer
eyn-puhr-sohns-kaa-muhr *single room*
eergisteren eyr-khis-tuh-ruhn
day before yesterday
eerste eyrs-tuh *first* a
eerste hulp eyrs-tuh hulp *first aid*
eerste klas eyrs-tuh klas *first class*
EHBO-kist ey-haa-bey-yoh-kist *first-aid kit*
eiland ⓒ ey-lant *island*
elke elk-kuh *each • every* a
en en *and*
Engels ⓔ eng-uhls *English (language)*
enkel eng-kuhl *ankle*
enkel eng-kuhl *only* adv
enkele eng-kuh-luh *some*
enkele reis eng-kuh-luh reys
one-way ticket
envelop en-vuh-lop *envelope*
eten ey-tuhn *eat*
euro/euro's sg/pl eu-roh/eu-rohs
euro/euros
exprespost eks-pres-post *express mail*

F

familie fa-mee-lee *family*
familienaam fa-mee-lee-naam
family name (surname)
fantastisch fan-tas-tis *great (fantastic)*

fax faks *fax • fax machine*
feestje ⑩ *fey*-shuh *party (entertainment)*
ferry *fe*-ree *ferry*
fiets feets *bicycle*
filmgevoeligheid
  film-khuh-*voo*-likh-heyt *film speed*
fitnesscentrum ⑩
  fit-nuhs-sen-trum *gym (place)*
fles fles *bottle*
flesopener *fles*-oh-puh-nuhr *bottle opener*
fooi foy *tip (gratuity)* n
fopspeen *fop*-speyn *dummy (pacifier)*
foto *foh*-toh *photo*
fotograaf foh-toh-*khraaf* *photographer*
fotografie foh-toh-khraa-*fee* *photography*
fototoestel ⑩ *foh*-toh-too-stel
  camera (photos)
fruit ⑩ fröyt *fruit*
fuif ⑧ föyf *party (entertainment)*

G

gaan khaan *go*
gaan ⑧ khaan *walk* v
gaan winkelen khaan *wing*-kuh-luhn
  go shopping
gangpad ⑪ *khang*-pat *aisle (on plane)*
garantie kha-*ran*-see *guarantee* n
garderobe khar-duh-*roh*-buh *cloakroom*
gas ⑩ khas *gas (for cooking)*
gauw khaw *soon*
geboortedatum
  khuh-*bohr*-tuh-daa-tum *date of birth*
gebouw ⑩ khuh-*baw* *building*
gebroken khuh-*broh*-khun *broken*
geel kheyl *yellow*
gehaast khuh-*haast* *in a hurry*
gehandicapt khuh-*hen*-dee-kept/
  khuh-*han*-dee-kapt ⑩/⑧ *disabled*
gehuwd khuh-*hewt* *married*
gekwetst khuh-*kwetst* *injured*
geld ⑩ khelt *money*
geldautomaat ⑧ khelt-*aw*-toh-maat *ATM*
gelukkig khuh-*lu*-kikh *happy*
geneeskunde khuh-*neys*-kun-duh
  medicine (study/profession)
genoeg khuh-*nookh* *enough*
gepensioneerde
  khuh-*pen*-syoh-*neyr*-duh *pensioner*
gescheiden khuh-*skhey*-duhn *divorced*
geschenk ⑩ khuh-*skhengk* *gift*
gesloten khuh-*sloh*-tuhn *closed • locked*
gestolen khuh-*stoh*-luhn *stolen*

geur kheur *smell* n
gevaarlijk khuh-*vaar*-luhk *dangerous*
gevoel ⑩ khuh-*vool* *feeling*
gevonden voorwerpen khuh-*von*-duhn
  vohr-wer-puhn *lost-property office*
gewone post khuh-*woh*-nuh post
  surface mail (land/sea)
gewoonte khuh-*wohn*-tuh *custom*
gezicht ⑩ khuh-*zikht* *face* n
gids khits *guide (person) • guidebook*
gisteren *khis*-tuh-ruhn *yesterday*
glas ⑩ khlas *glass (drinking/material)*
goed khoot *good*
goedkoop khoot-*kohp* *cheap*
goud ⑩ khawt *gold*
gram khram *gram*
grappig *khra*-pikh *funny*
gratis *khraa*-tis *complimentary (free)*
griep khreep *flu • influenza*
grijs khreys *grey*
groen khroon *green*
groente *khroon*-tuh *vegetable* n
groep khroop *band (music)* ⑧ *• group*
groot khroht *big*
grootmoeder *khroht*-moo-duhr
  grandmother
grootst *khrohtst* *biggest*
grootvader *khroht*-vaa-duhr *grandfather*
grootwarenhuis ⑩ ⑧
  khroht-*waa*-ruhn-höys *department store*
groter *khroh*-tuhr *bigger*
gsm khey-es-*em* *mobile (cell) phone* ⑧

H

haar ⑩ haar *hair* n
haar haar *her (possessive)*
halsketting *hals*-ke-ting *necklace*
hand hant *hand*
handdoek *han*-dook *towel*
handgemaakt
  hant-khuh-maakt *handmade*
handschoenen *hant*-skhoo-nuhn *gloves*
handtas *han*-tas *handbag*
handwerk ⑩ *hant*-werk *crafts • handicraft*
hangslot ⑩ *hang*-slot *padlock*
hard hart *hard (not soft)*
hart ⑩ hart *heart*
hartkwaal hart-kwaal *heart condition*
hebben *he*-buhn *have*
heen- en terugreis
  heyn-en-tuh-*rukh*-reys *return ticket*
heet heyt *(very) hot*

helft helft *half* n
helpen *hel*-puhn *help* v
hemd ⓝ hemt *shirt*
hersenschudding
  her-suhn-skhu-ding *concussion*
herstellen her-*ste*-luhn *repair* v
hetzelfde ⓝ huht-*zelf*-duh *same*
hier heer *here*
hij hey *he*
hitte *hi*-tuh *heat* n
hoed hoot *hat*
hoesten *hoos*-tuhn *cough* v
hoestmiddel ⓝ *hoost*-mi-duhl
  cough medicine
homo *hoh*-moh *gay (homosexual)*
homoseksueel hoh-moh-sek-sew-*weyl*
  homosexual n&a
hond hont *dog*
hongerig *hong*-uh-rikh *hungry*
hoofd ⓝ hohft *head (body)*
hoofdpijn *hohft*-peyn *headache*
hooikoorts *hoy*-kohrts *hay fever*
horloge hor-*loh*-zhuh ⓝ *watch* n
houden van *haw*-duhn van *like* v · *love* v
hulp hulp *help* n
huren *hew*-ruhn *hire (rent)* v
hut hut *berth (ship)* n
huur hewr *rent* n
huwelijksreis *hew*-wuh-luhks-reys
  honeymoon (trip)
huwen *hew*-wuhn *marry*
hydraulisch engineering hee-*draw*-lis
  en-zhi-*nee*-ring *water engineering*

I

identificatie ee-den-tee-fee-*kaa*-see
  identification
identiteitsbewijs ⓝ
  ee-den-tee-*teyts*-buh-weys *ID*
iedereen ee-duh-*reyn* *everyone*
ijs ⓝ eys *ice*
(room)ijs ⓝ (rohm-)eys *ice cream*
ijskast *eys*-kast *fridge*
ik ik *I*
inbegrepen in-buh-*khrey*-puhn *included*
incheckbalie in-*shek*-ba-lee
  check-in (desk)
indigestie in-dee-*khes*-tee *indigestion*
inenting *in*-en-ting *vaccination*
infectie in-*fek*-see *infection*
informatica in-for-*maa*-tee-ka *IT*
informatie in-for-*maa*-see *information*

ingang *in*-khang *entry* n
ingenieur in-*zhey*-nyeur *engineer* n
inlegkruisjes ⓝ pl in-lekh-*kröy*-shuhs
  panty liners
(een cheque) innen (uhn shek) *i*-nuhn
  cash (a cheque) v
inschrijvingsbewijs ⓝ
  in-*skhrey*-vings-buh-weys *car registration*
inspuiting *in*-spöy-ting *injection*
instapkaart *in*-stap-kaart *boarding pass*

J

ja yaa *yes*
jaar ⓝ yaar *year*
jas yas *coat* n · *jacket (casual)*
je yuh *you* inf sg
jenever yuh-*ney*-vuhr/zhuh-*ney*-vuhr ⓝ/ⓑ
  gin
jeugdherberg yeukht-*her*-berkh
  youth hostel
jeuk yeuk *itch* n
jij yey *you* inf sg
jongen *yong*-uhn *boy*
journalist zhoor-na-*list* *journalist*
jouw jaw *your* inf sg
juist yöyst *exactly*
jullie *yew*-lee *you* · *your* inf pl
jurk yurk *dress* n
juwelen ⓝ pl yew-*wey*-luhr *jewellery*

K

kaart kaart *map (of country/town)*
kaartje ⓝ *kaar*-chuh *ticket*
kaartjesautomaat *kaar*-chus-aw-toh-maat
  ticket machine
kam kam *comb* n
kamer *kaa*-muhr *room* n
kamernummer ⓝ *kaa*-muhr-nu-muhr
  room number
kamer te huur *kaa*-muhr tuh hewr
  vacancy (accommodation)
kantoorboekhandel
  kan-*tohr*-book-han-duhl *stationer*
kapper *ka*-puhr *hairdresser*
kapsel ⓝ *kap*-suhl *haircut*
kassa *ka*-sa *cash register*
kassier/kassierster ⓜ/ⓕ
  ka-*seer*/ka-*seer*-stuhr *cashier*
kasteel ⓝ kas-*teyl* *castle*
katedraal ka-tey-*draal* *cathedral*
katoen ⓝ ka-*toon* *cotton* n
keel keyl *throat*

kelner *kel*-nuhr *waiter*
kerk kerk *church*
kerkhof ⓝ *kerk*-hof *cemetery*
kermis *ker*-mis *fairground*
keuken *keu*-kuhn *kitchen*
kiespijn *kees*-peyn *toothache*
kiestoon *kees*-tohn *dial tone*
kiezen *kee*-zuhn *choose*
kind ⓝ kint *child*
kinderen ⓝ pl *kin*-duh-ruhn *children*
kinderoppasdienst
　kin-duhr-o-pas-deenst
　child-minding service
kinderzitje ⓝ *kin*-duhr-zi-chuh *child seat*
klacht klakht *complaint*
klant klant *client*
klassiek kla-*seek* *classical*
kleding *kley*-ding *clothing*
kledingzaak *kley*-ding-zaak *clothing store*
kleed ⓝ kleyt *dress* ⓑ · *rug* ⓝ
kleedhokje ⓝ *kleyt*-hok-yuh
　changing room (sport, individual)
kleedkamer *kleyt*-kaa-muhr *changing
　room (sport, communal)*
kleermaker *kleyr*-maa-kuhr *tailor* n
klein kleyn *short (height)* · *small*
kleiner *kley*-nuhr *shorter* · *smaller*
kleingeld ⓝ *kleyn*-khelt
　change (loose coins) n
kleinkind ⓝ *kleyn*-kint *grandchild*
kleinst kleynst *smallest*
kleur kleur *colour* n
kluis klöys *safe* n
knap knap *handsome*
knie knee *knee*
knoop knohp *button* n
koelkast *kool*-kast *refrigerator*
koekenpan *koo*-kuh-pan *frying pan*
koffer *ko*-fuhr *suitcase*
koffie *ko*-fee *coffee*
koffiehuisje *ko*-fee-höy-shuh *café*
koffieshop *ko*-fee-shop
　coffee shop (sells soft drugs)
kok kok *cook* n
koken *koh*-kuhn *cook* v
kom kom *bowl (plate)* n
kookpot *kohk*-pot *saucepan*
kop kop *cup*
kopen *koh*-puhn *buy* v
koplampen *kop*-lam-puhn *headlights*
korting *kor*-ting *discount* n
kost kost *cost* n
kosten *kos*-tuhn *cost* v

koud kawt *cold* a
kousen *kaw*-suhn *stockings*
kraantje ⓝ *kraan*-chuh *faucet (tap)*
krant krant *newspaper*
krantenzaak *kran*-tuh-zaak
　newsagency (selling newspapers)
krediet ⓝ krey-*deet* *credit* n
kredietkaart krey-*deet*-kaart *credit card*
kroeg krookh *pub (bar)*
kruidenierszaak kröy-duh-*neers*-zaak
　grocery shop
kunst kunst *art*
kunstgalerie kunst-kha-luh-*ree* *art gallery*
kurkentrekker *kur*-kuh-tre-kuhr *corkscrew*
kussen ⓝ *ku*-suhn *pillow*
kussensloop *ku*-suhn-slohp *pillowcase*
kwetsuur kwet-*sewr* *injury*
kwitantie kwee-*tan*-see *receipt* n

L

laat laat *late* adv
laatste *laat*-stuh *last (final)*
laken ⓝ *laa*-kuhn *sheet (bed)*
lang lang *long*
later *laa*-tuhr *later*
lawaaierig la-*waa*-yuh-rikh *noisy*
laxeermiddel ⓝ lak-*seyr*-mi-duhl *laxative*
leder ⓝ *ley*-duhr *leather* n
leeg leykh *vacant (empty)*
lekker *le*-kuhr *delicious* · *tasty*
lelijk *ley*-leyk *ugly*
lens lens *lens*
lente *len*-tuh *spring (season)*
lepel *ley*-puhl *spoon*
leraar/lerares ⓜ/ⓕ ley-*raar*/ley-*raa*-res
　teacher
lesbische *les*-bi-suh *lesbian* n
licht likht *light (colour/weight)*
licht ⓝ likht *light* n
lichtmeter *likht*-mey-tuhr *light meter*
liefde *leef*-duh *love* n
lift lift *lift (elevator)*
liften *lif*-tuhn *hitchhike*
links lingks *left (direction)*
linnen ⓝ *li*-nuhn *linen (material)*
lits jumeaux lee zhew-*moh* *twin beds*
loket ⓝ loh-*ket* *ticket office*
lopen *loh*-puhn *walk* v ⓝ · *run* ⓑ
luchthaven *lukht*-haa-vuhn *airport*
luchthavenbelasting
　lukht-haa-vuhn-buh-*las*-ting *airport tax*
luchtpost *lukht*-post *airmail*

luchtvaartmaatschappij
  lukht-vaart-maat-skha·pey *airline*
lucifers *lew-see-fers matches (for lighting)*
luid löyt *loud*
luier *löy-yuhr nappy (diaper)*
luisteren *löys-tuh-ruhn listen*
lunch lunsh *lunch*
luxueus luk-sew-*weus luxurious*

M

maag maakh *stomach*
maagpijn *maakh-peyn stomachache*
maaltijd *maal-teyt meal*
maand maant *month*
maandverband ⓝ *maant-vuhr-bant
  sanitary napkin*
maat maat *size* n
machinebouwkunde
  ma-*shee*-nuh-baw-kun-duh
  mechanical engineering
magnetron *makh-ney-tron
  microwave oven*
makelaarskantoor ⓝ
  maa-kuh-laars-kan-tohr estate agency
man man *man* n
mantel *man-tuhl coat* n
markt markt *market* n
matras ma-*tras mattress*
maximumsnelheid
  mak-see-mum-snel-heyt speed limit
me muh *me*
medicijn ⓝ *mey-dee-seyn
  medicine (medication)*
medicijnen mey-dee-*sey-nuhn
  medicine (study/profession)* ⓝ • *medicines*
meer meyr *more*
meer ⓝ *meyr lake*
meisje ⓝ *mey-shuh girl*
melk melk *milk*
mes ⓝ *mes knife* n
meter *mey-tuhr metre*
metgezel *met-khuh-zel companion*
metrostation ⓝ *mey-troh-sta-syon
  metro station*
meubilair ⓝ *meu-bee-leyr furniture*
microgolfoven *mee*-kroh-kholf-oh-vuhn
  microwave oven
middag *mi-dakh afternoon* ⓝ • *midday*
middagmaal ⓝ *mi-cakh-maal lunch*
middernacht mi-duh·r-nakht *midnight*
mijn meyn *my*
millimeter *mee-lee mey-tuhr millimetre*

minder *min-duhr less*
mineraalwater ⓝ mee-ney-*racl*-waa-tuhr
  mineral water
minuut mee-*newt minute* n
misselijkheid *mi-suh-luhk-heyt nausea*
missen *mi-*suhn *miss* v
mobiele telefoon moh-*bee*-luh
  tey-ley-fohn *mobile/cell phone*
mode *moh-duh fashion* n
modern moh-*dern modern*
moe moo *tired*
moeder *moo-duhr mother*
mond mont *mouth*
mooi moy *beautiful*
morgen *mor*-khuhn *morning* Ⓔ • *tomorrow*
motor *moh-tor engine*
muntstukken *munt-stu-kuhn coins*
museum ⓝ *mew-zey-yuhm museum*
muziek mew-*zeek music*
muziekwinkel mew-*zeek*-wing-kuhl
  music shop

N

na naa *after*
naald naalt *needle (sewing/syringe)*
naam naam *name* n
naar naar *to*
naast naast *beside*
nacht nakht *night*
nachtclub *nakht*-klup *nightclub*
nagelknipper sg naa-*khuhl*-kni-puhr
  nail clippers
namiddag *naa*-mi-dakh *afternoon*
nee ney *no*
nek nek *neck*
neus neus *nose*
niet-roken *neet*-roh-kuhn *nonsmoking*
niets neets *nothing*
nieuw neew *new*
nieuws neews *news*
noodgeval ⓝ *noot*-khuh va *emergency*
noorden ⓝ *nohr*-duhn *north* n
notitieboekje ⓝ noh-*tee*-see·-book-yuh
  notebook
nu new *now*
nummer ⓝ *nu*-muhr *number* n

O

ober *oh-buhr waiter*
ochtend ⓝ *okh*-tuhnt *morning*
olie *oh-lee oil (cooking)*

omhoog om·*hohkh* up
ondergoed ⓝ on·duhr·*khoot* underwear
ondertitels on·duhr·tee·tuhls subtitles
ongemakkelijk on·khuh·*ma*·kuh·luhk uncomfortable
ongeval ⓝ on·khuh·val accident
onmogelijk on·*moh*·khul·luhk impossible
ontbijt ⓝ ont·*beyt* breakfast
ontsmettend ont·*sme*·tuhnt antiseptic a
onze on·zuh our
oog ⓝ ohkh eye
oor ⓝ ohr ear
oorringen *oh*·ring·uhn earrings
oosten ⓝ *oh*·stuhn east n
op op on
openbare telefoon *oh*·puhn·bah·ruh tey·ley·*fohn* public phone
openbaar toilet ⓝ *oh*·puhn·baar twa·*let* public toilet
openingsuren ⓝ pl *oh*·puh·nings·ew·ruhn opening hours
opgewarmd op·khuh·*warmt* heated (food)
opnieuw op·*neew* again
op tijd op teyt on time
optreden op·*trey*·duhn gig
oranje oh·*ran*·yuh orange (colour)
oud awt old
ouders *aw*·duhrs parents
oude stad *aw*·duh stat old city
overmorgen *oh*·vuhr·mor·khun day after tomorrow
overvracht *oh*·vuhr·vrakht excess baggage

P

pak/pakket ⓝ pak/pa·*ket* package n • packet • parcel n
paleis ⓝ pa·*leys* palace
pantalon sg ⓝ pan·ta·*lon* trousers
panty *pen*·tee/pan·tee ⓝ/ⓑ pantyhose
papier ⓝ pa·*peer* paper n
papieren ⓝ pl pa·*pee*·ruhn paperwork
paraplu pa·ra·*plew* umbrella (rain)
parasol pa·ra·*sol* umbrella (sun)
parfum ⓝ par·*föy* perfume n
parkeren par·*key*·ruhn park (a car) v
paskamer pas·kaa·muhr changing room (shop)
paspoort ⓝ pas·pohrt passport
paspoortnummer ⓝ pas·pohrt·nu·muhr passport number
passagier pa·sa·*kheer* passenger
patisserie ⓑ pa·tee·suh·*ree* cake shop

pause *paw*·zuh intermission
pension ⓝ pen·*syon* boarding house • guesthouse
per (dag) puhr (dakh) per (day)
perron ⓝ pe·*ron* platform (train station)
personeel ⓝ per·soh·*neyl* staff
picknick pik·nik picnic n
pijn peyn pain
pijnlijk *peyn*·luhk painful
pijnstiller *peyn*·sti·luhr painkiller
pil pil pill
pin-automaat ⓝ pin·aw·toh·maat automated teller machine (ATM)
pincet ⓝ pin·*set* tweezers
plaatselijk *plaat*·suh·luhk local a
plak ⓝ plak slice n
plattegrond pla·tuh·*khront* map (of building)
plein ⓝ pleyn court (tennis) • square (town)
pleister *pley*·stuhr Band-Aid
politie poh·*leet*·see police
politieagent poh·*leet*·see·a·*khent* police officer
politiebureau ⓝ poh·*leet*·see·bew·roh police station
portemonnee por·tuh·mo·*ney* purse • wallet
post post mail (letters/postal system) n
postkaart *post*·kaart postcard
postkantoor ⓝ *post*·kan·tohr post office
postzegel *post*·zey·khul stamp (postage) n
potlood ⓝ *pot*·loht pencil
praten *praa*·tuhn speak
prijs preys price n
privé pree·*vey* private
proberen proh·*bey*·ruhn try (attempt) v
programma ⓝ proh·*khra*·ma program n
proper ⓑ *proh*·puhr clean a
prostituée pros·tee·tew·*wey* prostitute n
purper *pur*·puhr purple

R

raam ⓝ raam window
radio *raa*·dee·yoh radio
recept ⓝ rey·*sept* prescription
rechten ⓝ pl *rekh*·tuhn law (study/profession)
rechts rekhs right (direction)
rechtstreeks rekh·*streyks* direct a
rechtstreekse lijn rekh·*streyk*·suh leyn direct-dial
reddingsvest ⓝ *re*·dings·vest life jacket

regen *rey*-khuhn *rain* n
regenjas *rey*-khuhn-yas *raincoat*
reisbureau ⑩ *reys*-bew-roh *travel agency*
reischeque *reys*-shek *travellers cheque*
reisroute *reys*-roo-tuh *itinerary*
reisziekte reys-*zeek*-tuh *travel sickness*
rekening *rey*-kuh-ning
  account • bill • check n
rekenmachine *rey*-kuhn-ma-shee-nuh
  calculator
remmen *re*-muhn *brakes*
reservatie rey-ser-*vaa*-see
  reservation (booking)
reserveren rey-ser-*vey*-ruhn
  book (make a booking) v
restaurant ⑩ res-toh-*rant restaurant*
restauratiewagen
  res-toh-*raa*-see-waa-khuhn *dining car*
retourtje ⑩ ruh-*toor*-chuh
  return ticket
richting *rikh*-ting *direction*
rijbewijs ⑩ *rey*-buh weys *drivers licence*
rit rit *drive* n
rits rits *zip/zipper*
rivier ree-*veer river*
rockmuziek *rok*-mew-zeek *rock (music)*
rok rok *skirt*
roken *roh*-kuhn *smoke* v
rolstoel *rol*-stool *wheelchair*
roltrap *rol*-trap *escalator*
rolwagentje ⑩ *rol*-waa-khun-chuh *trolley*
romantisch roh-*man*-tees *romantic* a
rondleiding *ront*-ley-ding *guided tour*
rood roht *red*
roze *roh*-zuh *pink*
rug rukh *back (body)*
rugzak *rukh*-zak *backpack (rucksack)*
ruilen *röy*-luhn *exchange (general)* v
ruïnes rew-*wee*-nuhs *ruins*

S

saai saay *boring*
samen *saa*-muhn *together*
schaar sg *skhaar scissors*
schade *skhaa*-duh *damage*
schaduw *skhaa*-dew *shade*
scheerapparaat ⑩ *skheyr*-a-pa-raat
  razor (electric)
scheermes ⑩ *skheyr*-mes *razor (manual)*
scheermesje ⑩ *skheyr*-me-shuh
  razor blade
scheerschuim ⑩ *skheyr*-skhöym
  shaving cream

scheren *skhey*-ruhn *shave* v
schijf skheyf *disk*
schoenen *skhoo*-nuhn *shoes*
schoenenzaak *skhoo*-nuhn-zaak *shoe shop*
schoon skhohn *beautiful* ⑧ • *clean* a ⑩
schoonheidssalon skhohn-*heyt*-sa-lon
  beauty salon
schoonmaak *skhohn*-maak *cleaning*
schoonmaken *skhohn*-maa-kuhn *clean* v
schoonmoeder *skhohn*-moo-duhr
  mother-in-law
schoonvader *skhohn*-vaa-duhr
  father-in-law
schotel *skhoh*-tuhl *dish*
schouwburg *skhaw*-burkh
  theatre (building)
schrijven *skhrey*-vuhn *write*
seizoen ⑩ *sey*-zoon *season* n
seks seks *sex*
serveerster ser-*veyr*-stuhr *waitress*
servet ⑩ ser-*vet napkin*
short sg *short shorts*
shouder *skhaw*-duhr *shoulder*
sigaar see-*knaar cigar*
sigaret see-kha-*ret cigarette*
sim-kaart *sim*-kaart *SIM card*
sjaal shaal *scarf*
skisport *skee*-sport *skiing*
slaapkamer *slaap*-kaa-muhr *bedroom*
slaapwagen *slaap*-waa-khuhn
  sleeping car
slaapzak *slaap*-zak *sleeping bag*
slagerij slaa-khuh-*rey butcher's shop*
slapen *slaa*-puhn *sleep* v
slecht slekht *bad*
slechter *slekh*-tuhr *worse*
sleutel *sleu*-tuhl *key (door etc)*
slijterij ⑩ *sley*-tuh-rey
  bottle shop (liquor store)
slot slot *lock* n
sluiten *slöy*-tuhn *close* v
smeermiddel ⑩ *smeyr*-mi-duhl *lubricant*
snee ⑩ *sney slice* n
sneeuw *sneyw snow* n
snel snel *fast* a
snelweg *snel*-wekh *highway*
snijden *sney*-duhn *cut* v
sokken *so*-kuhn *socks*
souvenirwinkel soo-vuh-*neer*-wing-kuhl
  souvenir shop
spiegel *spee*-khul *mirror* n
sportwinkel *sport*-wing-kuhl *sports store*
stad stat *city • town*

stadhuis ⓝ stat·*höys* town hall
stadsbus stats·bus city bus
stadscentrum ⓝ stat·sen·trum
 city centre (downtown)
stadsplein ⓝ stats·pleyn main square
staking staa·king strike n
station ⓝ sta·syon station
stekker ste·kuhr plug (electricity) n
stil stil quiet
stoel stool chair n
stoeltjeslift stool·chuhs·lift
 chairlift (skiing)
stop stop plug (bath) n
storting stor·ting deposit (money) n
straat straat street
strand strant beach
strijkijzer ⓝ streyk·ey·zuhr
 iron (for clothes) n
stroom strohm current (electricity) n
student stew·dent student
stuk stuk broken down • faulty • out of order
suiker söy·kuhr sugar
suikerziekte söy·kuhr·zeek·tuh diabetes

T

taal taal language
taalgids taal·khits phrasebook
taksvrije winkel taks·vrey·yuh wing·kuhl
 duty-free shop
tandarts tan·darts dentist
tandenborstel tan·duhn·bor·stuhl
 toothbrush
tandpasta tant·pas·ta toothpaste
tandpijn tant·peyn toothache
tandzijde tant·zey·duh dental floss
tarief ⓝ ta·reef fare n
tas tas bag
taxistandplaats tak·see·stant·plaats
 taxi stand
te tuh too (much)
telefoneren tey·ley·foh·ney·ruhn
 telephone v
telefoon ⓝ tey·ley·fohn telephone n
telefoonboek ⓝ tey·ley·fohn·book
 phone book
telefooncel tey·ley·fohn·sel phone box
telefoongesprek ⓝ
 tey·ley·fohn·khuh·sprek phone call v
telefoonkaart tey·ley·fohn·kaart
 phonecard
televisie tey·ley·vee·see television
temperatuur tem·pey·ra·tewr
 temperature (weather)

tennisbaan te·nis·baan tennis court
tentoonstelling tuhn·tohn·ste·ling
 exhibition
terugbetaling tuh·rukh·buh·taa·ling
 refund v
terugkomen tuh·rukh·koh·muhn return v
theater ⓝ tey·yaa·tuhr theatre
theelepeltje ⓝ tey·ley·puhl·chuh teaspoon
thuis töys home
ticket ⓝ ti·ket/ti·kuht Ⓝ/Ⓑ ticket
tijdschema ⓝ teyt·skhey·ma
 timetable (general)
tijdsverschil ⓝ teyts·vuhr·skhil
 time difference
tocht tokht hike • tour • trek n
toegangsprijs too·khangs·preys
 admission (price)
toer toor tour (short, eg museum) n
toerismebureau ⓝ Ⓑ
 too·ris·muh·bew·roh tourist office
toerist too·rist tourist n
toilet ⓝ twa·let toilet
toiletpapier ⓝ twa·let·pa·peer
 toilet paper
tolk tolk interpreter
tolweg tol·wekh tollway
toneelstuk ⓝ toh·neyl·stuk
 play (theatre) n
tonen toh·nuhn show v
tot tot until
touringcar too·ring·kar coach (bus) n
traag traakh slowly
trap trap stairway
trein treyn train n
treinstation ⓝ treyn·sta·syon
 train station
trekken tre·kuhn hike v • hiking • pull v
trui tröy jumper (sweater)
tuin töyn garden n
tv tey·vey TV
twee twey two
tweede klas twey·duh klas second class n
tweepersoonsbed ⓝ
 twey·puhr·sohns·bet double bed
tweepersoonskamer
 twey·puhr·sohns·kaa·muhr
 double room

U

u ew you pol sg&pl
uw ew your pol sg&pl
uitgaan öyt·khaan go out

uitgaansgids öyt-khaans-khits *entertainment guide*
uitgang öyt-khang *exit* n
uitstappen öyt-sta-puhn *get off (bus etc)*
uitzicht Ⓝ öyt-zikht *view* n
universiteit ew-nee-ver-see-teyt *university*
uur Ⓝ ewr *hour*
uw ew *your* pol sg&pl

V

vacature va-ka-tew-ruh *vacancy (job)*
vader vaa-duhr *father*
vakantie va-kan-see *holidays • vacation*
valideren va-lee-dey-ruhn *validate*
van van *from*
vanavond van-aa-vont *tonight*
vandaag van-daakh *today*
veerboot veyr-boht *ferry* n
veertien dagen veyr-teen daa-khun *fortnight*
vegetariër vey-khey-taa-ree-yuhr *vegetarian* n
vegetarisch vey-khey-taa-ris *vegetarian* a
veiligheidsriem vey-likh-heyts-reem *seatbelt*
veilig vrijen Ⓜ vey-likh vrey-yuhn *safe sex*
ventilator ven-tee-laa-tor *fan (machine)*
ver ver *far*
verandering vuhr-an-duh-ring *change (general)* n
verband Ⓝ vuhr-bant *bandage*
verdieping vuhr-dee-ping *floor (storey)*
verjaardag vuhr-yaar-dakh *birthday*
verloofd vuhr-lohft *engaged (to be married)*
verloofde vuhr-lohf-duh *fiancé/fiancée*
verloren ver-loh-ruhn *lost*
verloving vuhr-loh-ving *engagement (to marry)*
vers vers *fresh*
verschillend vuhr-skhi-luhnt *different*
verschrikkelijk vuh-skhri-kuh-luhk *awful*
versnellingen vuhr-sne-ling-uhn *gears*
verstopt vuhr-stopt *blocked (drain/nose)*
verstuiking vuhr-stöy-king *sprain* n
vertalen vuhr-taa-luhn *translate*
vertraging vuhr-traa-khing *delay* n
vertrek Ⓝ vuhr-trek *departure*
vertrekken vuhr-tre-kuhn *depart*
vervelend Ⓑ vuhr-vey-luhnt *boring*
verwarmd vuhr-warmt *heated (place)*

verwarmingstoestel Ⓝ vuhr-war-mings-too-stel *heater*
verzekering vuhr-zey-kuh-ring *insurance*
vest Ⓑ vest *jacket (dressy)*
vest Ⓝ vest *jacket (casual)*
vestiaire ves-tyer *cloakroom*
vet vet *fat (food)* a
videofilm vee-dey-yoo-film *video tape*
vinger ving-uhr *finger*
vishandel vis-han-duhl *fish shop*
vissen Ⓝ vi-suhn *fishing* n
visum Ⓝ vee-zum *visa*
vlees Ⓝ vleys *meat*
vliegen vlee-khuhn *fly* v
vliegtuig Ⓝ vleekh-töykh *aeroplane (airplane)*
vlooienmarkt vloh-yuhn-markt *flea market*
vlucht vlukht *flight*
voedsel voot-suhl *food*
voedselvoorraad voot-suhl-voh-raat *food supplies*
voelen voo-luhn *feel (emotions/touch)* v
voet voot *foot (body)*
voetbal Ⓝ voot-bal *football (soccer)*
voetpad Ⓝ voot-pat *footpath*
vol vol *full*
volgend vol-khuhnt *next (following)*
volzet vol-zet *no vacancy*
voor vohr *before*
voornaam vohr-naam *first name*
voorschrift Ⓝ Ⓑ vohr-skhrift *prescription*
vorige voh-ri-khuh *last (previous)*
vork vork *fork*
vriend vreent *boyfriend • friend*
vriendin vreen-din *friend • girlfriend*
vrij vrey *free (available)* a • *vacant*
vrijgezel vrey-khuh-zel *single (person)*
vrijwilligen vrey-wi-li-khuhn *volunteer* v
vrijwilliger vrey-wi-li-khuhr *volunteer* n
vroeg vrookh *early* adv
vrouw vraw *woman*
vrouwelijk vraw-wuh-luhk *female* a
vuil vöyl *dirty*
vuilbak vöyl-bak *garbage can*
VVV Ⓝ vey-vey-vey *tourist office*

W

waar waar *where*
waardevol waar-duh-vol *valuable*
waarom waa-rom *why*
wachten wakh-tuhn *wait* v

Z

wachtkamer *wakht*·kaa·muhr
  waiting room
wagen *waa*·khuhn *car*
wakker maken *wa*·kuhr *maa*·kuhn
  wake someone up
wakker worden *wa*·kuhr *wor*·duhn
  wake up
wandelen *wan*·duh·luhn
  walk (go for a walk) v
wandelwagen *wan*·duhl·waa·khuhn
  stroller
wanneer *wa*·neyr *when*
warenhuis ⓝ Ⓝ *waa*·ruhn·höys
  department store
warm warm *hot • warm* a
warmwaterfles warm·*waa*·tuhr·fles
  hot water bottle
was was *laundry (clothes)*
wasmachine *was*·ma·shee·nuh
  washing machine
(iets) wassen (eets) *wa*·suhn
  wash (something) v
wasserette wa·suh·re·tuh *laundrette*
water ⓝ *waa*·tuhr *water* n
wattenproppen wa·tuh·*pro*·puhn
  cotton balls
wedstrijd wet·streyt *match (sport)*
week weyk *week*
weekend ⓝ *wey*·kent *weekend*
weg wekh *road • route*
wekker *we*·kuhr *alarm clock*
welke *wel*·kuh *which*
werk werk *job* Ⓑ *• task*
westen ⓝ *wes*·tuhn *west* n
wetenschap *wey*·tuhn·skhap *science*
wetenschapper *wey*·tuhn·skha·puhr
  scientist
wie wee *who*
wijn weyn *wine*
wijzen *wey*·zuhn *point* v
winkel *wing*·kuhl *shop* n
winkelcentrum ⓝ *wing*·kuhl·sen·trum
  shopping centre
winkelen *wing*·kuh·luhn *shop* v
(geld) wisselen (khelt) *wi*·suh·luhn
  change (money) v
wisselgeld ⓝ *wi*·suhl·khelt
  change (money given back) n
wisselkantoor ⓝ *wi*·suhl·kan·tohr
  currency exchange
wisselkoers *wi*·suhl·koors *exchange rate*
wit wit *white*

wittebroodsweken pl
  wi·tuh·brohts·wey·kuhn
  honeymoon (period)
wol wol *wool* n
woordenboek ⓝ *wohr*·duhn·book
  dictionary
woud ⓝ wawt *forest*

Z

zaak zaak *company (firm)*
zakdoek zak·dook *handkerchief*
zaken pl *zaa*·kuhn *business* n
zakenreis *zaa*·kuhn·reys *business trip*
zaklantaarn *zak*·lan·taarn
  flashlight (torch)
zakmes ⓝ *zak*·mes *penknife*
zee zey *sea*
zeep zeyp *soap*
zeldzaam *zelt*·zaam *rare (uncommon)*
zelfbediening *zelf*·buh·dee·ning
  self-service a
ziek zeek *ill • sick*
ziekenhuis ⓝ *zee*·kuhn·höys *hospital*
zijde *zey*·duh *silk* n
zijn zeyn *his (posessive)*
zijn zeyn *to be* v
zilver *zil*·vuhr *silver* n
zitje ⓝ *zi*·chuh *seat (place)* n
zoet zoot *sweet* a
zomer *zoh*·muhr *summer*
zon zon *sun*
zonder *zon*·duhr *without*
zonnebrand *zo*·nuh·brant *sunburn*
zonnebrandolie *zo*·nuh·brant·oh·lee
  tanning lotion
zonnebril sg *zo*·nuh·bril *sunglasses*
zonnecrème *zo*·nuh·kreym
  sunscreen (lotion)
zonsondergang zons·*on*·duhr·khang
  sunset
zonsopgang zons·*op*·khang *sunrise*
zoon zohn *son*
zout ⓝ zawt *salt* n
zuiden ⓝ *zöy*·duhn *south* n
zus zus *sister*
zuster *zus*·tuhr *nurse* n
zwaar zwaar *heavy (weight)*
zwanger *zwang*·uhr *pregnant*
zwart zwart *black*
zwart-wit (film) zwart·wit (film)
  B&W (film)
zwembad ⓝ *zwem*·bat *swimming pool*
zwemmen *zwe*·muhn *swim* v